Metaphoria
Metaphor and Guided Metaphor for Psychotherapy and Healing

Rubin Battino, M.S.

Mental Health Counseling
Adjunct Professor, Department of Human Services (Counseling)
Wright State University

Crown House Publishing
www.crownhouse.co.uk

First published by

Crown House Publishing Ltd
Crown Buildings, Bancyfelin, Carmarthen, Wales, SA33 5ND, UK
www.crownhouse.co.uk

and

Crown House Publishing Ltd
P.O. Box 2223, Williston, VT 05495-2223, USA
www.CHPUS.com

British Library Cataloguing-in-Publication Data
A catalogue entry for this book is available
from the British Library.

ISBN 1899836829

Library of Congress Control Number 2002107639

Printed and bound in the UK by
Bell & Bain Limited
Glasgow

To my grandchildren:

Eleanor Cecilia
Lily Jayne
Anabel Lark
Toma Kataoka
Miaki Kataoka

May their lives be stories full of wonder

Permissions

The author greatly appreciates permission to reproduce materials (exact citations given throughout the text) from the following sources:

Family Therapy Networker (Psychotherapy Networker)

O'Hanlon, W. H., (1994) "The third wave," *Family Therapy Networker*, Nov./Dec. pp. 19–29.

W. W. Norton & Company

Berg., I. K. and Dolan, Y., *Tales of solutions. A collection of hope-inspiring stories* (New York: W. W. Norton & Company, 2001).

O'Hanlon, W. H. and Hexum, A. L., *An uncommon casebook. The complete clinical work of Milton H. Erickson, M.D.* (New York: W. W. Norton & Company, 1990).

Miller, S. D. and Berg, I. K., *The miracle method. A radically new approach to problem drinking* (New York: W. W. Norton and Company, 1995).

Rosen, S., *My voice will go with you. The teaching tales of Milton H. Erickson* (New York: W. W. Norton and Company, 1982).

Watzlawick, P., Weakland, J. and Fisch, R., *Change. Principles of problem formation and problem resolution* (New York: W. W. Norton and Company 1974).

White, M. and Epston, D., *Narrative means to therapeutic ends* (New York: W. W. Norton and Company, 1990).

Riverhead Books (Penguin Putnam Inc.)

Remen, R. N., *Kitchen table wisdom. Stories that heal* (New York: Riverhead Books, 1996).

Remen, R. N., *My grandfather's blessings. Stories of strength, refuge, and belonging* (New York: Riverhead Books, 2000).

Jossey-Bass Publishers (John Wiley and Sons)

Haley, J., *Ordeal therapy. Unusual ways to change behavior* (San Francisco: Jossey-Bass Publishers, 1984).

Impact Publishers

Close, H. T., *Metaphor in psychotherapy. Clinical applications of stories and allegories* (San Luis Obispo, CA: Impact Publishers, 1998).

Crown House Publishing Ltd.

Berman, M., and Brown, D., *The power of metaphor. Story telling and guided journeys for teachers, trainers and therapists* (Carmarthen, UK: Crown House Publishing Ltd., 2000).

Irvington Publishers Inc.

Erickson, M. H., Rossi, E. L., and Rossi, S. I., *Hypnotic realities* (New York: Irvington Publishers Inc., 1976).

Brunner/Mazel (Taylor and Francis Group)

Gilligan, S. G., *Therapeutic trances, the cooperation principle in Ericksonian hypnotherapy* (New York: Brunner/Mazel, 1987).

Havens, R. A., and Walters, C., *Hypnotherapy scripts. A neo-Ericksonian approach to persuasive healing* (New York: Brunner/Mazel, 1989).

Kopp, R. R., *Metaphor Therapy. Using client-generated metaphors in psychotherapy* (New York: Brunner/Mazel, 1995).

Lankton, C. H. and Lankton, S. R., *Tales of enchantment. Goal-oriented metaphors for adults and children in therapy* (New York: Brunner/Mazel, 1989).

Lankton, S. R. and Lankton, C. H., *Enchantment and intervention in family therapy. Training in Ericksonian approaches* (New York: Brunner/Mazel, 1986).

Table of Contents

Foreword

Stephen Lankton

Introduction

Metaphors are the looms over which we stretch our experience. There is something about stories and metaphors that has a profound effect on listeners: they teach, inspire, guide, communicate, are remembered, and, most of all, are everywhere!

I see stories or complex metaphors as more than a description of one thing in terms of another. They are an altered framework within which listeners can entertain novel ways of experiencing. Metaphors play a central role in all learning and communicating. They mediate between feelings, thinking, perception, and behavior. They are the symbolic equivalent of sensation. I use the term to extend the story, analogy, and anecdotes as well, as they all act the same on consciousness. When a story is involved, it incorporates plot and character development and drama. These *entrain* conscious attention and provide an evermore profound manner of impacting listeners at an unconscious level.

Complex stories such as those in myths, epics, and legends created historical backdrops as well. I imagine that some people somewhere listened to a storyteller long ago as she told about Prometheus creating humans and stealing the fire from Mount Olympus for human use; how Zeus then created Pandora for revenge, and sent her to Earth. And the storyteller told how Pandora's curiosity led her to open that special box and release all human troubles—and, too, how in fright she shut the box just *before* hope was released.

Some of the listeners were concerned about the tattered fabric of their own lives. For some it was "worn thin," or in many ways "torn," for some their life had "faded," and for others it was drab or just old. And the listeners saw the storyteller's facial expressions as well as hearing the tale of Pandora. They saw a quick glance over there, a frown here, a questioning look there, and a smile here. And the listeners remembered: they thought about the origins of their own troubles and the need for courage—courage to look in the box of their life to find their own hope.

Elsewhere, other storytellers were remembered differently by their listeners. In the back of their minds people remembered hearing how characters invariably meet a god, confront a monster, overcome a challenger, complete a task, yield to a wise man, or ponder a riddle.

Listeners, just as do the protagonists within the stories, come to show jealousy, purity, wisdom, foolishness, piety, shame, doubt, or hesitation. They, like people everywhere, have been attracted to sirens who will ruin them, have exposed an Achilles' heel, are afraid to look into the box for hope or to take another risk, and are afraid to love or to cry. Yet the storyteller and the story help them to tap into their own resources and to cope with their own challenges in creative and personalized ways.

Myths retain a mystery and wisdom even though we may be too "enlightened" to believe. They also contain common sense and education. Homer's *Iliad* (c. 700 B.C.) tells of an episode in the Trojan War and the wrath of Achilles with its tragic consequences, including the deaths of Patroclus and Hector. But, too, Homer wove a tale that, perhaps inadvertently, explained how to launch a ship, talk to the other gender, prepare certain meals, negotiate a contract, and more.

Socialization

For better or worse, metaphors socialize us. We have "cultural myths" or "cultural metaphors" that infuse our growing minds with a nearly unexamined set of ideas. They soak into our minds as moisture penetrates a sponge. Without so much as a complaint, we can come to accept these so-called truths: "Men are strong, women are weak"; other religions or racial groups are better or worse; "God is on *our* side"; we should all act like Davie Crockett or Betty Crocker, James Dean or Marilyn Monroe, Superman, Rambo, or Madonna or *the* Madonna. Then, too, tales of our values bias what we believe about American justice, Native Americans, our unique history, our neighborhood, and even civilized progress.

Even the metaphor of "progress" has come to mean leaving things *behind* us, and has utterly obscured the idea of real growth, which means leaving things *inside* us. Metaphors and myths of progress tell us: For the want of a nail the shoe was lost (for the want of the shoe, a horse, a rider, a battle, a kingdom etc.). And, from within the cultural cage, we cannot evaluate reality for ourselves. Yet, at the same time, we are told via still other stories, other metaphors, that we can indeed evaluate reality for ourselves.

There are also cultural metaphors that concern even our biological attributes and address characteristics such as red hair, green eyes, long fingers, blonde hair, fatness, skinniness, and so on. There are children's metaphors that guide or tease out self-image. We hear labels such as Pinocchio, "Anna-Rexia," and Gumby as children. We have family metaphors that include everything from "I can fix anything" and "our family is never good at math" to an idea that our family name can determine our occupation. And, of course, there is the favorite family "sphincter" (Berne, 1972, p. 164) that develops from repeated attention focused on how life is a "thrill to the heart," or "a pain in the butt," or "a constant upset," a "pain in the neck," "pisses me off," or "oh, my aching back." Metaphors are everywhere and they influence our being from cradle to grave, from our expectations to our attitudes and to our visceral experience.

Discovery and inspiration

But metaphors do even more. Let's remember Dr Carl Jung, who pointed out the fact that even when our senses react to real phenomena—sights, and sounds—that they are then somehow translated from the realm of reality into that of the mind. That is, as our sensation happens, the experience has been affected or absorbed subliminally without our conscious knowledge, and ideas well up later from the unconscious as a sort of afterthought. These ideas may appear in the form of a dream or an inspiration. As a general rule, the unconscious aspect of any perceptual event is revealed to us in dreams, where it appears not as a rational thought but as a *symbolic* image, that is, a metaphor. In other words, our discoveries and inspirations are neither more nor less than the residual processing of perceptions in areas that are related metaphorically to our novel observations and conceptions.

Consider the view of heaven before the Renaissance. To put this in a proper historical perspective, it is helpful to realize that this was the time of the Second Crusade (1147–49). The ideology of this crusade was preached by St Bernard of Clairvaux after the Christians lost at Edessa (1144) to the Turks. This was around the time that Saladin captured Jerusalem for Islam (1187) and built the wall we still see today in the "old city." In this time frame a Persian poet and mathematician named Omar Khayyam (1050–1122) said that all we ever know is a reflection in a shadow box with the sun at the center.

> *We are no other than a moving row*
> *Of Magic Shadow-shapes that come and go*
> *Round with the Sun-illumined Lantern held*
> *In Midnight by the Master of the Show …*

He wrote mathematical studies and participated in a calendar reform, but he is best known for *The Rubáiyát of Omar Khayyam*, a collection of epigrammatic quatrains that express an apparently hedonistic philosophy. The point in relating this, however, is that a heliocentric view of the universe was first proposed as a metaphor. And this was several hundred years before Copernicus, Kepler, Galileo, and Brahe set the world on fire with the same idea, but with telescopes to back it up!

In still another great moment, Kekulé in 1847 had a dream of a snake swallowing its tail. Friedrich August Kekulé von Stradonitz (1829–96) was a German organic chemist. He was a professor at Bonn who is most noted for his representation of the molecular structure of benzene as a ring. Such rings are the basic structural feature of many organic and all aromatic compounds. While all of us as modern chemistry students are simply given such details, Kekulé came to the realization of the structure of benzene in a dream—that is, a metaphor. Once again an inspiration that changed the world came first via metaphor.

And then there is the Scottish novelist, poet, and essayist Robert Louis Stevenson (1850–94), who got the idea for Dr. Jekyll and Mr. Hyde in a dream. But more mysterious still is that he claimed that the dreaming was done by "Brownies." Four plays written with W. E. Henley (1885) had little success, but the adventure novel *Treasure Island* (1883) and *A Child's Garden of Verses* were very popular. In 1886 came two of his best-known works, *Kidnapped*, an adventure tale set in Scotland, and *The Strange Case of Dr. Jekyll and Mr. Hyde*. Stevenson claimed that all of these, including that science-fiction thriller with moral overtones, was a story told to him by his internal "Brownies."

But, years before, Archimedes (c. 287–212 B.C.) had another historically enlightening experience from metaphoric insight. Archimedes sat in a tub of water pondering, for Heredes II, how to determine the composition of a crown presumably made of gold. Archimedes was a Greek mathematician, physicist, and inventor. His reputation in antiquity was based on several mechanical contrivances, such as, "Archimedes' screw," which he is alleged to have invented. One legend states that during the Second Punic War he protected his native Syracuse from the besieging armies of Marcus Claudius Marcellus for three years by inventing machines of war, such as various ballistic instruments including the catapult, and, perhaps more interestingly, mirrors that set Roman ships on fire by focusing the sun's rays on them. His best-known experience was that of realizing how his body displaced an exact amount of water that was determined by his body's composition—and that a quantity of gold would do the same. Thus, the metaphor of his body in the bath would lead to theories of density and displacement (and incidentally prove that the king had indeed been cheated in the manufacturing of that "gold" crown). Archimedes was inspired to invention through his metaphor.

The artist is a receptacle for emotions that come from all over: from the sky, from the earth, from a scrap of paper, from a passing shape, from a spider's web. Consider the works of Pablo Picasso (1881–1973), the Spanish artist. Or consider the writer Henry Miller (1891–1980), who stated, "I didn't have to think up so much as a comma or a semicolon: it was all given, straight from the celestial recording room. Weary, I would beg for a break, an intermission, time enough, let's say, to go to the toilet or take a breath of fresh air on the balcony. Nothing doing."

Indeed, the psychologist Timothy Leary (1920–99), a one-time Harvard psychologist, stated that science itself is all metaphor (Leary, 1980). We should see not just individual breakthroughs of scientists and artists as metaphor and metaphor-derived, but the entire fabric of science itself as metaphor. After all, does not science attempt to describe the universe in terms other than what it in fact is?

Many do not realize that Isaac Newton was the best-known pupil of René Descartes. These men are individually or collectively considered the "parents" of modern science. Descartes, who was not a believer in the occult, "nevertheless attributed all of his philosophic ideas to images which appeared to him either in dreams or when he was in the hypnagogic state just before awakening." (Mishlove, 1993, p. 51). In fact, he stated that an angel had informed him in a dream that mathematics was the only true method of knowing reality. Thus, mathematics was the only thing to believe in and, unless the mathematical relationship could be proven, nothing should be believed. Ironically, he came to this conclusion by a message from an angelic visitor in a decidedly nonmathematical dream (Kafatos & Nadeau, 2000, p. 120)!

Consciousness

Consciousness can change experience. Neural net models of the mind began in 1943, and identified nets with circles and nets without. That is, those without circles have no feedback and reverberation and cannot continually activate. Unfortunately, these nets are the ones that have been studied the most. This is much like the way we developed our worldview. It is the metaphor developed by science and that of Newtonian mechanics. We forget to study the change created by the very act of studying! In our civilization we come to think in terms that are born out of linear causation, objective observation, external truth, reductionism, and specialization.

Experts of the mind are not usually experts of the body. Children are nowadays often unaware of the question: "Which came first—

the chicken or the egg?" But it is possible or even likely that neither came first—the world of cause and effect is an illusion. The world of experience and metaphor is "real."

Yet experience is often recognized as sequential—we live in a world with a dimension of time. Currently most of us are aware of four or five dimensions of experience on this planet. We know we can exert control over three of them: length, width, depth. Time is a fourth dimension, over which we feel no control but which we believe carries us along. And consciousness is perhaps our fifth dimension, which in some invisible manner gives rise to the feeling we each have of a unique and basically enduring identity.

I can mention Grandma, and you become aware of a familiar face, a tone of voice, maybe a setting, a smell of a kitchen on a holiday, and so on. But how does this occur? This is called the *binding problem*. My words bind your experience—they *entrain* experience. My story, my metaphor, binds your experience and your "cause-and-effect" is set in motion.

This is in part due to the fact that we can monitor only 150 nerve cells at once. This is probably the result of language limitation. The human mind has been developing in hominids for 10 million years. Yet the development of language seems to be only in the last 100 thousand years. Knowledge as we relate it to language has not developed in parallel to the growth of the size of the brain. Rather, knowledge appears to have mushroomed in growth after the size of the brain stopped its evolutionary expansion and, in fact, declined in average size in modern *Homo sapiens*. It is as if growth in mass equals smaller increase in knowledge, and no growth in mass equals more increase in knowledge.

With respect to metaphors of the mind, we use the more recent technologies as our way to "best" describe brain and mind activities. While at present we often speak in computer terminology of "retrieving experience" or "programming our mind," in an earlier era we used to speak in terms of astronomy, as in this example from Charles Sherrington (University of Edinburgh 1937–38 lecture): "The great topmost sheet of the mass, that where hardly a light had twinkled or moved, becomes now a sparkling field of rhythmic flashing points with trains of traveling sparks hurrying hither and thither. The brain is waking and with it the mind is returning. It is as if the Milky Way entered upon some cosmic dance. Swiftly the head mass becomes an enchanted loom where millions of flashing shuttles weave a dissolving pattern though never an abiding one; a shifting harmony of sub-patterns."

Now, we like to speak of the mind as a computer. By using the computer metaphor many feel we are advancing to an understanding of the brain and maybe the mind. But I want to remind readers to be wary of these metaphors. We create computer neural networks that consist of fewer neurons than those in a frog. These are only a couple of thousand neurons at most and therefore the number is more closely related to the brain of a slug, or a cockroach, and most certainly a brain smaller than that of a cat. The mind is far more complex—10 billion neurons—than that of the largest parallel processing computers we now design. All computer metaphors of the brain should be considered extremely inadequate and must be held in suspicion. The best metaphor to describe our mind or our brain has not yet been spoken! Beware. "The mind of the thoroughly well-informed man is a dreadful thing. It is like a bric-à-brac shop, all monsters and dust, with everything priced above its proper value." Thus spoke the Anglo-Irish playwright and author Oscar Wilde (1854–1900), in *The Picture of Dorian Gray* (1891/1974, Chapter 1).

Therapy

Finally, the discussion of metaphor comes to the arena of personal change and professional therapy. History, culture, art, science, and human growth all hinge on the magic of metaphor. Naturally, there is a manner for using it that will facilitate therapeutic change. Perhaps modern clinicians owe Milton Hyland Erickson, M.D., of Phoenix, Arizona, the ultimate gratitude for the use of storytelling in therapy. His pioneering work, more than any other, has triggered the revolution in effort and thinking that has brought the use of therapeutic metaphor to light.

Erickson wrote "The Method Employed to Formulate a Complex Story for the Induction of an Experimental Neurosis in a Hypnotic Subject" in 1944. In the discussion he shows that the use of a story whose content parallels that of the client's neurosis will indeed bring the experiential material closer to consciousness for the subject. He concluded correctly that these stories can exert significant influences upon the behavior of hypnotic subjects. Furthermore, Erickson speculated that the *method* by which the story is told may be even more important than its content. In this warning we find an essential caveat for therapists. That is, training and supervision are essential for the acquisition of new skills and techniques. Excellent sources of material may make it possible for therapeutic metaphors to be constructed, but written material will fall short of the goal of honing perception and skill in verbal delivery.

Metaphors work because the mind is metaphoric. It holds attention due to drama—material presented out of sequence. It creates experience because people live in a world of ambiguity. It leads to change when properly conducted, because experience can be elicited, associated, linked, and eventually conditioned to occur in novel ways and in novel situations. Consciousness will generally follow the plot line and stick to the need for resolution of the drama of a story (no matter how minimal), and yet the mind listens to plot while the unconscious responds to the experiences retrieved. As a result, images, ideas, affects, and urges can be elicited and basically brought into play to better assist a client in personal or interpersonal adaptation.

Therapeutic metaphors and longer stories are (1) not to be used at random, (2) built with constrained or guided elaboration of ambiguity that is chosen to work effectively for the unique listener, and (3) used to impart known experience into domains in which listeners have no information or insufficient experience. Context gives meaning to metaphor, and while clients can make no subjectively adequate response they will have an increasing need for some kind of response. When the context of therapy is conducted correctly, its meaning will have an opportunity for an admixture of relevant experience, memory, and perception. This means, ultimately, that internal and external events can come to be linked to therapeutically useful feelings, ideas, behaviors, and complex patterns.

There are many different ways to go about using metaphor that include everything from talking, bibliotherapy, and cinema, to extramural assignments and physical activity. There are also many types of goals for the use of metaphor in therapy. At first one might think the entire matter is too overwhelming to embrace. But that is just why a book like *Metaphoria* is so appropriate.

Metaphoria

Metaphors (1) provide a cluster or gestalt of associations, (2) resist reduction, (3) facilitate thinking, (4) are more compelling than structured language, and (5) are more easily assimilated. Elaborations are limited by constraints of perceptual experience: biological, social, personal. Metaphors allow for new models and concepts of life. They are the principal structures by which psychological change and growth can occur. They are how the mind transforms itself! *Metaphoria* is the most complete overview and reference book to date on the various approaches to metaphor.

Rubin Battino's motivation for writing this book is to present an accurate and comprehensive guide for the existing ideas and literature concerning metaphor or storytelling in therapy. In this new millennium, this is the first book to embrace such a courageous goal. I am thrilled to say that Battino has succeeded in his effort. Not only is *Metaphoria* comprehensive in scope, but it is also very readable. At several points in the book readers feel they are sitting around a fire with Rubin and hearing his opinions and detailed summaries of all the contributors in the area of metaphor.

Maybe I failed to mention a story about a therapist with a great deal of experience who attempted to put his own expertise into a presentation. Laying aside his personal opinions, he attempted to be balanced and fair about the professional colleagues he knew. He spoke about the skill, the contribution, the value, and the intricacies of each colleague. At times it seemed he had to resort to storytelling, or, more precisely, he chose to entrain his listeners with tales that enchanted them. Sometimes, he presented examples of his colleagues' ideas, and at other times he perfectly articulated teaching their contributions to the field and the details of their approaches. His listeners—people from universities and private training institutes, competitors, young hero-worshippers, trained professionals seeking direction, and experienced clinicians needing a comprehensive overview for reference—all of them came to listen. All of them walked away after the experience, enriched. All of them realized that they were enhanced and stimulated by this therapist's ideas and his grasp of the ideas of others. There was no competition, no ego, no games. All there was, in the therapist's recitation, was value. All there was was learning. All there was was accurate details, footnoted backup, and creative examples.

Rubin Battino, a long-time colleague of mine, has done just this in his magnificent work. Is this volume about metaphor worth the time to buy and read? Absolutely! In fact, it is a must-buy and a must-read book. There are so many ideas about the use of metaphor in professional circles that it would be nearly impossible for an individual therapist to look at and review all of it. Furthermore, there are dozens of authors and clinicians who are ever so insistent that their material be accurately represented. I am but one of those authors. And I can say from my personal experience that Rubin Battino has accomplished the task of accuracy, comprehensiveness, and brevity everywhere throughout this book.

Here is a glimpse of what you find within. Battino reviews the literature and covers every imaginable angle of metaphor in therapy, whether they be spoken or enacted metaphors. He provides numerous examples and at all times speaks to you, the reader, as a person who is a colleague and collaborator. His freshness and honesty are unparalleled, and his grasp of the subject matter is uncanny. Readers will know how and why to construct all manner of therapeutic metaphor, and can act with confidence, knowing what sorts of responses clients will create. From creation of metaphors to rapport, from application to specific case illustrations, this book is a chest of golden treasures. It will shine for some time to come.

—Phoenix, AZ
February 2002

Bibliography

Berne, E., (1972), *What do you say after you say hello?* New York: Grove Press.

Erickson, M. H., (1944), "The method employed to formulate a complex story for the induction of an experimental neurosis in a hypnotic subject," *Journal of General Psychology*, 31, pp. 67–84.

Kafatos, M. C. and Nadeau, R., (2000), *The conscious universe: parts and wholes in physical reality* New York: Springer, p. 120.

Leary, T., (1980), "An interview with Timothy Leary," *Contemporary Authors*, Vol. 107, No. 24, September.

Mishlove, J., (1993), *The roots of consciousness: the classic encyclopedia of consciousness studies* Tulsa, OK: Council Oak Books, p. 51.

Sherrington, C. S., (1937), Lectures. University of Edinburgh (1937–8). Also see: Sherrington, C. S., *The brain and its mechanism* Cambridge: Cambridge University Press.

Stevenson, R. L. and "Brownies." See, e.g., Elwin, M., *The strange case of Robert Louis Stevenson* (London: Macdonald & Co., Ltd., 1950), p. 199, where RLS is quoted commenting on *Olalla* and *The Strange Case of Dr. Jekyll and Mr. Hyde*: "both ... were in part conceived by 'the little people who manage man's internal theatre'—the 'Brownies,' 'who do one-half my work for me while I am fast asleep, and in all human likelihood, do the rest for me as well, when I am wide awake and fondly suppose I do it for myself'."

Wilde, O., (1891, 1974), *The Picture of Dorian Gray* Oxford: Oxford University Press, Chapter 1.

Preface

When I was asked to consider writing a book on the subject of metaphor, my first reaction was that there were several books already available. (This project was recommended to the publisher by John Roberts, Ph.D.—thank you, John.) I thought about the project at odd moments—in one of those the title of this book, *Metaphoria*, popped into my head. Somehow, this invented word caught my imagination with its hints of euphoria, metamorphosis, passion, and moments of delight. Once I had this working title, the book became an established entity, just waiting for an opportune time to put words to paper. This preface is being written in the lakeside town of Mondsee, Austria. The "opportunity" is that my wife, Charlotte, is singing in the Berkshire Choral Festival in Salzburg, with rehearsals and accommodations in Mondsee. So, while she vocalizes and rehearses, I write (or tour!).

For a while, I felt that "Metaphoria" was sufficient as a title, until I decided that an explanatory subtitle was needed. This is: "Metaphor and Guided Metaphor for Psychotherapy and Healing." The word "guided" connects with my work in guided imagery, and the phrase "guided metaphor" is an accurate description of the ways I use metaphor in a structured manner for both psychotherapy and healing. With this extended title the book had to be written.

There are a number of good books on metaphor (see Chapter 1 for a guide to these books). How is the present book different? The major difference arises from my many years in academia—this book is written more in the style of a textbook or primer on the subject than a collection of case studies with some theory thrown in. That is, the book is designed to systematically teach the reader new to the field how to construct and use metaphors in a variety of circumstances. In addition, the style and content of the book are influenced by my training in and practice of Ericksonian psychotherapy and hypnosis. Milton H. Erickson, M.D., was a master storyteller and his ability to weave helpful ideas into his stories is legendary. I have been much influenced by his work. The accompanying audio material for this book provides an illustration of metaphors for a variety of purposes, and also a guide to their delivery.

Chapter 1 deals with definitions and a survey of the literature. Throughout the book illustrations of relevant uses of metaphor are given by using both published metaphors and those created by me. Since metaphors are basically stories using words, Chapter 2 is a systematic summary of appropriate language forms and usage—just what words, phrases, and grammatical structure will enhance the content of a metaphor? There is a section on language-rich metaphors.

Metaphors are stories, and you need to be a good storyteller to use them effectively. Chapter 3 is then concerned with the *delivery* of metaphors. This involves material on rapport building as a basis for connected communication. Theatricality is important, as well as the discipline of speech and communication. Chapter 4 covers the basic structure of a metaphor—what are the essential elements and how are they combined? This chapter recognizes that there are many storytelling styles. There is a section on themes for basic metaphors.

A special feature of the book is the analysis of published metaphors that is presented in Chapter 5. Using a two-column format, parts of several published metaphors are critiqued and analyzed. Alternate ways of saying the same thing more effectively are also given. Metaphors can involve a complex structure as in multiple-embedded metaphors; these are treated separately in Chapter 6 on advanced metaphor, which also contains several literature and author examples.

Richard R. Kopp's Metaphor Therapy is such a significant contribution, basically a paradigm shift from therapist-generated to client-generated metaphors, that an entire chapter (7) is devoted to describing his pioneering work. This chapter includes a critique and some alternate ways of doing Metaphor Therapy.

Chapter 8 describes the author's guided-metaphor approach. This is based on guided imagery, Metaphor Therapy, and the author's experience as a hypnotherapist. This chapter also includes a workbook for structured writing on guided metaphor.

The next group of chapters connects metaphor with a number of therapeutic approaches. Reframing, or the art of changing the meaning of an event or idea or memory, is discussed in Chapter 9. This chapter starts with a discussion of first-order and second-order change, or the nature of change. Chapter 10 deals briefly with the uses of metaphor in psychotherapy and hypnotherapy. Ambiguous-function assignment (Chapter 11) and ordeal therapy (Chapter 12) are special applications of metaphor.

Solution-focused therapy as practiced by Steve de Shazer and his colleagues generally involves the use of the "miracle question," a special application of the "as-if" frame. Pretending is an inherent part of listening to and being engrossed in a story—Chapter 13 covers this aspect of metaphor. Narrative therapy (see Chapter 14) was developed by Michael White and David Epston and is a creative and effective way of using a person's own story to help them. The elements of narrative therapy work are presented.

Many of the "art" therapies (Chapter 15) are variants of metaphor in media other than words. There is a section on guided-metaphor art therapy. Chapter 16 is a specialty chapter on psychodrama and metaphor written by my guest contributor Joan Chappell Mathias, M.D. There are illustrations and a discussion of psychodrama.

In Chapter 17 the uses of metaphor for healing are presented, particularly the use of guided metaphor. The use of stories for preparation for surgery and other invasive interventions is the subject of Chapter 18. A major use of metaphor has been in the search for meaning and in spiritual practices (Chapter 19). Two examples are given in the lives and experiences of Viktor E. Frankl, M.D., and Douglas Mawson, Ph.D. Chapter 20 is on rituals and ceremonies with definitions and illustrations of different kinds of ceremonies. Finally, Chapter 21 is a summarizing chapter ending in a closing metaphor. There is an extensive list of references.

Special thanks are due to my friend and colleague Howard H. Fink, Ph.D., whose helpful comments and suggestions improved the manuscript, and whose enthusiastic support was always evident. Jane Chernek-Shaw did all of the rough typing and graciously adapted to my requirements. Bridget Shine, editor, sustained me through many of the ups and downs in the process of writing this book—her considerate support was and is gratefully appreciated.

Your comments are always welcome
(email address: rubin.battino@wright.edu).

Rubin Battino
Yellow Springs, Ohio
Fall 2001

Contributors

Rubin Battino, M.S.
He has a private practice in Yellow Springs, and also teaches courses for the Department of Human Services at Wright State University where he holds the rank of Adjunct Professor. This book is based on one of those courses. He has over ten years of experience as a volunteer facilitator in a Bernie Siegel-style support group for people who have life-challenging diseases and those who support them. Also, he has many years of experience in individual work with people who have life-challenging diseases. He is President of the Milton H. Erickson Society of Dayton, and co-author with T. L. South, Ph.D., of *Ericksonian Approaches: A Comprehensive Manual*, a basic text on Ericksonian hypnotherapy and psychotherapy. His other books from Crown House Publishing include *Guided Imagery*, *Coping*, and *Meaning*. He is currently Professor Emeritus of chemistry at Wright State University.

Joan Chappell Mathias, M.D.
Dr Mathias received her M.D. in England and worked as a G.P. in a slum-clearance estate in north London before qualifying as a psychiatrist in order to specialize as a psychotherapist. Her training included Balint groups at the Tavistock Clinic, a full analysis with the late Dr J. L. Rowley, and work with the Family Planning Association. Encouraged by the late Joshua Bierer, she trained in encounter, bioenergetic analysis, Gestalt therapy, NLP, transactional analysis, and finally in psychodrama. She is now a Distinguished Member of the ANZ (Australia/New Zealand) Psychodrama Association (ANZPA), with Max Clayton being her primary trainer.

In 1970 she and her husband Norman moved to New Zealand, where she worked in the Hospital Psychiatric Service, was visiting psychiatrist to the Women's Prison in Christchurch, and supervised in Marriage Guidance, the City Mission, and Life Line.

Although she is retired now and living in Tauranga, she is sought out for supervision by a chaplain, workers in the Dual Diagnosis and Alcohol and Drug Treatment Services, and by experienced members of the ANZPA seeking accreditation as trainers, educators, and practitioners in Psychodrama.

Chapter 1

Introduction

1.1 A brief history of the use of metaphor

The tribe gathers around the fire. It is night and the sparks that fly upward mimic the stars. The sparks last for moments, the stars are eternal, slowly moving across the sky in their daily trek, their yearly changes. Backs are cold and faces and hands are warm in the glow of the fire. In the ever-changing patterns of flame and glowing embers there is mystery and myth and the world of dreams. Enchantment. And the Old One tells once again the story of their origin, how the world began, how man was formed, how this tribe came about. And there is great comfort and wonder in hearing the old stories. Each member of the tribe is part of the story, is the continuing story. This is who they are. It is also who we are—simply a story, words strung together, connections with our past, our present, and our future. Words and stories ...

Stories are transformative. When you listen to or read or observe a story unfolding there is a magical transformation into the world of story, its events, and its participants. You become "entranced" in the tale. Your boundaries extend beyond your body to the limitless "out there" of the imagination. You fill in the details out of your uniqueness, your memories and connections. The story may take place in a forest or a city or a room—the forest is your forest, as is the city and the room. We all know what a forest is—trees and undergrowth and open spaces. Your forest may be all evergreen, or all deciduous, or some unique personal combination. Is the forest flat or hilly, does it have a stream or a river, is it winter or summer, are there animals and insects and flowers, are you alone or are others present? Such a simple word, "forest." The magic, the power of a story, a word, an image, a metaphor, is in the detail that you realize about it in this moment. This book is about the transformative power of words consciously used as metaphors for therapy and healing.

"Read me a book." "Tell me a story." Most stories at this time are the retelling in some medium of those created by a writer. It is rare to experience a spontaneously generated story. The medium controls the amount of detail explicitly presented. Printed stories generally allow the most variation in the recipient's mind. Illustrated printed stories are more restrictive in presenting specific images. Listening to a story is much like reading one, except for the reader's delivery, which highlights particular words and phrases. Theater is more restrictive in the way the words are spoken, in the movements and body expressions of the actors, and in the visual constraints of the sets. Movies and television restrict even more with the images chosen by the director. There is less left to the imagination and more is controlled.

It is my contention that the most effective use of metaphor, of stories, is in the *precise use of vague language*. All poets know this. It is no mistake that the great epics and sagas of many cultures are in poetic form. This holds for *The Iliad* and *The Odyssey* as well as for the Bible and other religious writings. The poet knows the art of the minimal use of precise words to create an image or evoke a feeling. Too much detail confines the reader. What about the myriad details in *Look Homeward Angel* or *Moby Dick*? Although the reader may be overwhelmed with descriptive words, each reader still interprets all of those details in her own way.[1] Sufficient information is needed to match your client's language, interest in detail, and own personal story; or to utilize her own self-descriptive metaphors.

The history of humanity is a story that is manifested in many ways. There are the oral traditions of preliterate man, whereby significant tribal stories were learned verbatim and passed on for thousands of years, as in the case of the Australian Aborigines. The accuracy of those oral-tradition stories is quite incredible. When all you have to rely on is remembering stories to tell over and over again, then that is what storytellers do. Since it is easier to remember rhymed poetry, or even blank verse, many of these old stories were in poetic form. In fact, the language forms of poetry have much in common with the language forms of metaphor. The writings and

---

[1] To avoid awkward constructions the feminine pronoun will be used in odd-numbered chapters, and the masculine in even-numbered chapters.

sayings, and particularly the parables, of all religions are rich in metaphor. God and the Great Spirit or other deities are mostly described indirectly by metaphor rather than directly. In Judaism you cannot even speak or write the name of God. Through all ages wandering storytellers (troubadours in the Middle Ages) were always welcome for their diversions and their news.

Joseph Campbell (1968) has written about the " hero's journey," a particular kind of story that appears to be universal. The Hero sets out on a quest for either personal enlightenment or advantage, or for some communal benefit. After many adventures involving "Heroic" challenges and deeds, the heroine wins through to her personal goal or that of the tribe. The difficulties of the journey are many, as are the obstacles in everyone's life. The retelling of these stories provides a comfort to ordinary people in identifying with the hope of success. The hero's journey also becomes a rite of passage into manhood or womanhood in many cultures. Is the modern involvement of many with the superheroes of sports a current re-enactment of the hero's journey? Most probably. Of course, there has been an evolution in particular in Western cultures over who is considered to be a hero, and what deeds are considered heroic. We have Nobel laureates, and sports stars, and selfless people like Mother Theresa and the Dalai Lama, but rarely political leaders in modern times.

1.2 Some definitions

When searching for definitions I always like to start with my treasured copy of the second edition of *Webster's New International Dictionary*, unabridged. For me, the very *weight* of this tome adds value to the definitions therein. The word "metaphor" is a noun, and comes from the French *metaphore*, the Latin and Greek *metaphora*, and from the Greek *metapherein*, which means to carry over, to transfer, as in its roots of *meta*, meaning beyond or over, plus *pherein*, to bring or bear. So in this sense a metaphor is something that is brought or carried over or beyond. In the context of rhetoric it is defined as the use of a word or phrase literally denoting one kind of object or idea in place of another by way of suggesting a likeness or analogy between them (the ship *plows* the sea; a volley of oaths). A metaphor may be regarded as a compressed *simile*, the comparison implied in the former (a marble brow) being explicit in the latter (a brow white like marble). The only synonym listed is the word "comparison," although the reader is also directed to the word "trope." The rhetorical definition of this latter word is: "The use of a word or expression in a different sense from that which properly belongs to it, for giving life or emphasis to an idea; also, an instance of such use; a figure of speech." Tropes are chiefly or four kinds: *metaphor, metonymy, synecdoche,* and *irony*.

Continuing with this merry chase of definitions, metonymy (whose Latin and Greek roots mean changing a name) is: "Use of one word for another that it suggests, as the effect for the cause, the cause for the effect, the sign for the thing signified, the container for the thing contained etc. (Darkness was the *saving* of us, for the *cause of saving*; a man keeps a good *table*, instead of good *food*; we read *Vergil*, that is, his poems; a man has a warm *heart*, that is, warm *affections*." The roots for *synecdoche* indicate that it means to receive with or jointly, and the rhetorical definition is: "A figure of speech by which a part is put for the whole (fifty *sail* for fifty *ships*), the whole for a part (the smiling *year* for *spring*), the species for the genus (*cutthroat* for *assassin*), the genus for the species (a *creature* for a *man*), the name of the material for the thing made, etc."

The word " irony" comes from the Greek for "dissimulation," a bit different from the previous words. Three definitions are given: "1. Dissimulation; ignorance or the like feigned to confound or provoke an antagonist. 2. A sort of humor, ridicule, or light sarcasm, which adopts a mode of speech the intended implication of which is the opposite of the literal sense of the words, as when expressions of praise are used where blame is meant; also, the figure of speech using this mode of expression. 3. A state of affairs or events which is the reverse of what was, or was to be, expected; a result opposite to as if in mockery of the appropriate result; as the *irony* of fate." *Simile* is defined rhetorically as: "A figure of speech by which one thing, action, or relation is likened or explicitly compared in one or more aspects, often with *as* or *like*, to something of different kind or quality; an imaginative comparison ('Errors, like straws, upon the surface flow'; 'Reason is to faith as the eye to the telescope.')."

4

Finally, with respect to definitions, it is commonly said that when you are using metaphors you are telling "stories." The word "story" has its roots in the Latin *historia* or history. Definitions of *story* include: "1. a. An account or recital of some incident or event. b. A report; an account; a statement; as, the man's *story* was not convincing. c. An account of the career of a particular individual, or of the sequential facts in a given case; also, a group of facts, told or untold, having a particular significance in respect of some person or thing, as, the *story* of my life; the *story* of a mine. d. An anecdote, especially an amusing one; as, his speech contained several good *stories*. 2. In literature: a. A narrative in either prose or verse; a tale, especially a fictitious narrative less elaborate than a novel. b. The intrigue or plot. 3. A fib; a lie; a falsehood. 4. Tradition; legend; as, to live a *story*."

In his later years it was said that a significant amount of Milton H. Erickson's teaching was via the telling of stories. He had an enormous fund of these "teaching talks" (Rosen, 1982) and was adept at adapting them to individual clients and audiences. He also did symbolic metaphoric teaching via activities such as taking quite a bit of time and effort to pick up a rock near his wheelchair and to suddenly throw it at someone. The "rock" was a realistically painted piece of Styrofoam. He didn't need to emphasize the message of "things are often not what they appear to be."

1.3 The power of metaphor

I recall a radio interview with Isaac Bashevis Singer, the Nobel Laureate for literature. Singer was asked about his own writing style. In reply, he was essentially critical of "modern" novelists who were too analytical and too much in the heads of their characters. He said that these authors were forever *telling* the reader what was going on in their characters' minds, and also what were their feelings and motivations. Singer said that he was basically a storyteller, and that he let the *stories* of his characters convey what was going on inside of them. So Singer left a great deal up to the imagination of the reader. The making and creating of connections within the reader's/listener's mind is the power of metaphor. The artfully constructed metaphor permits the listener to develop her own unique interpretation. This, then provides an alternate way of perceiving her own reality. Rather than being stuck on one response, the metaphor opens up the possibility of alternate responses, many of which may be more appropriate and healthful.

Combs and Freedman (1990) devote an entire chapter (pp. 27–43) to a "Batesonian Perspective," based on the work of Gregory Bateson (1979). Kopp (1995) writes about Bateson's ideas (pp. 97–9) and builds on them in his Epilogue (pp. 170–3), where he considers that Bateson's ideas serve as a fundamental theoretical basis for the effectiveness of metaphor. Bateson (1979) proposed that mind and nature are unified within a single principle, that of "the pattern that connects." He maintained that *metaphor* is the pattern that connects, i.e. a pattern that characterizes the evolution of all living organisms. Bateson stated that patterns within a person that connect are *first-order connections*; and that *second-order connections* are external, i.e. between people and things. Metaphoric structure identifies the pattern that connects two different things. Kopp (1995, p. 99) states:

> Metaphor, does, in fact, point to a resemblance between two different things. The two things compared in a metaphor *can* be both different *and* similar because their difference and similarity involve different levels of comparison. The fact that a metaphor is false as a *literal* statement does not address or pertain to the way in which it is true as a correspondence of similar pattern or organization.

Kopp also states (1995, p. 99):

> ... the "pattern that connects" is a "nonlinear" resemblance of pattern and organization between two things that are different when considered as discrete entities belonging to two different "linear" logical classes.

Thus, metaphors are characterized by nonlinear causal chains—in other words, the patterns that connect are *not* logical. We close this discussion of Bateson's work with several quotations from Combs and Freedman (1990), with the page citation at the end of each quotation:

• ... Bateson argues persuasively that in mind all is metaphor. (p. 30)

- We can never definitively know anything about external reality. The best we can do is to seek more and more workable metaphors for it … (p. 30)
- … the metaphor is not of the same logical type as the idea it represents. A metaphor can point to an idea, but it can never BE the idea. (p. 31)
- Because metaphor is indirect, multidimensional, and multi-meaningful, it is a communication form that incorporates some randomness. (p. 39)
- … stories are how a mind connects individual bits of data. (p. 42)
- … each person is his own central metaphor. (p. 43, part of "metalogue" written by Mary Catherine, Bateson's daughter)
- … telling stories is a natural technique for evoking resources in clients. (p. 53)
- The indirectness of metaphor allows clients to try out a new perceptual frame without having to decide consciously whether to accept or reject it. (p. 68)

Words, stories, images, imagination, as-if, and dreams allow safe explorations of new ideas, new feelings, new connections, new ways of being in the world. There are fairy tales and fables and myths and heroic journeys in which we can participate vicariously. The magic of all these metaphoric activities lies in the fact that the mind finds it hard to distinguish "reality" from "fantasy." How real is it really? When you imagine *it*, whatever *it* is, *it* takes on its own reality. These ideas, used effectively, can be and are effective change and healing agents.

There is a line in Robert Burns's "To a Louse. On Seeing one on a Lady's Bonnet at Church" that goes:

O wad some Pow'r the giftie gie us
To see oursels as others see us!

To see ourselves as others see us, to step outside our mind/body boundaries, to get perspective, a new vantage point—this is the power of metaphor.

1.4 A brief guide to books on metaphor

There have been quite a variety of books published on metaphor, particularly as applied to its use in psychotherapy. This section is a brief guide to those books with my comments on each. Each book has good things to offer in its own way. Many of these books will be referred to in more detail in later chapters. There is a general reference list at the end of this book. (The following is arranged by date of publication.)

Martin Buber, *Tales of the Hasidim* (1947)
Buber's book begins with (p. 1): "The purpose of this book is to introduce the reader to a world of legendary reality." The Hasidic movement was founded by the Baal Shem Tov (1700–60), and the core of Hasidic teachings is the concept of a life of fervor, or exalted joy. These tales are in two books: those of the early masters followed by those of the later masters. They are full of mysticism, wisdom, and wonder, with a richness of metaphor that is inspirational.

Viktor E. Frankl, *Man's Search for Meaning* (1959, 1962, 1984)
Frankl's remarkable story is not technically *about* metaphor: it *is* a metaphor. It is the story of one man's search for meaning during his time in the Nazi concentration camps of World War II. In fact, the story of the rest of his life (Frankl, 1997; Klingberg, 2001) continued that search. His life and his works have had a profound effect on millions of readers.

Sheldon B. Kopp, *Guru. Metaphors from a Psychotherapist* (1971)
After a general introduction in Part I, Kopp discusses in separate chapters, under the heading "An Enchantment of Metaphors", metaphors from primitive religion, Judaism, Christianity, the Orient, ancient Greece and Rome, the Renaissance, tales for children, science fiction, and the "Now Scene." There are many illustrative metaphors in this erudite book. The perspective is that of becoming a guru via the use of metaphor. Kopp's many books are well worth studying and are rich in the use of metaphor. He was a storyteller. You may particularly enjoy reading *If You Meet the Buddha on the Road, Kill Him!* (1972).

David Gordon, *Therapeutic Metaphors* (1978)
Gordon's book was the first that really popularized the use of therapeutic metaphors. He comes out of an NLP (neuro-linguistic programming) background and the book reflects this. The material on the nature and structure of metaphor is quite good, as are the sections dealing with language usage. There are many illustrative metaphors, a good list of references, but no index. This is the book to read first in a serious study of metaphor.

Sidney Rosen, *My Voice Will Go With You* (1982)
The subtitle of this book is, "The Teaching Tales of Milton H. Erickson." These tales have been edited by Rosen and also have his illuminating commentary. Erickson was a master storyteller and did much of his psychotherapy via these tales. This is a rich source, and will be utilized later in this book. If you are interested in Erickson's work, look at the guide to his complete clinical cases by O'Hanlon and Hexum (1990), which is quite useful.

Stephen R. Lankton and Carol H. Lankton, *The Answer Within* (1983)
The Lanktons did the first careful analysis of multiple embedded metaphors, a complex construction in which several metaphors are built into one consciously designed story for a client. They call this the multiple-embedded-metaphor framework and, "We define framework as an association of one or more related metaphors and bundles of experience that results in specific attitudes and influences perception" (p. 247). Their chapter on this subject (pp. 247–311) discusses the structure and characteristics of this framework, as well as giving several examples.

Lee Wallas, *Stories for the Third Ear. Using Hypnotic Fables in Psychotherapy* (1985)
This collection of stories is based on Erickson's work. There are nineteen elaborate stories, and each is for a particular type of client, such as a paranoid personality, a client with separation-anxiety disorder, and an obese client. There is a foreword by Sidney Rosen.

Philip Barker, *Using Metaphors in Psychotherapy* (1985)
Barker's book is solidly based with many useful case illustrations with suggested metaphors. There are metaphors for developmental problems, conduct disorders, emotional and family problems. There is a useful chapter on the delivery of metaphors.

Joyce C. Mills and Richard J. Crowley, *Therapeutic Metaphors for Children and the Child Within* (1986)
Mills and Crowley's book is specifically written for developing and using metaphors therapeutically with children. To this end there is good background information relevant to child therapy. In Part II they give the basics of this kind of work in a three-level model of communication: (1) storyline; (2) interspersed suggestions; and (3) interweaving. There are case illustrations with metaphors. They include in their Chapter 8 the use of the artistic metaphor, and in Chapter 9 cartoon therapy. A delightful and useful book.

William H. O'Hanlon, *Taproots. Underlying Principles of Milton Erickson's Therapy and Hypnosis* (1987)
This book contains a relatively brief but good description of the use of metaphors from an Ericksonian perspective.

Carol H. Lankton and Stephen R. Lankton, *Tales of Enchantment* (1989)
The subtitle of this book is "Goal-Oriented Metaphors for Adults and Children in Therapy." This is a detailed book about the design and construction of metaphors for particular purposes for each client. They emphasize the importance of gathering sufficient information to build a metaphor as part of a total treatment plan. There are many examples for specific classes of cases, such as metaphors for affect, attitude, behavior, family-structure change, self-image thinking, and children. This book is a valuable resource.

Ronald A. Havens and Catherine Walters, *Hypnotherapy Scripts. A Neo-Ericksonian Approach to Persuasive Healing* (1989)
This book is a collection of hypnotherapy scripts. These scripts are a good model for learning about this type of work. There are complete scripts in various categories, such as affirming the self, alleviating unwarranted fears, developing spontaneity, and improving performance. In addition, there are five "general-purpose" metaphors.

D. Corydon Hammond, *Handbook of Hypnotic Suggestions and Metaphors* (1990)
This edited tome put out by the American Society of Clinical Hypnosis contains almost endless contributions for many conditions on the uses of metaphor and suggestion in the context of a hypnotic session. The contributors are experts in their respective areas and the metaphors are both useful and adaptable.

Michael White and David Epston, *Narrative Means to Therapeutic Ends* (1990)
The jacket blurb for this book states:

> The authors start with the assumption that people experience problems when the stories of their lives, as they or others have invented them, do not sufficiently represent their lived experience. Therapy then becomes a process of storying or re-storying the lives and experiences of these people. In this way narrative comes to play a central role in therapy.

Drawing on the theories of the French philosopher Michel Foucault, they develop their ideas and their system for doing therapy based on the client's story. White and Epston's approach is a significant paradigmatic shift in how therapy is done—more on this later.

Gene Combs and Jill Freedman, *Symbol, Story and Ceremony Using Metaphor in Individual and Family Therapy* (1990)
This important book on metaphor starts with the contributions of Milton H. Erickson to the use of metaphor in clinical practice, and

those of Gregory Bateson to the *theory* of how metaphor works. The Batesonian perspective is particularly clarifying. There is then a systematic approach to the construction of metaphors, as well as the use of symbols and ceremonies in doing therapy. There are many case examples and illustrations.

Lee Wallas, *Stories that Heal. Representing Adult Children of Dysfunctional Families Using Hypnotic Stories in Psychotherapy* (1991)
This is a continuation of the style of stories in her preceding book, but now keyed to developmental stages, such as normal autistic phase, separation and individuation, Oedipal phase, puberty etc. The emphasis of the stories is on reparenting.

Richard R. Kopp, *Metaphor Therapy. Using Client-Generated Metaphors in Psychotherapy* (1995)
In my readings about the use of metaphor in psychotherapy and healing I found this book to be the most significant since it turned my thinking around 180 degrees with respect to how to use metaphor therapeutically. All of the other books cited in this section are about how the therapist can construct metaphors to deliver to a client. Of course, this is based on client-supplied information, and is tailored to that particular person. Kopp listens for the metaphors that a client relates about her own life, and then simply suggests that she can change that metaphor to get what she wants. So, this is working *within* the client's own story or stories. Kopp also gives details about how to similarly use metaphoric memories. There are many examples. Kopp's approaches will be given much room later in this book (see Chapter 7). There is a connection to narrative therapy.

Henry T. Close, *Metaphor in Psychotherapy. Clinical Applications of Stories and Allegories* (1998)
Close's book has many illustrative metaphors for particular cases. They are quite cleverly constructed. Since he is an ordained minister, there is a distinct religious slant to some of the metaphors.

George W. Burns, *Nature-Guided Therapy* (1998)
Burns has integrated nature as a psychotherapeutic and healing metaphor into his practice. He also calls his approach "ecopsychotherapy." Via a "Sensory Awareness Inventory" and specific assignments involving interactions with nature he has added an extra dimension to this work.

Rubin Battino and Thomas L. South, *Ericksonian Approaches: A Comprehensive Manual* (1999)
These authors present two chapters on basic and advanced metaphors (with illustrations) from an Ericksonian perspective. Some of the metaphors are on an accompanying audiotape.

Michael Berman and David Brown, *The Power of Metaphor. Story Telling and Guided Journeys for Teachers, Trainers and Therapists* (2000)
This is an excellent source of metaphors that have been developed from a shamanic perspective and background. If that is your interest, this is a useful book.

Rubin Battino, *Guided Imagery and Other Approaches to Healing* (2000)
The stories told in a guided-imagery session are metaphors for healing. This book is a systematic development of guided imagery and contains many illustrations. The audiotapes accompanying this book are useful not only for the content, but as a guide to delivery.

There is no listing of relevant websites—if you wish to explore the Internet for information on metaphor, a search engine will produce many, many "hits."

1.5 Varieties of metaphors

The previous section was a brief guide to books on the subject of metaphor. There are also many articles on the subject, which means that there is a great variety of metaphors, how to construct them, and how to use them for different purposes. Within this book metaphors will be explored for psychotherapy, for helping people with mental or psychological concerns, and for healing. The emphasis in almost all of the cited books is for the use of metaphors for psychotherapy.

Before touching on the use of metaphor for healing it is useful to make a few distinctions. The word "disease" applies to a physical ailment or condition such as a broken bone, an infection, or a cancer. Diseases can be "cured," that is, broken bones can be set, infections can be treated with antibiotics, and cancers can go into remission or disappear via the use of surgery, radiation, and chemotherapy. An *illness* has to do with the *meaning* you give to your disease. Thus, an illness is how you *feel* about the disease, and this is controlled by your upbringing, your social group, your family, and your religious and spiritual beliefs. Illnesses are *healed*, where the healing applies to understanding, accepting, or being comfortable with the physical disease. You can continue to "fight" the physical manifestations of the disease while you are at peace with yourself and in balance or harmony with your life. You would then be working in a partnership with your body and your beliefs, rather than in some adversarial mode. It is not uncommon that healing is accompanied by a physical improvement.

The use of metaphor for healing has been in use from early times in tribal stories and shamanic rituals. It has been said that the history of medicine until about the 1950s, with the advent of controlled and double-blind studies, is the history of the placebo effect. A neutral or known ineffective substance or treatment is given to a patient with the suggestion (implied or direct) that she will be helped, and she is helped remarkably frequently. In fact, one of the purposes of a double-blind study is to separate the placebo effect from the intervention effect—how much is due to each? The placebo effect typically is in the 30 to 70 percent effectiveness range. The level of belief and conviction of the deliverer of the placebo is directly connected with its effectiveness. The placebo can then be considered to be a metaphor for the healing connection. (See Battino, 2000, for the connection between the placebo effect and guided imagery for healing.)

Guided-imagery work uses "images" for healing—these are *personal metaphors* developed in conjunction with the client. The healing agent may be some fierce predator (all of this within the mind) that seeks out and destroys cancer cells; it can also be a personal angel who gently persuades with loving kindness the cancer cells to leave the body; a marching band may surround and escort the cancer cells away; or a wise "helper" may teach the immune system how to function more effectively. These are all healing metaphors.

Art and movement therapies use visual and physical metaphors to help clients. The play therapy done with children is essentially metaphoric, as is the acting in psychodrama. Group therapy may even be considered to be metaphoric. In fact, we can consider to be metaphoric any therapeutic approach in which the client goes within her own mind and gets involved in the "as-if" game. Can this also be said of the transformative powers of theater, movies, opera, poetry, and books? Yes.

1.6 Metaphors for learning and exploration

This section contains three of Erickson's teaching tales taken from Rosen (1982) with a page citation at the end of each. Then there will be one of my stories, followed by some brief concluding comments.

Learning To Stand Up

We learn so much at a conscious level and then forget what we learn and use the skill. You see, I had a terrific advantage over others. I had polio, and I was totally paralyzed, and the inflammation was so great that I had a sensory paralysis too. I could move my eyes and my hearing was undisturbed. I got very lonesome lying in bed, unable to move anything except my eyeballs. I was quarantined on the farm with seven sisters, one brother, two parents, and a practical nurse. And how could I entertain myself? I started watching people and my environment. I soon learned that my sisters could say "no" when they meant "yes." And they could say "yes" and mean "no" at the same time. They could offer another sister an apple and hold it back. And I began studying nonverbal language and body language.

I had a baby sister who had begun to learn to creep. *I* would have to learn to stand up and walk. And you can imagine the intensity with which I watched as my baby sister grew from creeping to learning how to stand up. And you don't know how *you* learned how to stand up. You don't even know how you walked. You can *think* that you can walk in a straight line six blocks—with no pedestrian or vehicular traffic. You don't know that you *couldn't* walk in a straight line at a steady pace!

You don't know what you do when you walk. You don't know how you learned to stand up. You learned by reaching up your hand and pulling yourself up. That put pressure on your hands—and, by accident, you discovered that you could put weight on your *feet*. That's an awfully complicated thing because your knees would give way—and, when your knees would keep straight, your hips would give way. Then you got your feet crossed. And you couldn't stand up because both your knees and your hips would give way. Your feet were crossed—and you soon learned to get a wide brace—and you pull yourself up and you have the job of learning how to keep your knees straight—one at a time and as soon as you learn that, you have to learn how to give your attention to keep your hips straight. Then you found out that you had to learn to give your attention to keep your hips straight and knees straight at the same time *and* feet far apart! Now finally you could stand having your feet far apart, resting on your hands.

Then came the lesson in three stages. You distribute your weight on your one hand and your two feet, this hand not supporting you at all [E. raises his left hand]. Honestly hard work—allowing you to learn to stand up straight, your hips straight, knees straight, feet far apart, this hand [right hand] pressing down hard. Then you discover how to alter your body balance. You alter your body balance by turning your head, turning your body. You have to learn to coordinate all alterations of your body balance when you move your hand, your head, your shoulder, your body—and then you have to learn it all over again with the other hand. Then comes the terribly hard job of learning to have *both* hands up and moving your hands in all directions and to depend upon the two solid bases of your feet, far apart. And keeping your hips straight—your knees straight and keeping your mind's attention so divided that you can attend to your knees, your hips, your left arm, your right arm, your head, your body. And finally, when you had enough skill, you tried balancing on one foot. That was a hell of a job!

How do you hold your entire body keeping your hips straight, your knees straight and feeling hand movement, head movement, body movement? And then you put your one foot ahead and alter your body's center of gravity! Your knees bent—and you sat down! You got up again and tried it again. Finally you learned how to move one foot ahead and took a step and it seemed to be good. So you repeated it—it seemed so good. Then the third step—with the same foot—and you toppled! It took you a long time to alternate right left, right left, right left. Now you could swing your arms, turn your head, look right and left, and walk along, never paying a bit of attention to keeping your knees straight, hips straight. [pp. 47–9]

He Will Talk

A lot of people were worried because I was four years old and didn't talk, and I had a sister two years younger than me who talked, and she is still talking but she hasn't said anything. And many people got distressed because I was a four-year-old boy who couldn't talk.

My mother said, comfortably, "When the time arrives, then he will talk." [pp. 58–9]

Swimming

Learning by experience is much more educational than learning consciously. You can learn all the movements of swimming while you're lying on your belly on a piano stool. You can establish your rhythms, breathing, head movement, arm movements, feet movements, and so on. When you get into the water, you only know how to dog paddle. You have to learn to swim in the water. And when you have learned that, you have got a learning.

Learning experientially is the most important thing. Now, we have all learned while we are going to school that we should learn consciously. You did things unconsciously, in relationship to the water.

17

And you learned to roll your head, paddle with your hands, and kick with your feet in a certain rhythm—in relationship to the water. And any of you who are not swimmers don't know, can't describe to me, the feeling of your feet in water, the feeling of water on your hands, the suction of the water as you turn your body right and left in the Australian crawl, for example.

When you swim on your back you know about this. How much attention do you pay to the spring of the water under your back as you swim backwards? If you have ever gone skinny-dipping, you will find out what a horrible drag a bathing suit is. The water skips over your skin so much more easily when you are in the nude. And the swimming suit is definitely a handicap.

I am not concerned with how much any of you learn about hypnosis here in this room, because all of you know, from time to time—in that neither-here-nor-there period, when you are not asleep and not awake—you learn a whole lot, in that hypnagogic state, about hypnosis. I used to like to awaken in the morning, have my feet hit the floor as I opened my eyes, and my wife always liked to take fifteen to twenty minutes to wake up slowly, gradually. My blood supply goes instantly to my head. Her blood supply goes very slowly. We all have our own individual patterns. How many times do you have to go into a trance, maybe a dozen times, until you lose interest in watching the experience yourself?

Have you ever taken a swim in the Great Salt Lake? It looks like water, and feels like water. I knew ahead of time that I couldn't swim in it. I wondered what would happen if I tried to swim. I had all the understanding of the lake being supersaturated salt water. But I had to have the experience of trying to swim before I could figure out what would happen to a swimmer who tried to swim. And most hypnotic subjects want to understand as they experience. Keep the experience separate. Just let things happen. [pp. 163–4]

Learning to Write

One of the joys of being a grandparent is to be able to re-live those great adventures of childhood that we all passed through without being aware of the incredible things we were learning. How did we master the complex coordination needed to be able to crawl, to pull one's self up, to stand, to fall, to walk? One step at a time, one teeter, one adjusting of the tension in this muscle and that one. A step or two towards mommy, five steps to daddy and being lifted into the air, laughing, smiling, with that special baby giggle. Then, just walking, and running, and climbing, and standing on your head looking between your legs. How did that all happen, all that complicated coordinated movement? And, watching a grandchild grow is reliving, one muscle, one step, one fall at a time.

I am writing this now, ink flowing from a pen, arm moving, wrist, fingers moving these, oh, so precise ways, forming letters, words, sentences. And, can you remember what letter you wrote first? Was it an A with its two straight lines touching and a bar across the middle? Sort of like two poles touching. Or was it an H with the two parallel (more or less!) vertical lines and the bar connecting? O's were sort of easy to draw—just a circle. Was it flat on one side or more oval in shape? And the letters were big, and the lines scraggly and uneven. Yes, that is an A, and that is an O, and that is an E. T's were quite easy to draw—just a line with a hat.

Slowly differentiating, learning the names of each letter, recognizing them in books. Just one letter at a time. And when did you start putting the letters together, to make words? Recognizing that group of letters as CAT or HAT. The real thrill was having someone write your name—DAVID or BOB or ELLEN or JANE. Those marks are me! What excitement. Lines on a piece of paper are you. Other lines are animals and people and objects like trees and balls. Do you recall at all the magic of writing, of words on paper that were the same (or were they?) with the images in your head, the objects you played with, the people you knew?

Words are magic, and isn't magic using special words like "abracadabra" to do extraordinary things? The magic is that the words on the page, the words in your head, connect you to the real things out there. The words are how you know.

And, there are words for feelings and states. "Mama" is a person, "No" is quite different. "I hurt" is different again. Slowly, slowly, words become more than the representation, the connection, to things. Words are also feelings—happy, sad, hungry, cold, warm, loved.

Words are what and who we are, or are they? The metaphor of metaphors. And, how much have you learned today?

Words, words, words, and the images they call to mind. Metaphors all. This chapter ends with a special metaphor, stated by Jean Valjean at the end of his life in the musical *Les Misérables*. He said: "To love another person is to see the face of God."

Chapter 2

Language for Metaphor

2.1 Introduction

Metaphors are stories and stories are words strung together in grammatical patterns. Is there a specific language for metaphor? If there is, it is poetry, since the power of a story is enhanced by the use of poetic language. Indeed, many of our classical epics are narrative poems, and much of our religious writings are also poetic. If this chapter is about language usage for metaphor, then it follows that the chapter should be about writing poetry. The metaphors in the books cited in the previous chapter are more prosaic, as is almost all metaphoric usage in therapeutic and healing sessions. So we, too, will be concerned with prose in this chapter, although some space will be devoted to poetry.

Since there is so much in common between hypnosis, guided imagery, and metaphor, it makes sense for the serious student of metaphor to obtain training in hypnosis. Within the United States the three most reputable sources of training in hypnosis (in the author's judgment) are: (1) the Milton H. Erickson Foundation, Inc. (3606 North 24th Street, Phoenix, AZ 85016-6500; (602) 956-6196); (2) institutes affiliated with the Milton H. Erickson Foundation—write or phone the Foundation for a list; and (3) the American Society of Clinical Hypnosis (2200 East Devon Avenue, Suite 291, Des Plaines, IL 60018-4534; (312) 645-9810).

Chapter 5 on "Language Forms" in Battino and South (1999) is an excellent resource for learning about language usage for hypnosis. There is a shorter version of this chapter (see Chapter 7, "Language for Guided Imagery") in the author's book on guided imagery (Battino, 2000). This chapter is adapted (with permission) from the latter book, but with an emphasis on language specifically for metaphor. Of course, another way to prepare to become a metaphorist (made-up word—these can be used for special effect to surprise, confuse, or extend) is to take courses in short-story and poetry writing. Both can be helpful and are useful disciplines. There are also storyteller groups and courses/workshops.

Metaphors are generally of two types: general or generic ones that any audience would find useful or entertaining; and specific ones that are designed for a particular purpose for an individual (or couple or family or group). Hypnotic language forms are of more use for the former group since the language is deliberately vague. For a particular person you use story elements and language that are unique to that person—the story is for him. This does not mean that artfully vague language cannot be used in specific ways. An example involving relaxation can help here. If walking in the woods is a particularly relaxing experience (or image) for you, then you would be tempted to use this as a way to get your client into a relaxed and recipient state. But what if your client was raised in the city and had no sense of the woods as being safe and peaceful? Or your client may have had a traumatic experience in the woods as a child, such as getting lost or being assaulted. The woods, then, would be wonderfully relaxing for you, but frightening for your client. If at all possible, the metaphor needs to be client-specific. In fact, it is best to elicit and use the client's own metaphor for relaxation, and his own words.

Since it may be difficult at times to elicit sufficient specific information from a client about what works for him, the artful use of indirect language is necessary. Language for metaphor for a general audience needs to be open, vague, and permissive. This chapter will explore systematically the structure of such language. In large part this style of language usage was popularized by Milton H. Erickson, M.D., through his use of indirect language for hypnosis. It has been said that Erickson was a master of the *precise* use of *vague* language. We especially emphasize both "precise" and "vague" in this description. By precise we mean *conscious* choice of the exact word(s) for a particular purpose. But the words are vague in the sense of comparing "going for a walk in the woods" to "going somewhere that is safe for you." The word "somewhere" is open and vague and the listener creates or finds that place. I have a sense of what "safe" means to me, but your idea of safety is unique to you and your experience.

Another way to examine these ideas is to use the transformational-grammar concepts of surface and deep structures. As a class exercise we state, "Jo(e) hurt me," and after the students have considered their reaction to this sentence for one minute, we ask them: (1) Is Jo(e) male or female? (2) Is the "hurt" physical or mental? (3) What is the relationship (husband, wife, significant other, relative) between Jo(e) and "me"? (4) Who is "me"? The sentence "Jo(e) hurt me" is an example of a *surface structure* that contains only the partial meaning of the communication. The full linguistic meaning is in the *deep structure* and may be a sentence such as, "My husband Joe hurt me by holding onto my left arm very tightly." This sentence is more specific and detailed and could probably be made even more complete. Yet the *real* meaning (internal reality) for this woman is well beyond the deep-structure sentence, since it incorporates (a) her physical sensations, (b) her memories of other similar incidents of hard contact, (c) her memories of related incidents, (d) the words that she uses to describe the experience to herself, and (e) her entire life's experiences and memories to that point in time.

When we attempt accurate communication using language, we can at best use deep structures. The implied "but" here is that even deep structures are only an approximation of the real meaning to the listener. In fact, *the meaning of any communication is the response that you get*. It is the nature of language that you can only hope that the response is connected to your intention in the communication. How many times have you been misunderstood or had to repeat yourself, particularly when you thought you were being very clear?

Fortunately, good metaphoric language is more often surface structure rather than deep structure. When you are designing a metaphor for a particular person, you specifically incorporate their words and phrases and images into your delivery. If they are known, you also use words that are part of their *representational system*, i.e. whether their way of being in the world can be described as primarily visual, auditory, or kinesthetic.

Another way of emphasizing the importance of vague language is to consider the differences in your experiences of reading a novel, listening to it on audiotape, or seeing/hearing it as a movie. How many times has a movie made from a favorite book disappointed you because they didn't get the characters or the scenes just "right," i.e. the way that you pictured the scene in your mind, and heard the dialogue in your mind? Good novels and short stories are successful because they provide only sufficient information for you to fill in the details.

There are three more common mistakes in *general-audience* guided imagery, or guided metaphor, or metaphoric helping audiotapes. A good tape is usually built around just one image. Poor tapes use too many ideas and images. After all, if fifteen minutes is a good length for a session, there just is not sufficient time to develop more than one image. A related idea is that most deliverers talk too much and too continuously. (This is also a common problem with neophyte hypnotherapists.) The listener needs time to develop his image and a response. In transformational grammar the search for response and meaning is called a *transderivational search*. Effective tapes and deliveries incorporate both short and long pauses. The last common mistake is to incorporate music into the tape—the music may be too loud and intrusive, and it may be of a style and from a period that is foreign to the client. Tastes in music differ so much that it is best to leave the music out. If music is important for your client, then he can play his own special music in the background using separate equipment. It is my practice to not use music. (I know that some effective and respected designers of tapes feel rather strongly about the incorporation of music. In fact, Belleruth Naparstek uses a composer who composes music specifically for each of her tapes.)

Practitioners of neuro-linguistic programming (NLP) have contributed much to the systematic study of language. Some accessible NLP sources are Lewis and Pucelik (1982) and McLauchlin (1992). For a more linguistically oriented approach read Bandler and Grinder (1975) and Grinder and Bandler (1976). A recent comprehensive book on NLP by Bodenhamer and Hall (1999) has excellent extended material on the NLP language model (Part II, pp. 135–243), including material on hypnotic language forms, as well as story, metaphor, and analogy.

2.2 *Delivery*

The effective delivery of guided imagery goes beyond the rapport-building skills discussed in the next chapter, but necessarily builds on those skills. For effective communication, insofar as possible, you still need to speak your clients' language the way that they do—this is pacing. It always helps to incorporate particular words or phrases that they use (but beware of exact mimicry). Your session notes should record idiosyncratic language usage for future utilization. When you are starting out in this field, it really helps to listen to many different people to develop a sense of how they deliver their material. In fact, in the initial stages you may wish to copy the delivery style of someone you particularly like. When I was learning how to do hypnosis in the Milton Erickson style, I consciously copied many of his mannerisms to later adapt them to my own style. It is also the case that students in my workshops tend to mimic my style initially—there is nothing wrong with learning in this way. (This is a problem only if you stay stuck in someone else's style.)

It certainly helps to have experience on the stage or in front of students to sharpen your speaking/acting skills—I have been fortunate to have a background as a professor of chemistry and many years in community theater. For example, actors and actresses have long known the value of the dramatic pause. Timing is central to all comedic routines: just think of the way that Cary Grant used pauses and double-takes in *Arsenic and Old Lace*. Pauses are a way of … adding … emphasis … to words … and phrases. Read the previous sentence aloud with and without the pauses indicated by the ellipses, and play with varying the length of each pause. We earlier mentioned the concept of a transderivational search wherein you search internally to find the deep structure for your own meaning or interpretation of a particular word or phrase. Pauses allow the client time to carry out such transderivational searches. The most common problem in delivery with neophytes in metaphor and guided imagery and hypnosis is that they talk non-stop. It's almost as if they were afraid to give up control or direction or lose their train of thought. If you err at all, then do it on the side of more and longer pauses. Again, the client's *internal* work is what is important in the use of metaphors—give him the *time* to develop his own responses.

When you develop a metaphor script, it is important to mark by underscoring or capitalization or boldface the words and phrases you wish to emphasize in your delivery. In fact, it would be useful to have two or three levels of emphasis. In the delivery itself, particular words or phrases are marked by loudness or softness of delivery, speed of speaking, adding a musical quality, pauses, and intonation. How many interpretations can a good actor give to Hamlet's "To be or not to be?"? This is the art of delivery. If your client's eyes are open and he is looking at you, then body language can be used for marking. Dragging out a word can mark it: yessss … The human ear is sensitive to the source of a sound, so you can use *voice locus* for marking. With practice, you can even "pitch" or "throw" your voice in a particular direction. Certainly, you could also shift your head position. Within limits, using slang, an accent, and ungrammatical usage can also mark words and phrases. Puns and rhymes and homonyms and well-known quotes and confusion can all be used for marking.

In the interspersal technique you weave especially significant words and phrases into your conversational flow as a way of marking them. In some way, these interspersed words and phrases seem to slide right by the conscious mind, but are heard by the unconscious or inner mind since they are different, out of context, or out of the ordinary. And how surprised will you be about the changes that have already occurred?

Analogical marking uses nonverbals to mark out particular words and phrases as separate messages. If your client has his eyes open, you can use natural movements, such as head nods or tilts or other body movements to mark. A movement like a head nod can be associated with a word like "comfort" to anchor it. If eyes are closed, then this is done using voice dynamics.

Quotes are a useful way to add emphasis as in, "My minister once said, 'God is always with you.'" I particularly like to quote Jean Valjean in the musical *Les Misérables* as saying, "To love another person is to see the face of God." I also like to quote the psychologist Wyschogrod, who said, "Life poses a peculiar problem—to become who you are."

Suggestions and presuppositions can be embedded within questions. (More will be written later in this chapter about the importance of presuppositions, which imply the existence of some state or feeling.) Some examples are:

"Just how comfortable are you, now?"

"And this, too, will pass, will it not?"

"What haven't you done yet that you can do?"

"And, just being relaxed ..."

It is, of course, important to be congruent in your delivery. The word "fast" is spoken quickly, the word "soft" softly, the phrase "and you can sense that ..." with conviction, and "I believe in miracles" in a way that conveys your deep inner commitment. If you do not believe what you say, will your client believe or be helped? (As a point of irreverence here, I quote Flanders and Swann from their song "The Reluctant Cannibal," who said: "Always be sincere—whether you mean it or not!" As another aside, the interesting thing about flattery is that it appears to make people feel good, even when they are doubting the speaker! The readers of this book are a select and wonderful group ...)

2.3 Words

In terms of impact some words are "more equal" than others. This section presents classes of such words. (Again, much is owed to NLP for this organization.)

a. Nominalization

When a verb or "action" word is converted into a noun or "static" word, this is a nominalization. Consider the difference between "I am a cancer victim" and "Cancer is victimizing me." Also, "I am depressed" or "I am in depression" versus "I wonder what is depressing me." Nominalizations seem to be cast in concrete, and when you think of yourself in nominalizations the situation appears hopeless.

Bernie Siegel's statement, "Cancer is not a sentence, it is just a word" denominalizes "cancer" within the context of word play. Since depression is a common concomitant of life-challenging diseases, it is important to denomalize this state by saying "I wonder how you are (have been) depressing yourself." The denominalization opens the possibility of change. Denominalization involves converting a noun into a verb.

b. Unspecified verbs

In a sense, no verb is completely specified in terms of an action. There are particular verbs that are sufficiently vague to be useful. Some of these are: know, learn, understand, feel, change, wonder, do, think, and fix. The listener fills in the specifics. Some examples are:

"And you may wonder just how much you can learn."

"Change is easier to do than you think."

"Just in what specific ways will that be fixed?"

"And you can feel the change starting."

"The body knows just how to do that."

Some of these sentences use an unspecified referential index in words like that, how, learn, know, body etc. That is, these words do not have a specific reference. A good example is the word "it" as in, "It really will help."

c. Causal connections

These constructions exist in compound sentences where a connection is implied or stated between one thing and another. There are three levels of connection. The weakest is using the word "and" as in:

"You are paying attention to your breathing, and becoming even more comfortable."

The next strongest linkage uses words related to time, such as, while, during, as, when, and soon:

"As you pay attention to your breathing, you become more comfortable."

"Soon your breathing will slow down, while you relax even more."

The strongest level of causal connection uses real causal words— makes, causes, forces, and requires:

"As your breathing slows, it makes you calmer."

"While you pay attention to that spot on the wall, it makes your eyes blink more."

Start these causal connections with something that is already going on like sitting, blinking, or breathing, and then connect that to another condition. (This is an example of pacing and leading.)

d. Mind-reading

This is a form of pacing and leading that involves some guesswork based on reading body language, plus concentrated listening:

"I wonder what you are hearing/feeling/saying to yourself now."

"You are probably feeling a little nervous/scared/anxious/tense right now."

e. Lost performative

Evaluative statements are made in this speech pattern, but it is not known who makes the statement. The favorite generalization is "it":

"It's not important just how fast you relax."

"It is good to be at peace with yourself."

f. Modal operators of necessity

These words imply particular actions and lack of choice. Here are some of them: will/won't, can/can't, should, have to, must, no one, and necessary. One of Loretta LaRoche's favorite admonitions is, "Don't should on yourself!" She also refers to people who are "must-erbators":

"And, you should do that, shouldn't you?"

"You must never give in/give up hope/cry/be weak/trust people ..."

These words tend to be an inheritance from our upbringing, can be part of the unfinished business or "garbage" in our lives, and can be successfully challenged—many people are just not aware of how much control the "shoulds" have over their lives.

g. Transitional words

These are words that connect or link: *and, as, while,* because, become, could, but, might, makes, may, causes, wonder, if, then, what, how, beginning, will, allow, and when. The first three are italicized since they are the ones you will use most frequently. You generally start with a truism—something the person can't deny— and then bridge to an action or thought you wish to occur. Examples are:

"And, as you pay attention to your breathing, your eyes can softly close/you become more relaxed/you become calmer/your breathing softens."

"As you sense the way that your chair supports you, and as you are aware how your feet touch the floor, you relax even more."

"While you pay attention to the sounds of the air conditioning, your breathing becomes deeper and more regular."

"While one part of your mind is busy analyzing this, the other inner part of your mind is peaceful and calm."

h. Meaningful words

These words mean nothing in themselves, but are powerfully vague in leading people into doing inner searches. Here are some meaningful words: hopes, dreams, talents, resources, sensations, memories, thoughts, beliefs, unconscious, inner mind, love, learning, loving, genuine, really, try, and yet. These wonderfully vague words can be deliberately inserted into your metaphor since they allow your listeners to fill in their "real" meaning to themselves. The word " try" is a special case since it implies *not* succeeding:

"Just try harder, won't you?"

"Please try to be calmer."

Use "try" consciously. Some examples of using meaningful words are:

"Try doing that, now, but don't change yet."

"Dreams can be so helpful."

"Your unconscious mind really knows how much you are learning."

"Pleasant memories are a wonderful resource."

"And how much have you learned from your hopes and dreams?"

"Deep beliefs are so sustaining."

i. "Or" and the illusion of choice

The word "or" presupposes the occurrence of one or more events:

"You can close your eyes now *or* in a few moments."

"I don't know whether you will be more relaxed now *or* in a minute or two, as you continue to breathe calmly."

"Your head can stay still *or* move to either side or back and forth."

There appears to be a choice, but some action is presupposed.

j. Awareness predicates

Words such as know, realize, notice, aware, find, and understand presuppose the rest of the sentence. Their use reduces to *whether* the listener is aware of the point you are now making. Examples:

"And you are aware now of noticing those changes."

"You really know, you realize, just how relaxed you are now."

"Did you understand all of what has already happened for you?"

These awareness predicates bring the communication to the point of whether your client is aware of the message(s) in the sentence.

k. Adverbs and adjectives

These can be used to presuppose a major clause within a sentence. Some choices are deeply, readily, easily, curious, happily, and simply:

"Have you wondered how easily this happened?"

"Just simply, easily, deeply, relaxing ..."

"How curious are you about the changes that are happening so easily?"

l. *Commentary adverbs and adjectives*

These are related to (k), but presuppose everything after the first word. Some good ones are innocently, happily, luckily, necessarily, usefully, fortunately, and curiously:

"Happily, relaxing is easy."

"Fortunately, your innermost thoughts are yours alone."

"Necessarily, people do change and change is the order of life."

"Usefully, you've already learned how to relax deeply."

m. *Now*

Although this word can be overused, the immediacy of its meaning makes it potent. You may have already noticed how frequently "now" has been used in examples. Generally, its use is more effective following or preceding a pause: "And ... now ... just relaxing even more." A more complete example to make this point, now, is: "And you can know, now, how to use this word, now, in the middle of a sentence for emphasis, or at the end for definitive action, now." To paraphrase Alexander Lowen, "To know your mind, you need to mind your no, ... now."

n. *That's right*

This was a favorite phrase of Milton Erickson's and it peppered much of his trance work—that's right, isn't it? "That" is an ambiguous word with many possible referents in a given sentence—it can mean almost anything. That's right, yes it is. Be cautious in its use, yet you'll find yourself frequently using it ...

2.4 Suggestions, implications, and presuppositions

The relaxed state, like the hypnotic trance, is a highly suggestible state, and clients are more open to suggestions at that time. It is even presumed by some that communications to a relaxed person bypass the conscious mind and are "heard" by the inner or unconscious mind. This means that your words take on extra meaning, must be chosen carefully, and with conscious intent. Also, the unconscious mind tends to interpret words *literally* as in thinking of a "rest room" as a place to rest.

a. Suggestions

Suggestions may be delivered to a relaxed person directly or indirectly. Contrast the following two sentences:

"Close your eyes and relax."

"And, breathing softly and easily, calmly, becoming even more comfortable."

Ericksonian hypnotherapists tend to use indirection more than direction, finding it effective and gentle and respectful. Yet you always need to know your client and adapt your language appropriately. (It should be noted that Erickson himself could be rather forceful and direct on occasion.)

Contingent suggestions imply a causal connection. "The more you pay attention to your breathing, the more relaxed you will become." At some point the listener makes the connection between the two ideas, and then acts as if the second statement were true. This has the form of "when this ... then that."

Open-ended suggestions are those that emphasize choice and are deliberately vague. (Recall that a major difficulty with many metaphors is that they are too specific.) Open-ended suggestions are like master keys that can open many doors.

"And, I don't know just when, or whether, your eyes will comfortably close, and you'll…"

"Within your mind, now, you can safely drift off to your special place."

"And, you don't need to know how those cancer cells are being eliminated, just sense their departure."

"Your immune system will pick just the best and most efficient way to destroy those weak and aberrant cells."

With respect to indirect suggestions we can quote Erickson, Rossi and Rossi (1976, p. 269):

> With indirect suggestions, however, subjects usually do not recognize the relation between the suggestion and their own response. There thus can be no questions of voluntary compliance with the therapist's suggestion. If a response does take place, then it has been mediated by involuntary processes outside of a subject's immediate range of awareness. This involuntary mediation of responses is what we use to define the genuineness of trance behavior.

b. Implications

Again, let us quote from Erickson, Rossi, and Rossi (1976, p. 59) before giving some examples:

> For Erickson, psychological implication is a key that automatically turns the tumblers of a patient's associative processes into predictable patterns without awareness of how it happened. The implied thought or response seems to come up automatically within patients, as if it were their own inner response rather than a suggestion initiated by the therapist. Psychological implication is thus a way of structuring and directing patients' associative processes when they cannot do it for themselves.

"If you sit down, then you can relax."

"When you take few deep breaths and let your eyes defocus, you will be even calmer."

"Before you start relaxing, you ought to be comfortable."

"I don't know just how, or how fast, your healing will occur."

The implication is generally made up of three parts: (1) a time-binding introduction of some kind; (2) the implied/assumed/intimated/hinted suggestion; and (3) some sort of behavioral response to signal when the implication has been accomplished.

c. Presuppositions

O'Hanlon (1987) has defined a presupposition as "... the use of language, actions, and situations that necessarily involve certain antecedents or consequences." O'Hanlon (1987) also states, "Presupposition is a form of language in which certain ideas or experiences are presumed without ever being directly stated." The power of presuppositions is that they cannot be ignored and—if used correctly—create expectations for change that are outside or beyond the conscious mind. (See Battino and South (1999) for an extended treatment on the use of presuppositions.) Study the following examples for what is presupposed:

"Gloria had a good day."

"I liked the way you did that."

"Doctors can be very helpful."

"If you meditate every day, you will be helped."

"When she takes a nap in the afternoon, she feels better."

"When you eat properly, too, you are more comfortable."

"Fortunately, you have a good medical team/family support/group of friends."

"Where is the heating pad?"

"That wasn't the last bottle of pills, was it?"

"Just how much change/healing/comfort/learning is possible?"

d. Overloading

A speech pattern using lots of "ands" linking together many items has as its goal the overloading of the conscious and/or unconscious mind to ease into another state. "As you sit there and pay attention to your breathing and listen to the clock and feel the support of your chair and move a little when you need to and let your eyes defocus and observe passing thoughts, how soon will you be deeply, deeply relaxed?" You just stack one set of realities/truisms on another until the mind just gives up and heeds the last suggestion.

e. Nongrammatical language

Since the human mind automatically fills in missing elements or gaps in speech and visual images, you can use this idea to confuse, disorient, embed messages etc. This work must be subtly done. Examples follow:

"Being is or was, soon, and now ... change."

"Before you relax even more ... during ... while these thoughts ... helpful ... friendly ... aren't they not now ... but then ... for you ...."

"Ain't just ain't the way to get now what you want for yourself ... it ain't ... is."

"And, you do not know, no you do not, exact how to change/heal/learn/get what you want, but, ... when but?"

"The moving finger is right as it writes in your rite, right? As you changed/found/got/discovered, and that is no right, or it is, yes?"

"By the dawn's beginning to sense those changes have changed what is to what was, but when and how soon is the past with all of this deep as a well behind you?"

You can certainly have fun with these nongrammatical change statements. They are effective, as Gilligan (1987, p. 244) states:

> ... non sequiturs will have maximum hypnotic effect [read: metaphoric effect] when (1) they are delivered meaningfully (2) by a speaker assumed and expected to speak rationally and relevantly (3) in a context where the listener trusts the integrity of the speaker.

The "shock" value of these statements means that they have to be used sparingly.

f. Language involving time

Consider the following sentence:

> As you change, now, thinking about all of the new things you've already learned about yourself, then, and how, will you have already begun your healing process, even while you continue to progress even more, now?

Using time-related words and grammatical tense to confuse and presuppose that what you want has already occurred and all you need to do is discover and ratify it, or continue the already ongoing processes, is the power of this style. The use of time-related language takes practice.

2.5 Negation

As you read this, close your eyes if you will, and do not think about a pink polka-dotted zebra ... Human brains are wired such that you first have to create an image of the pink polka-dotted zebra before you can blank out that picture and, even then, the blanking out may not be perfect. Grinder and Bandler (1981, p. 67) state, "No single pattern that I know of gets in the way of communication more often than using negation. *Negation only exists in language* and does not exist in experience." (Emphasis in original.) And, you will now learn how to use negation, will you not?

a. Double negatives and tag questions

Double negatives generally require a pause for processing before it is understood that an affirmative is intended, and there are residuals of one of the negatives as the other is not heard. "Don't stop doing …" "This is not never going to happen." "When you do not know what you really know, change can happen rapidly." "Do not not be careful in using a 'no' to be a 'not'." This last sentence also plays on confusion generated by the homonyms of "no" and "know," and "not" and "knot".

Tag questions, at the end of a sentence, reinforce what came before, even if the tag is a negation.

"And you can, can you not?"

"And you will, won't you?"

"You won't do it until your inner self is ready, will you not?"

"And, you really do not know how fast you will, do you?"

"You probably cannot get yourself fully comfortable, can you?"

"It is all right to relax, is it not?"

"And how has that healing process started already, has it not?"

Practice, practice, practice, will you not?

Milton Erickson liked to establish rapport and minimize resistance in the first session by saying at an appropriate time, "Please be sure to not tell me anything that you do not wish to tell me." This is an elegant way to reassure a client, even though the embedded message is, "You can tell me anything—the choice is yours."

b. *Apposition of opposites*

This consists of two opposing concepts or experiences that are juxtaposed within the same sentence or context. This is partly a confusion technique, yet the apposition also reinforces the tag concept or experience. Examine:

"And you can remember to forget, can you not?"

"I wonder if you really wish to remember to forget, or forget to remember."

"As that toe itches a bit more, your comfort will increase."

"As that slight tingling appears, you know that the healing continues."

"Learning to unlearn can be very useful."

"Thinking about that relationship, just how much warmth can you find in coldness."

"As you sit there, comfortably immobile, your mind can safely wander to a safe haven."

In an *oxymoron* the opposites are in a single phrase:

"How quickly can you slow down and escalate the decrease of that discomfort."

"As you blindly look at yourself, what is it you are not seeing?"

"Sometimes it is quicker to crawl."

"And just how smooth can your life be on that rocky road?"

c. *Not knowing and not doing*

In this language pattern, the "not" is ignored, resistance is bypassed, and the client acts as if only positive statements were made. Some of Milton Erickson's statements from Erickson, Rossi, and Rossi (1976) with page numbers in parentheses follow:

"You don't have to talk or move or make any sort of effort. You don't even have to hold your eyes open." (p. 23)

"You don't have to bother to listen to me because your unconscious can do that and respond all by itself." (p. 24)

"Now the important achievement for you is to realize that everyone does not know his capacities. (Pause) And you have to discover these capacities in whatever slow way you wish." (pp. 36–7)

"You don't know when you're going to change your rate of breathing [or whatever]." (p. 154)

"You don't need to know [whatever] for when the occasion arises, your unconscious will supply that knowledge." (p. 198)

And you don't know, now, how much you have learned already about negation, have you not?

d. Truisms and the "yes set"

In using the "yes set" you make a series of statements and questions whose obvious answer is "yes"—that is, they involve truisms. This establishes rapport, for you are affirming what the client already knows or experiences. Then the client will continue to be in a receptive and affirmative state of mind to other things that you say. These are statements like, "Today is Tuesday, isn't it?" "And you are sitting on a straight-back chair." "Your husband's name is Harry?" "There are a lot of books in this room, aren't there?" "It was raining this morning, wasn't it?" "And how soon do you think you will be deeply relaxed?" "Your healing sense is strong today." The last two sentences are part of your opening suggestions. It is generally useful to begin a metaphoric session with truisms to connect the person to the present and his environment and his bodily senses.

41

e. Ambiguity

The word "ambiguity" applies to the case where there is more than one deep structure to a surface structure—there is some doubt and uncertainty. Puns may be used for their ambiguity.

Phonological ambiguity occurs where words have the same sound sequences, but different meanings. These are homonyms such as knows/nos/nose, dear/deer, way/weigh, weight/wait, rein/reign/rain, there/their, bare/bear, road/rode, and to/too/two. In addition, the English language has many individual words that sound the same and have the same spelling, but have different meanings—it is the context that supplies the meaning. Some examples are moon, hold, comber, ship, tire, cow, card, bowl, die, train, fast, and founder. Can you hold something fast to you while you are moving fast? Or can you train a dog on a train? A sentence like, "To know how to say no may be the right rite for you when you write baring your deepest thoughts." Use these ideas sparingly and consciously.

Syntactic ambiguity occurs when the syntactic function of a word cannot be uniquely determined by the listener from the context in which the word is used. Some examples from Bandler and Grinder (1975, p. 233) are:

"… flying planes can be dangerous."

"… investigating FBI agents can be dangerous."

"… they are murdering peasants …"

Another form is the nominalization of a noun:

"The touching woman …"

"The running leader …"

"The feeling of the chair …"

Punctuation ambiguity is a nongrammatical form where two unrelated sentences or ideas are connected by a word that can reasonably fit into both parts.

"Now you can notice your hand me that paper."

"You can take that turn around your life."

"When you're at the store away what you have learned."

"The clerk gave you the change that has already begun."

2.6 Binds

Binds and double binds have been well discussed by Erickson, Rossi, and Rossi (1976, pp. 62–76) and by Erickson and Rossi (1979, pp. 42–9). The former book gives good definitions (pp. 62–4):

> A bind offers a free choice of two comparable alternatives—that is, whichever choice is made leads behavior in a desired direction. Therapeutic binds are tactful presentations of the possible alternate forms of constructive behavior that are available to the patient in a given situation. The patient is given free, voluntary choice between them; the patient usually feels bound, however to accept one alternative.

> Double binds, by contrast, offer possibilities of behavior that are outside the patient's usual range of conscious choice and control … The double bind arises out of the possibility of communicating on more than one level. We can (1) say something and (2) simultaneously comment on what we are saying … What is a bind or double bind for one person may not be for another.

Although the idea of binds and double binds may appear to be simple, their construction and delivery are not. Some examples follow:

"Would you like to deeply relax in this chair or that one?"

"Would you like to work on your healing imagery now or in a few minutes?"

"Would you like me to read your bedtime story to you now or after your bath?"

"When do you think your eyes will get heavier and close?"

"Just how soon will your special healing light begin its work?"

"Those old sensations of pain will safely and easily change to a mild tingling in how many minutes?"

"It doesn't really matter what your conscious mind does, because your inner mind will do just what it needs to in order to achieve that analgesia/anesthesia/relaxation/healing force/body cleansing."

A central characteristic of all binds is an illusion of choice. This is fostered frequently by mentioning all possible responses: "Your eyes may close now, or they may close in a minute or two, or they may become softly defocused." "Change may come about momentarily or in a few minutes, or at 10:16 P.M. this evening or, even, sometime after that." "This discomfort may increase temporarily for a moment, or it may stay the same, or it may have already significantly decreased."

2.7 Poetry

Snyder (1971) wrote a book entitled *Hypnotic Poetry*—this is a reprint of a book originally published in 1930. Snyder placed poetry on a continuum from hypnotic (or what he also called hypnoidal or spell-weaving) to intellectualistic. The latter appeals to the intellect and appears to require analysis and cogitation on the part of the listener. He indicated that, although there appear to be some readers who can achieve a kind of self-hypnosis simply in reading to themselves, spell-weaving is generally manifested when the poetry is read aloud. Of course, the ability of the reader, the venue, and the expectational atmosphere are also important factors. What Snyder found was that there were certain poems whose actual structure and choice of words and imagery were more conducive to hypnoidal states than others. Some of these poems (with the poet in parentheses) are "Auld Lang Syne" and "John Anderson, My Jo" (Burns); "Kubla Khan" and much of *The Rime of the Ancient Mariner* (Coleridge); much of *The Rubáiyát of Omar Khayyam* (Fitzgerald); "The Elegy" (Gray); "La Belle Dame Sans Merci" (Keats); "The Long Trail" (Kipling); "Sea-Fever" (Masefield); "Annabel Lee" (Poe); and "O Captain! My Captain!" (Whitman).

In analyzing for the commonalities in hypnotic poetry, Snyder found (p. 37) "... a peculiarly effective stimulus consists of words which fix the subject's attention by their rhythmic sound and make a simple suggestion on which the subject concentrates without any great mental activity." He found that hypnotic poems have the following characteristics in common:

1. An unusually perfect pattern of sound, which tends to be soothing. In fact (p. 42), "Hypnotic poems in general give us heavy stresses falling regularly at half-second intervals, and so ornamented that the rhythmically inclined listener has his attention drawn to the sound rather than the sense."

2. There is in these poems a freedom from abrupt changes, which can break the spell, and this especially means freedom from ideas that might compel mental alertness.

3. The poems contain a certain vagueness of imagery (p. 42). "The pictures presented in these hypnotic poems have such soft, shadowy outlines that one may fill in the details to suit one's fancy or let the picture remain hazy. They foster an idle, dreamy state of consciousness like the preliminary stage of hypnosis."

4. There are fatigue-producing elements, i.e. what Rossi calls "depotentiating habitual mental frameworks." These include verbal difficulties (p. 45). "Paradoxical though it sounds, we may yet have to accept the view that in the early stages of a hypnotic poem, a foreign word, an obscure phrase, or any slight difficulty that causes fatigue from strain on the part of the listener may actually promote the ultimate aesthetic effect at which the artist aims."

5. Another characteristic is the use of a refrain or of frequent repetition. (Think of the repetition of "nevermore" in "The Raven.")

6. Finally, these hypnotic poems tend to use suggestion on the entranced listener, the suggestions sometimes having a posthypnotic effect. In fact, the key suggestive sentence comes near the end after "… there has been a long preliminary soothing of the listener's senses by monotonous rhythmic 'passes'." (p. 48)

With Snyder's observations in mind, you can consider incorporating poetic language forms into your metaphors. Recall that some stories are "prose" poems and that many epic tales are in fact in poetic form. Poems and poetic language seem to stick in the mind more easily than straight prose. Poetic images enrich any tale or metaphor. Practice speaking poetically.

2.8 Some language-rich metaphors

In this section are a number of illustrations of the language of metaphors. They are presented in three parts: poems and poem fragments, adages, and some short pieces.

a. Poems

The Road Not Taken
Two roads diverged in a yellow wood,
And sorry I could not travel both
And be one traveler, long I stood
And looked down one as far as I could
To where it bent in the undergrowth;

Then took the other, as just as fair,
And having perhaps the better claim,
Because it was grassy and wanted wear;
Though as for that the passing there
Had worn them really about the same.

And both that morning equally lay
In leaves no step had trodden black.

Oh, I kept the first for another day!
Yet knowing how way leads on to way,
I doubted if I should ever come back.

I shall be telling this with a sigh
Somewhere ages and ages hence:
Two roads diverged in a wood, and I—
I took the one less traveled by,
And that has made all the difference.

– Robert Frost

Mending Wall
...
He only says, "Good fences make good neighbors."
Spring is the mischief in me, and I wonder
If I could put a notion in his head:
"Why do they make good neighbors? Isn't it
Where there are cows? But here there are no cows.
Before I built a wall I'd ask to know
What I was walling in or walling out,
And to whom I was like to give offense.
Something there is that doesn't love a wall,
That wants it down." I could say "Elves" to him,
But it's not elves exactly, and I'd rather
He said it for himself ...

– Robert Frost

Birches
When I see birches bend to left and right
Across the lines of straighter darker trees,
I like to think some boy's been swinging them.
...
One could do worse than be a swinger of birches.

– Robert Frost

The Tuft of Flowers
...
"Men work together." I told him from the heart,
"Whether they work together or apart."

– Robert Frost

Precaution

I never dared be radical when young
For fear it would make me conservative when old.

— Robert Frost

Parting

My life closed twice before its close;
It yet remains to see
If Immortality unveil
A third event to me,
So huge, so hopeless to conceive,
As these that twice befell,
Parting is all we know of heaven,
And all we need of hell.

— Emily Dickinson

In a place of stillness,
The one who thinks
hears the whisper of the heart.
In a place of trust,
The one who cures,
heals.
In a place of acceptance,
a stone
can explode
into a butterfly.

— Rachel Remen and Vivekan Flint

Hippocratic Oath

May I escape
The shame, inadequacy, self-judgement and self-doubt
my teachers have taught me.
May I trust
That my love is as needed as my knowledge.
May I remember
in me, the limitations of every man.
May I be open
to know my darkness and true to what light I have.
May I be used
as a blessing and a friend to life.

— Rachel Remen, M.D.

Mother Knows Best ...
Don't talk
about your troubles.
No one loves a sad face.
O Mom.
The truth is
cheer isolates,
humor defends,
competence intimidates,
control separates,
and sadness ...
sadness opens us to each other.

– Rachel Remen, M.D.

They say that good intentions
pave the road to hell
if a thing is not worth doing
it's not worth doing well.

– R. D. Laing

Now
if not forever
is
sometimes
better than never

– R. D. Laing

My mother loves me.
I feel good.
I feel good because she loves me.
I am good because I feel good.
I feel good because I am good.
My mother loves me because I am good.
My mother does not love me.
I feel bad.
I feel bad because she does not love me
I am bad because I feel bad
I feel bad because I am bad
I am bad because she does not love me
she does not love me because I am bad.

– R. D. Laing

What do you do with these poems? They are so artfully vague, and yet explicit. Good poems lead you inside to search your heart and memories. Good poems challenge you to find *their* meaning(s) in *your own* life. What are the connections? How do they apply? How have these words changed your perceptions? You can give clients specific poems to read; you can just recite them *meaningfully* at an appropriate time in a session; you can incorporate poems or poetic fragments into your metaphors; and you can yourself wax poetic within the stories you tell. The preceding are poems that have special meaning for me and that I have used from time to time.

b. Adages

Our inherited wisdom has been pithily summarized in adages, wise sayings, aphorisms, and in proverbs. They are the punch lines of stories, fables, jokes, poems. In the preceding section Remen's "sadness opens us to each other," and Laing's "if a thing is not worth doing, it is not worth doing well" are examples. In fact, good metaphors are strewn with these significant statements, and frequently end with them. A sampling of some of the ones I recall (and use) follows with the author (or the person I heard it from) in parentheses.

One hand washes the other. (Anna DeCastro Battino)

Never go empty-handed [when you visit someone]. (Anna DeCastro Battino)

Cancer is not a sentence, it is only a word. (Bernie Siegel)

It is never too late to have a happy childhood.

You can never touch without being loved.
You can never give without receiving.
You can never love without receiving love.

Living well is the best revenge.

The present is called that for it is a special gift.
When you hug a tree it grows better.
When you hug a child they grow better.

You may have to believe the diagnosis, but you do not need to believe the prognosis.

Smell that flower.
Watch that cloud.
Touch that tree.
Taste, really taste.

There is no such thing as failure, there is only feedback.

Life is full of "elses." What else is there?

These adages are but *common sense*, are they not? And common sense is our heritage of practicality. Use sparingly, but wisely. The last chapter in Battino's book on guided imagery (2000, pp. 301–17) has an extensive collection of special sayings from a number of authors.

c. Some short metaphors

Stories, stories, stories. In this section I cite a few from three special people. The first group is from Rachel Naomi Remen's *Kitchen Table Wisdom* (1996). (Also, see her recent book (2000), *My Grandfather's Blessings*.)

All real stories are true. Sometimes when a patient tells me their story, someone in their family will protest. "But it didn't happen quite that way, it happened more like this." Over the years I have come to know that the stories both these people tell me are equally true, equally genuine, and that neither of them may be "correct," an exact description of the event much as a video camera might have recorded it. Stories are someone's experience of the events of their life, they are not the events themselves. Most of us experience the same event very differently. We have seen it in our own unique way and the story we tell has more than a bit of ourselves in it. Truth is highly subjective.

All stories are full of bias and uniqueness; they mix fact with meaning. This is the root of their power. Stories allow us to see something familiar through new eyes. We become in that moment a guest in someone else's life, and together with them sit at the feet of their teacher. The meaning we may draw from someone's story may be different from the meaning they themselves have drawn. No matter. Facts bring us to knowledge, but stories lead to wisdom.

The best stories have many meanings; their meaning changes as our capacity to understand and appreciate meaning grows. [pp. xxvii–xxviii]

If we think we have no stories it is because we have not paid enough attention to our lives. Most of us live lives that are far richer and more meaningful than we appreciate. [p. xxix]

In my experience, a diagnosis is an opinion and not a prediction. What would it be like if more people allowed for the presence of the unknown, and accepted the words of their medical experts in this same way? The diagnosis is cancer. What that will mean remains to be seen.

Like a diagnosis, a label is an attempt to assert control and manage uncertainty. It may allow us the security and comfort of a mental closure and encourage us not to think about things again. But life never comes to a closure, life is process, even mystery. Life is known only by those who have found a way to be comfortable with change and the unknown. Given the nature of life, there may be no security, but only adventure. [p. 67]

It is actually difficult to edit life. Especially in regard to feelings. Not being open to anger or sadness usually means being unable to be open to love and joy. The emotions seem to operate with an all-or-nothing switch. I never cease to be impressed by the capacity of some ill people to live life more fully than most, to find more meaning and more depth, more awe in the ordinary. Perhaps it is because they have allowed the events of their lives to take them to some extraordinary highs and lows. Meeting people there is a choice. [p. 203]

Martin Buber's *Tales of the Hasidim* (1947) contains many gems. Here are three:

At the Pond

After the maggid's death, his disciples came together and talked about the things he had done. When it was Rabbi Schneur Zalman's turn, he asked them: "Do you know why our master went to the pond every day at dawn and stayed there for a little while before coming home again?" They did not know why. Rabbi Zalman continued: "He was learning the song with which the frogs praise God. It takes a very long time to learn that song. [p. 111, Book 1]

Comparing One to Another

Someone once told Rabbi Mendel that a certain person was greater than another whom he also mentioned by name. Rabbi Mendel replied: "If I am I because I am I, and you are you because you are you, then I am I, and you are you. But if I am I because you are you, and you are you because I am I, then I am not I, and you are not you." [p. 283, Book 2]

Dying and Living

As a comment to the words in the psalm: "I shall not die but live," Rabbi Yitzhak said: "In order to really live, a man must give himself to death. But when he has done so, he discovers that he is not to die—but to live."

Milton Erickson was a master storyteller. Here are two from Rosen's Book (1982):

Style

My daughter came home from grade school and said, "Daddy, all the girls in school bite their nails and I want to be in style too." I said, "Well, you certainly ought to be in style. I think style is very important for girls. You are way behind the girls. They have had a lot of practice. So I think the best way for you to catch up with the girls is to make sure you bite your nails enough each day. Now I think if you bite your nails for fifteen minutes three times a day, every day (I'll furnish a clock) at exactly such-and-such an hour, you can catch up."

She began enthusiastically at first. Then she began beginning late and quitting early and one day she said, "Daddy, I'm going to start a new style at school—long nails." [p. 145]

A Card Trick

One of my hypnotic subjects at Worcester said, "I don't like to do this trick. It gives me a terrible headache. I think you ought to know about it though." He said, "Go into a drugstore and buy a deck of cards. Open it. Take out all the jokers and extra cards." Then he said, "Shuffle the deck thoroughly, half a dozen times, and cut it and shuffle it again. Deal the cards face up, one at a time, and then turn them over." Then he said, "Pick up these cards, shuffle them again and deal them back side up." And he named the cards in the exact order back side up. He had placed them face up and then turned them over.

Then he showed me. You bought a pack of cards with cross lines and little squares on the back. The squares are not cut truly. He said, "All I had to do was to remember a quarter of a square miss-ing here, a quarter missing there on another card. I just remem-bered fifty-two cards. And it always has given me a terrible headache—and it took long, hard practice to do it!" He had used that in working his way through school. He had earned a lot of money that way.

It really is amazing what people can do. Only they don't know what they can do. [pp. 196–7]

This section has presented a number of metaphors as poetry, adages, and stories. They all bear analyzing as to language usage, and they all bear studying. As an exercise, you can consider which of the previous offerings you would use with current or past clients. You can also make a list for each offering of the kinds of clients and concerns they can help. How would you adopt or mod-ify Erickson's stories, for example, to your own particular style?

2.9 Summary

Even this abbreviated introduction to language for metaphor may appear to be too extensive, but it is the foundation for this work. This will become abundantly evident in the chapter where we do a detailed linguistic analysis of some published guided-imagery scripts. A metaphor needs to be self-contained: that is, if it needs an explanation to be understood, then it has not been properly constructed. The art of the language of metaphor is that the listener makes the connections internally. Also, remember that good stories convey their message(s) more by actions than by intellectualization or descriptions of events and thoughts.

At this point, you may feel a bit overwhelmed by all of the material. Do not despair: just as it took you a while to learn how to swim or ride a bike or drive a car or learn a foreign language, before you know it, you will know without even knowing how you know what you know even if at times you wanted to say "no." Practice, practice, practice! Remember that learning theory states that new knowledge begins with a state of confusion. So, if you feel confused now …

Chapter 3

Delivery of Metaphor

3.1 Introduction

There is a story about a Joke Club whose members had been together for a long time and who shared a repertoire of beloved old jokes. In fact, these special jokes were so familiar to the members that they were given numbers or symbolic names. For example, #15 was a favorite and the mere stating of "15" by a member would result in gales of laughter. "Harry" was another favorite. A new member, who had a wonderful fund of jokes, frequently got laughter when he spun out a tale and oozed out the punch line. One day he decided on brevity and just said "Harry." There was no response. Being puzzled he said, "When you guys say "Harry" or a number, everybody laughs. What did I do wrong?" A kindly member took him aside and explained that it was his delivery—he just hadn't delivered "Harry" right!

Well, the above is a hoary old tale, but still contains that germ of truth—the story, the metaphor, may be great, but with a lousy delivery there is no *connection*. This chapter contains many ideas for improving your delivery. How do you become a good story-teller? Well, you can read stories, write them, listen to them, join a storytellers' circle and perhaps "apprentice" with them, take lessons or courses in communications and/or theater, and practice. There are many opportunities to tell stories and use metaphors—you just may not be aware that you are doing this already. At this writing I am reading Rachel Naomi Remen's new book (2000), *My Grandfather's Blessings*, and it is a superb collection of *her* stories. Yet, many of them could be adapted to *your* needs.

3.2 Rapport-building skills

Whenever I teach a course on guided imagery or psychotherapy, I always include a section on rapport-building skills. For some participants this is a refresher; for others it is new material. For the purposes of this book, I have adapted and summarized the material (with permission) to be found in more detail in earlier books (Battino and South (1999), Battino (2000)).

Before you can effectively work with someone, rapport has to be established. Your client must trust you and have confidence in you. There are some people you just automatically trust, and there are others whom you somehow distrust. How can you maximize useful rapport with your clients so that the cooperative work of their getting what they want will be enhanced? *Establishing rapport is something that can be learned*. In this section we will teach you the basic skills of rapport building and provide exercises for practicing and honing those skills.

It will always be the case that some people are "naturally" better at rapport building than others. Yet we all learned those incomparably harder skills of walking, talking, and writing. Remember that the early stages of learning any new skill involves confusion and awkwardness as well as a sense that "something" is not just right. Practice helps. Giving the people you work with the congruent sense of having your "unconditional positive regard," that you are there for them and with them during the session, and that they have your undivided attention, is the foundation on which *all* change work is based.

We exist and function in the world in terms of our proprioceptive senses, and also in terms of language. We function in many different contexts, cultures, subcultures, and even mini-subcultures. If, as an American, say, you meet another American abroad, there is an automatic feeling of recognition. If the two of you were both white, black, or Hispanic, then another level of recognition would occur. If you shared the same religion, region of the country, sex, university, town, relatives etc., the feeling of comfortableness around each other would increase even more. The closer the match, the greater the sense of rapport, of connection, of existing in the world in the same way.

An ethical objection may be raised with respect to being "genuine" when you are working with someone. You cannot be other than yourself. If you adapt your behavior for the advantage of your clients, isn't that ethical and responsible behavior? If shifting the way that you phrase your speech to be closer to that of the client helps build rapport, what can be wrong with that? In fact, not to do so would be irresponsible since you should be free to do whatever you *ethically* can to help people.

Carl Rogers pioneered the approach of giving the client your "unconditional positive regard." He meant a number of things by this. First and foremost is that your clients should know from your congruent behavior that you are there for her, that you are concerned about her wellbeing, and that you will do whatever is ethically possible for her within the therapeutic context. Almost everyone has something about him/her that is likable, and with which he/she can make some connection. Clients should have your undivided attention during a session since this is *their* time. There is no place in working with clients for imposing your belief systems, your politics, your religion, your sexual preferences etc. on them. If your belief system gets in the way of working with a particular client, then you must refer that client to someone else who would be comfortable with her. This "unconditional positive regard" is the foundation for all therapeutic and healing relationships. A surgeon may possess remarkable technical skills, but even those skills can be enhanced by the belief of the patient that the surgeon is there for her and the patient is not just another "case."

a. Gathering information

How much do you need to know about a client to help her? The answer is "just enough." Healing work needs to be done in cooperation with the person's physician or with the knowledge that the person is currently under conventional medical care. I use a simple form that obtains vital information such as address, phone numbers, family etc., and then leaves one half of the page for, "briefly describe your concerns and what I can help you with." A ten- to thirty-minute discussion will usually provide sufficient information to devise interventions to help the client. Direct inquiry is also useful.

Some therapists indicate that doing healing work is 95 percent gathering information and 5 percent interventions. My philosophy is that, since you cannot design an intervention without information, it is important to gather *just enough*. You can always gather more information later if it is needed.

Body language is an important channel of information and it is important to "read" your client. This means being aware of facial expressions, voice quality, posture, movements, and breathing patterns. Of course, this should be done without its being obvious. Pay special attention to incongruencies between verbal and non-verbal messages. With practice, you can read bodies automatically and with peripheral vision.

b. Representational systems

We function in the world in terms of language. As we have experiences, we describe those experiences for ourselves in words, which are then stored along with other sensory inputs such as images, sounds, sensations, and odors. A number of observers have pointed out that people *tend* to have a *primary* representational system that they favor, such as auditory, visual, or kinesthetic (bodily sensations). NLP (neuro-linguistic programming) practitioners have done the most with this concept, although the literature appears to be ambiguous as to its validity. As with many other ideas in psychotherapy, the concept of representational systems can sometimes be useful. If it works for you with a particular client, then use it.

Language can be limiting if your vocabulary is limited in some way. For example, there are some cultures whose language has words only for the numbers one and two. They can only count: one, two, many ... There are cultures that have words to describe only a limited number of colors, so they can describe what they see only in terms of those words. The full spectrum of colors may be out there, but if the only words you know are black, white, red, and green, then your reality is circumscribed by those words. The cross-cultural significance of how different peoples use time, space, and language can be found in the works of anthropologists such as E. T. Hall (see Hall, 1959, for example). We are bound by our culture, our words, and our language.

Since the meaning of any communication is the response that you get, it is important to be exquisitely sensitive to how your clients react to what you say and do. You may intend one thing by the content of your language and your delivery, but your client may be understanding something quite different. *When in doubt, ask.* Of course, much marital and family discord comes from misunderstandings that arise from habits of hearing in a particular way. Language is important to communication, and it is also important in terms of establishing rapport.

Assume for the moment that everyone does have a preferred representational system, that is, everyone tends to perceive and record reality primarily in visual, auditory, or kinesthetic terms. The senses of taste and smell are important, but are used less frequently in terms of language than the three mentioned. Table 3.1 lists words and phrases that are typically used by people whose representational system preference is auditory, visual, or kinesthetic. In addition, the table shows some words that are generally "neutral" or *unspecified* with respect to representational systems.

Table 3.1 Typical words and phrases used in each representational system

Visual	Auditory	Kinesthetic	Unspecified
see	say	handle	think
picture	tone	firm	sense
clear	feedback	force	judging
visual	tune	build	assume
imagery	sounds good	handy	allows
point out	talk	push	learn
focus	hear	grasp	motivate
eye	tempo	hard	thought
look	shout	reach	discover
view	scream	solid	aware
draw	rhythm	pull	decide
appear	musical	feel	agree
perceive	rings a bell	shape	believe
show	tell	hold	develop
movie	sounds like	take apart	evaluate
delight	strike a note	grind	realize
blurred	said	thrust	know
foggy	spoken	nail down	understand
keep your eye on it	sound the alarm	concrete	internalize

These words are in general predicates or process words—verbs, adjectives, and adverbs that people use for communication. As you practice with representational systems other words will come to mind.

A person tends to stick to one representational system, although within given contexts and normal word usage she may switch around. It is sometimes difficult to figure out a person's primary representational system. When in doubt, be sure that your communication involves the use of *all three* systems. It makes good sense when doing general metaphoric work to use all three representational systems as far as possible. By careful observation, you may find that you get stronger responses using one system rather than another.

The usefulness of the idea of representational systems is that it lets you "speak the same language" as your client. You can then "be in touch," "be on the same wavelength," "be in tune," "have the same grasp," "be in step," "see eye to eye," "see things the same way," "have the same image/vision/picture," "be on the same footing," "sound the same" etc. There is therefore something *simpatico* about the way that you speak and exist in the world. You are literally speaking the same language as your clients when you join their representational system.

One use of the concept of representational systems is in establishing rapport with your clients. Another is in enlarging their worldview. If you have a client who is primarily visual, for example, she may be missing out on two-thirds of the possible ways of experiencing the world. Sex for such a person may be unsatisfactory since she is "seeing" rather than feeling. Music may not be as impactful since she would be seeing an orchestra play rather than really experiencing (hearing) the sounds. One way of expanding representational systems is by the process of *overlapping*. You, as therapist, can describe an experience such as walking in the woods by first talking about what it is that you see, and then adding sound and feeling to the description so that the senses "overlap" from one to the other. The other senses are then connected to sight. For example, you might say, "As you look around in the woods and see the trees and leaves and path, you can also be aware of the sounds that your shoes make as you walk over the path and how it feels differently to walk on leaves or dirt or stones. Taking a close look at the bark of a large tree, you can see the various shades of brown and the texture, and running your fingers over the bark, just feel the places where it is rough and smooth, and listen to the scratching noises as your fingers rub on the bark, or your clothing brushes up against it as you look so keenly at the tree."

Representational-system exercise

This exercise can be done in dyads or triads. If done in dyads, the *A* person engages the *B* person in conversation, perhaps in the form of an initial interview, and elicits information. In the course of this conversation, *A* attempts to discover *B*'s preferred representational system. Once you think that you know what that system is, then you match the system and observe *B*'s responses. A powerful check on this is to switch to other representational systems and observe *B*'s responses. Does "violating" *B*'s preferred system make *B* appear uncomfortable, pull back, or ...? After five minutes, switch roles. When the second person has finished this part of the exercise, then the two people should process what has happened. Ask for each other's experiences during the process. Feedback is important to calibrate what you have done. If you don't know, ask. *A* might say, "When I said this, you responded that way. What was going on then?"

When the exercise is done in triads, person *C* has two roles. The first is that of observer of both *A* and *B*. The second is that of adviser to *A*. *C* can whisper comments to *A* or pass notes to *A* about things to try or do or observe. *C* can also take notes. When all three participants in the exercise have had an opportunity to try the three different roles, then they can process what has occurred together.

Identifying representational systems can be difficult and, as in any new learning, requires practice. You can train yourself to be sensitive to representational systems by *listening* to the radio, television, movies, conversations in cafeterias and other public places, and within your family. Once you are aware that people can have a preferred representational system, you will find this phenomenon everywhere. This is also prevalent in books and other writings since authors also have preferred systems. If you look and listen for them, you will find them.

As another exercise, you can practice *overlapping* in dyads once you know each other's representational system. Overlapping not only helps enlarge your clients' experiences of the world, but, in the process of your doing this for your clients, *your* world experience will also be enriched. A "blind" walk, a "deaf" walk or a touching with hand-in-glove experience will really emphasize the power of representational systems.

c. Pacing and leading

A good place to observe natural pacing behaviors is in a shopping mall. All you have to do is observe the way people interact with each other. For example, two people walking along together generally walk with the same stride and rhythm. Two people standing and conversing will generally stand in mirror images of each other. If one of the pair is leaning against a wall, then the other will, too. If one has his head slightly cocked to the right, then the other will have her head slightly cocked to the left. If one speaks loudly, softly, rapidly or in a special cadence, then the other is likely to speak in the same pattern. It is a general observation that couples who have been married for a long time (to each other!) tend to "look" alike. What we are perceiving here is that they tend to stand, walk, sit, posture, and use the same, if not similar, facial expressions. We take these similarities to mean that they "look" alike when we are experiencing the way that they fit into the world as a totality of their postures, movements, and expressions. Adopted children grow to "look" like their "parents." These children certainly "sound" like their parents! Since each person fits uniquely and unconsciously into the world in terms of her postures, movements, expressions, and speech, one way of establishing a subtle rapport with her is for you to *also* fit into the world in the "same way," and to communicate this sense of oneness to her. First, we will discuss verbal pacing, then physical pacing, and finally the use of pacing in leading. This will be followed with some exercises.

Some of the characteristics of speech include: tempo, loudness, speed, rhythm or cadence, accenting, regional or cultural accents, and breathiness. It is common knowledge that people from the same culture, subculture, and even mini-subculture have identical speech patterns. *Verbal pacing* means to match your client's speech patterns in some way so that she feels more comfortable in your presence. Generally, *you need to match in only* one *characteristic* such as volume or rhythm for this rapport to become apparent. It is important not to mimic or match too closely, since this will be detectable by the client and taken as a manipulation or an insult.

Pacing must be subtle. Pacing should be done in such a way that it is perceived outside of conscious awareness and not directly in consciousness by the client. If a client speaks rather loudly, you do not have to shout with her, but just *increase* the *normal* volume of your voice. Some people speak exceedingly fast or slow. This may be difficult for you to duplicate directly, but you can duplicate this by *crossover pacing* by using finger or toe movements or slow head nods to match the rate of speech. These other movements in a different system will be perceived outside of awareness. With verbal pacing, you literally want to "speak" your client's language in some way so that you both fit into the world similarly.

Physical and postural pacing have to do with matching your client's movements or postures in some way. Again, you do not have to match all movements and postures. It is only necessary to match the *general* way the other person is sitting in a chair, or to tilt your head to the right just a bit if she is a head tilter, or to nod your head a bit if she is a nodder, or move one of your feet if she is a foot tapper or wiggler. Exact mirroring can be detected and will be taken as an intrusion or mocking. Physical pacing should be subtle, not exaggerated.

Pacing a client's breathing pattern is perhaps the most effective, and yet the most subtle, way of fitting into her world. Breathing is such a basic pattern of existence that matching it is a profound experience. Babies do this automatically when placed on their mothers' bosoms. In doing metaphoric work it is important to pace your speech to the breathing patterns of your client. This is a fundamental axiom for this kind of communication. In some cases it may be necessary to match breathing patterns in a crossover form. Of course, you should not stare at the bosom of your female client to pick up her breathing pattern, particularly if you are a male therapist. Breathing patterns can be picked up via peripheral vision, or by observing the small movements in clothing, in the shoulders, or in the abdomen. Subtle observation and matching are always better.

Being aware of body language is an important part of the science of being an effective therapist and healer, since it is not possible to do verbal and physical pacing without reading body language. Knowledge of body language is not only useful to pacing, but is also important in terms of being aware of your client's emotional state and changes in that state. Since the meaning of any communication is the response it gets, be aware of what *you* might be reading into your client's body language. Check out any meaning or interpretation before jumping to conclusions. A smile may not mean happiness. A grimace may not mean pain. A "blank" face may not mean being somewhere else. Gestalt therapy teaches you to look for incongruities between verbal and body communications. For example, the client may be verbally stating that she is "open" to new ideas while her arms and legs are crossed. Some of these incongruities may be usable in certain contexts or they may be ignored; however, there is no substitute for paying exquisite attention to your client.

One of the major uses of pacing is to then be able to *lead* your client into other states, feelings, or postures once you have paced them. When you have matched the walking pattern of a companion, you can then get her to increase or decrease her stride or pace by simply varying yours. When you have matched the breathing rate of your client, you can get her to breathe faster or slower by modifying your own breathing rate. This, of course, has obvious uses. You can literally lead someone out of a depression by first pacing, and then changing your bodily and verbal patterns.

Pacing and leading exercises
This verbal pacing exercise can be done in dyads or triads. Person A and person B stand or sit or stand back to back so that they are making contact with their backs and can sense each other's breathing as well as feel the vibrations generated in speaking. If C is available, then C will observe and provide feedback on the accuracy of the pacing. A says something—one short sentence works well here. It might be something like, "My name is Harry and I am feeling a bit uncomfortable about doing this exercise." It is B's task

to repeat *A*'s statement to *A*'s satisfaction that *B* has their speech patterns accurately paced. Alternate several times doing this before moving on to practicing with someone else. Both *A* and *C* can coach *B* in how to do better. Being back to back rules out visual cues and forces you to concentrate on your hearing. *B* can also practice matching *A*'s breathing patterns while doing this exercise. Once you are aware of individual speech patterns you can even mentally rehearse matching people during ordinary conversations since this mental rehearsal actually activates your vocal cords and other relevant speech structures within your body. In practice you will be pacing representation systems, as well as speech patterns at the same time!

A second verbal pacing exercise is also done in dyads or triads. *A* is the client, *B* is the therapist, and *C* is the observer. In the framework of carrying out an initial interview with a client, find out what happens when you pace her speech patterns and when you deliberately "violate" her speech patterns. If pacing will lead your client to be more comfortable in your presence, then deliberately *not* pacing will "drive" her away. *A* and *B* switch roles (or *C*, too) and repeat the exercise. After everyone has had a chance to practice all parts, then process what went on. It is important to find out how your client reacted to the things you did. Now that you have had some success at pacing, do the exercise again, but this time consciously *lead* the client by changing one aspect of her speech patterns. Observe carefully what occurs so you can do this better and better. The body-posture exercise is done in a similar fashion with dyads or triads. It is the therapist's task to mirror in a subtle way some aspect of the client's body posture, to "violate" that mirroring, and to observe what happens. Once you have successfully learned to mirror body postures (and you need to do only one at a time), then use this postural pacing to *lead*. Get the client to shift positions or change movements. You can sometimes subtly lead a client out of an emotional state by just shifting your body posture. Test this.

As a final exercise, put the pacing of representational systems, speech patterns, and body postures together so that you actually remember and match in *all* channels of communication. This exercise can be done in dyads or triads. Remember to process the exercise afterwards and to ask your "client" about internal states he/she experienced during the exercise. People daily demonstrate pacing and leading—all you have to do is be sufficiently aware to observe this.

d. Eye accessing cues

The observation of eye movements when you are working with someone can be of use. There is much controversy in the literature about the validity of eye accessing cues. My own approach is that if you are aware of a consistent pattern of eye movements in your client, and that the pattern matches the NLP assertions about this phenomenon, then you can use them in appropriate contexts. One assertion is that people tend to have a consistent association of an eye movement down and to their own right when accessing kinesthetic states internally. The pattern for most right-hand/left-brain individuals is shown in Figure 3.1. You are *looking at* this person. When a person looks up and to the left she is accessing stored mental images or pictures, V^R. When she looks up and to the right she is constructing a mental image or picture, V^C. Looking straight left is accessing internal auditory messages, A^R. Looking straight right is constructing sounds, A^C. Down right is for kinesthetic states—from memory or current (K); and down left is for talking to yourself, A^D. Check these out for yourself to convince yourself of their validity. Some people demonstrate a mirror image of the patterns shown in the figure. It is sometimes difficult to ascertain an individual's eye accessing patterns. For Figure 3.1, V^R = visual recall; V^C = visual construction; A^R = auditory recall; A^C = auditory construction; K = kinesthetic; and A^D = auditory "digital," i.e. talking to yourself.

There is a practical aspect to knowing about eye accessing cues: it is useful to know what your client's internal states are and what she is feeling or doing mentally while she is talking or listening to you. Is she looking at old pictures in her head, talking to herself, listening to someone talking to her in the past, or accessing (kinesthetic) feelings? You can seem like a mind-reader when you ask "What are you seeing now?" You can practice eye accessing cues by observing your clients' responses, by observing performers in the movies and on television, and by observing people in casual conversations. If eye accessing cues make sense to use, then use them.

Figure 3.1. Eye accessing cues

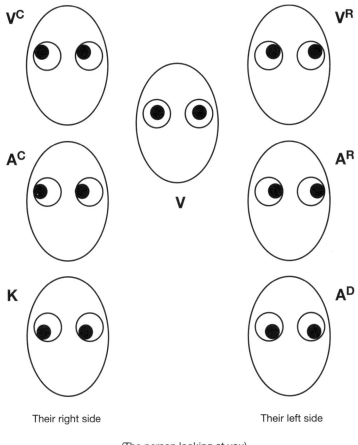

V^C   V^R

A^C   A^R

V

K   A^D

Their right side   Their left side

(The person looking at you)

(Young, 1999)

e. Anchoring

Anchoring is a word used in NLP and other disciplines to mean the *obtaining of a conditioned response by an associated stimulus.* Anchoring is any stimulus that elicits a consistent response. In one sense, you cannot not anchor in any interaction with another person. A typical culturally installed anchor is the handshaking response. Someone raises her right hand toward you and you automatically start raising your own hand.

Anchors may be placed by touch, sound of voice, cue words, hand movements, odors, tastes, body postures, voice location, physical surroundings, or other stimuli. It is well known, for example, that students do better on exams given in the same lecture hall in which they received instruction. Just being in the same room aids in the recall of the lecturer's words or writings and other associated material. Sitting in the same seat helps even more.

In working with a client the easiest stimulus to use is that of touch. Touch has an additional advantage in that there is a *kinesthetic override* that appears to operate so that touch is more powerful for most people than other stimuli. The sense of smell is perhaps the most powerful stimulus to memory since it bypasses consciousness, but it doesn't lend itself to convenient use in a therapeutic situation! Since the physical arrangement of your office is under your control, use this to position yourself and your client in such a way that it is both convenient and natural to be able to reach over casually and touch a shoulder or a knee or an arm or a hand. However, *permission* should be obtained before touching a client. Since it is important to be able to reproduce a kinesthetic anchor *exactly*, you should pick a location that is easy to reach and easy to touch in *exactly* the first way you touched it. Knuckles are useful. It is also important to reproduce exactly the amount of pressure used. Remember that the sense of touch varies in sensitivity depending on the part of the body touched. Fingertips and hands are much more sensitive than the middle of the back or the thigh. So you need more precision to reproduce a kinesthetic anchor on the hand than on the shoulder. Generally, use a hand or an arm or a shoulder for anchors.

There are several rules for effective anchoring. They are:

- Have your client access the desired experience which you wish to anchor as powerfully and as fully as possible. She will probably need to be verbally guided to do this.
- "Insert" your stimulus at the moment of fullest expression or the most intense response. Timing is crucial here. Use your senses to detect the peak experience by paying attention to breathing, facial color and tone, pulses etc. Behave congruently with the type of response you are seeking. It is usually convenient to place the anchor lightly as the client starts to access

the desired state, and then to slowly increase the pressure of the anchor as the client gets deeper into the desired state. Remember that these are always *gentle* pressures, and that small and subtle changes are readily detected.

- Be sure that the stimulus can be repeated *exactly*.
- Always *test* to be sure that your anchor works. "Triggering," that is, touching the anchor, should get the response that you originally anchored. Observe!

One of the simplest uses of anchors in your office is to have a "storytelling" chair, i.e. one chair that you use for this purpose only. The client will automatically know when she sits in that chair that it is time to relax and listen. Some therapists use a particular voice tone or delivery style that says this is a story time. It could also be the way that you sit or hold your head. (Some hypnotists use a separate hypnosis chair.)

The most important things about the concept of anchoring are that it does exist and that people are capable of one-trial learning. Once you are aware of this, then you can use it in appropriate contexts.

Anchoring exercises
Practice with anchoring is best done in dyads. One person is the operator and the other is the person having the anchor installed, i.e. the subject. As the operator, be sure to control the physical space arrangements with your client. (You don't want to stretch awkwardly to place an anchor.) For the first exercise, have your client access a pleasant or happy experience and then anchor it. Test by triggering the anchor outside of the client's awareness by engaging her in casual conversation. As a second exercise, you will be anchoring two experiences, one of which is the opposite of the other. These could be pleasant and unpleasant, happy and sad, a good meal and a bad one etc. The two anchors could also be used for an undesired behavior, and a desired one, or a present state and a desired state. Once the two anchors have been installed, then trigger both at the same time and observe what happens. You can influence the outcome by using slightly more pressure on the desired/positive state than the other one. It is also useful to contrast the "positive" state with a *mildly* "negative" one, since you do not want to traumatize the subject!

3.3 The utilization approach

In many ways the *utilization approach* (Zeig, 1999) is the heart of the famous psychiatrist and hypnotherapist Milton H. Erickson's approach in working with clients. He accepted clients as they were and then moved on from there. It was said of Erickson that a client never knew what Erickson would do when the client entered his office. Erickson felt that every client was unique and deserved to be treated in a unique way. For example, if a client is a devout Catholic and you are an atheist, you can still help the client by working within her belief system *since yours is not germane.* (Remember, if *your* belief system gets in the way, then you *must* refer the client.) If you are a Republican and your client is a dyed-in-the-wool Democrat, then use that information. If your client believes in past lives and you don't, or vice versa, then use that information and belief system to help the client. Of course, being aware of belief systems and cultural patterns is extremely important in doing cross-cultural work.

One of Erickson's most quoted observations involves the Greek thief Procrustes, who was in the habit of kidnapping people. He kept them in an iron bed. If they were too short for the bed, he stretched them to fit the bed. If they were too tall for the bed, he cut them down to size! By too rigorously applying any given approach, you are in danger of becoming a Procrustes.

In the utilization approach, you simply accept and utilize the client's observable and nonobservable behaviors and beliefs. By nonobservable we mean paying attention to what the client says about herself. Pacing these behaviors establishes rapport, and leading them moves the client along. Everyone is unique. In delivering metaphors the story needs to be within the belief system and knowledge of the client. The story "utilizes" her background and what she brings into the consultation. In a sense, effective psychotherapy and storytelling is a form of verbal judo in which you use the client's strengths (who she is) as a lever to help her.

Utilization exercise
This can be done in dyads or triads. In a triad the third person is an observer and commentator and assistant to the operator. The

framework for this exercise is to hold an intake interview with the client, paying attention to and noting her uniqueness. Then, using that uniqueness, devise and deliver a therapeutic or healing metaphor. You can take a few minutes after the initial interview to make notes about the content of the metaphor.

3.4 Theatricality

It undoubtedly helps to be an actor or an actress if you are to be a storyteller. How many ways can you say "yes" or "no," and in how many ways can you alter your body posture to emphasize each of these words? How much can you convey by a tone or a gesture? How well do you use pauses and inflections? When do you make eye contact, and when do you not? How frequently do you modulate your voice in normal speech? Do you come from a family where all is spoken in monotones with rigid postures, or do you come from a flamboyant family used to large gestures and oratory? Training in the theater and speech and communication can increase your range in delivery.

The *principle of requisite variety* came out of the discipline of cybernetics. Basically, it states that in any complex system the component with the most variability controls. A two-person interaction is quite complex. So, if you have more *variability* than your client, if you have many ways of communicating from softly compassionate to forcefully commanding, you will then be able to help your clients more effectively than a nonreactive deadpan therapist. Controlled and conscious variability is what is needed. There needs to be a conscious design to your delivery. Theatricality can help.

And theatricality also means that stories need some element of drama and suspense. This is what makes a story interesting and engages the attention of the listener. Heroines face challenges and obstacles; heroes face daunting adversaries; heroic deeds are done within the fantasy land of a story. Certain aspects are "bigger than life," and yet life itself is so challenging that the ordinary may be all that is needed. "Her life is a soap opera." "His life is a crazy adventure." Drama may be larger than life, but it cannot stray too far from the truth, from real lives.

Do not forget the power of poetry, the magic of images and words, a phrase, the moment caught in a line. Reading Dylan Thomas and connecting with his passion for words, or Robert Frost and the down-to-earth simplicity of his language and stories, provides models for poetic usage.

3.5 Informed consent?

How do you arrange to tell your clients stories? You can do it in a natural way by saying, "You know, that reminds me of a story," or "I had a client named John who ..." or "When I was in college I ..." or "I read about this person the other day ..." or "Did you see that movie/play/TV show or read that book/magazine article/story in the paper?" There are many ways to segue gracefully into telling tales.

In terms of "informed consent" I like to simply tell my clients that I am a storyteller and frequently tell stories during sessions. In fact, I continue, many of my clients like the stories and frequently find useful things in them. I may even say that some of my stories are true and some are made up. Generally, it helps to prepare your clients for storytelling.

What about personal disclosure, stories about yourself? There are schools of therapy who maintain that you should never talk about yourself, or tell personal details—this would destroy the client–professional relationship, and take the therapist out of the objective observer/clinician role. To divulge or not? When a personal story is relevant, not only is there no harm in telling it, but the sharing of a personal experience can serve to establish a closer rapport with the client, and show a level of concern and empathy that objective distance cannot. Remember that your story is not told as a catharsis for you, but as a vehicle to provide more choices for your client. If your personal story is too heroic and seemingly beyond the reach of your client's current capabilities, then the story is not appropriate. The story needs to be isomorphic in some elements, and show your struggles and doubts in finding your way. These can be elements of luck and mystery. Everyone has stories and you are, indeed, a collection of such stories. They define who we are. Personal disclosure in this way needs to be subtle and not intrusive.

Much has been written about the wounded healer. In David Spiegel's support groups for women with fourth-stage metastatic breast cancer, one of the brilliant things they did was to have as a co-leader a woman who was in remission for breast cancer, but who had herself undergone some regimen of surgery, chemotherapy, and radiation. The wounded healer is a witness to humanity, to life's capriciousness, and to learning from adversity. There is an understanding with another wounded person that goes beyond simple facts: there is empathy and compassion and caring and being in the world in the same way. An obvious caution is that the wounded healer is a witness, partially a model, and certainly not an advocate. For example, each and every one of the alternative therapies for cancer has helped some people to attain remissions, some quite long-term. Such a person can bear witness to how this particular treatment/regimen has helped her, but if she pushes what she did as the *exclusive* way to health she loses her witness status, and can cause harm.

In the last section of this chapter I tell some personal stories.

3.6 *Some personal stories*

In the following stories about myself, in one long metaphor, I deliberately intersperse poor language usage since I would like the reader to learn about metaphor by confronting good and bad storytelling. So, this is a study piece ...

Rubin stories

You know, I've often wondered who I am, what I am, and if I've accomplished anything worthwhile in my life. How do you ever really know these things? If your parents loved you, and you knew this deep inside in your core being, then that was some kind of validation of your value, your self-worth. I sort of knew this when I was growing up. Sort of, since my parents weren't overt huggers or people who said, "I love you," openly. I just had to infer that they loved me or were proud of my accomplishments. Mostly, I thought I was a source of aggravation, and for a long time I believed that this aggravation was the source of my mother's many illnesses and operations. It was only much later that I was able to separate fact from belief—it takes a long time to recognize your parents as real independent individuals, with their own histories and troubles and imperatives, and joys. Did I have a happy childhood? The best I can say now is "probably." And how was yours, I wonder? Well, to continue …

When I was in graduate school I tried my hand in acting with the Duke Players. I was already into rehearsals when I realized with something of a shock that I had the lead role in Pirandello's *Right You Are, If You Think You Are*. The role was that of the cynical commentator and philosopher Lamberto Laudisi. Somehow, I did that part well, and I sent some good reviews back home. No word at all. When I visited a few months later, neither my mother nor my father commented on my acting. I was crushed, because in those days I did many things with the secret hope that they would praise me. Who was I?

Many years later my oldest brother told me that my father carried those clippings in his wallet and would proudly show them to friends, family, and business acquaintances. Yet never a word to me. Is secret love and pride helpful? Only when it is let out. I learned this after my father's death. Perhaps, better late than never.

Most of my professional life has been spent as a professor of chemistry. Science was the center of my life for a long time, and still plays a significant role. The dreams of all young scientists reach to the Nobel Prize at some time. I realized early that I was not of that caliber, but might still make a contribution that would earn me a reputation. As a young untenured instructor and assistant professor, I had much doubt about myself and my work. This is not to say that I did not routinely work very hard, putting 60 to 70 hours each week into my science. Did it matter? Was I any good? As a researcher? As a teacher? I just didn't know.

And then, one day, I overheard a conversation between two of my colleagues. One of them was telling the other how much he admired something about me. Wow! It was about something *he* couldn't do, and that I appeared to do easily. I never found out what this "something" was, but coming from a tenured faculty member who I admired, this was something like a miracle. I did a lot of soul-searching. There was that not-so-good, scared, not really competent image I had carried internally for so long, I almost cherished that image as who I really was, and then this external evaluation. To see ourselves as others see us can be both devastating and transforming. Which to choose? Is the external evaluation always more objective? We are judged so often in so many areas and ways that being judgmental of ourselves becomes a way of life. A real quandary. How do I, how did I, develop an inner sense of who I was and am?

I finally came to the conclusion of getting as much objective external information as I could, and then treating it all with some levity. To be able to laugh at one's self is the height of wisdom, and sanity. If I had just been diagnosed with a catastrophic disease, how many of these old judgments would matter? And, in the face of those evaluations, was I ever anyone else but myself, human, fallible, and basically a decent person? Different now than I was then, for the only people who do not change are dead, figuratively or literally.

Carl Hammerschlag is fond of saying, "When you speak from the heart you speak the truth." And, when you live from the heart ...

I don't know what you will make out of these personal stories. They are mine, and I've enjoyed listening to your stories. With enough stories we can erect a very tall building. Thanks for listening.

How much of the previous would you change, and in what ways? Do you have your own parallel personal stories? Is there too much personal disclosure or not enough? Can you imagine telling one of your clients this story or variants based on it? Is it too specific? not vague enough? too personal? not poetic enough? too much in one representational system? Can you imagine the client this story was told to, and write a description of her and the concern(s) the story addressed?

Thanks for listening ...

Chapter 4

Basic Metaphor—Structure and Development

4.1 Introduction

There are as many styles of metaphor as there are storytellers. Is the metaphor simple or complex, direct or indirect, with a straightforward message or one embedded in riddle like a Zen koan, plain or dramatic, neutral or moralistic, realistic or mythical, ordinary or heroic, general or specific, client- or therapist-generated, or one involving real people or spirits or animals or objects or fantastical beings? There are obviously many choices in the construction of a metaphor, just as there are in the content and delivery. Stories have beginnings, middles, and ends, with the middles expandable for whatever complex development is deemed necessary. The simple version may be that used by good lecturers: tell them what you are going to tell them, tell them, and then tell them what you've told them. A related approach is the sandwich method of criticism wherein you say something nice or praise the listener, state your criticism, and then end with something nice again. Whatever the format, the metaphor needs to engage the listener's attention, i.e. it needs to be dramatic, a *good* story.

Zeig (1980) has given eight reasons for the value of anecdotes (or metaphors) in therapy. They are: (1) anecdotes are nonthreatening; (2) anecdotes are engaging; (3) anecdotes foster independence— the person needs to make sense of the message and then come to a self-initiated conclusion or a self-initiated action; (4) anecdotes can be used to bypass natural resistance to change; (5) anecdotes can be used to control the relationship; (6) anecdotes model flexibility; (7) anecdotes can create confusion and promote hypnotic responsiveness; (8) anecdotes jog the memory—"They make the presented idea more memorable." Anecdotes are also respectful and gentle.

4.2 The four elements of a metaphor

Using a metaphor involves four basic elements. They are: (1) gather information; (2) construct the metaphor; (3) deliver the metaphor; and (4) some kind of closure. Each element is treated separately in what follows. (This material builds on Battino and South (1999) with permission.)

1. Gather information

Two kinds of information are needed before constructing appropriate metaphors. The first is about the presenting concern, and the second is related to obtaining sufficient personal information so that the metaphors can be tailor-made. These two aspects will be discussed separately. Please note that I use the word "concern" rather than the word "problem" since the former is less threatening and more open to solutions. This choice represents my bias towards solution-oriented therapy, rather than problem-oriented therapy.

a. Information about the problem
In a chapter on "negotiating the problem," Cade and O'Hanlon (1993) give a useful list of questions designed to clarify the presenting concern. The questions are followed by some commentary. (To avoid awkward constructions, I will use "problem" in some of this section.)

(1) *When* does the problem occur? Are there any patterns or regularities in the occurrence of the problem, i.e. only on weekends, in the evening, at midnight etc.?

(2) *Where* does the problem occur? Is there a pattern as to particular locations where the problem occurs or does not occur? Is it never at work and only in the kitchen, for example?

(3) What is the *performance* of the problem? What would an objective observer see when the client had the problem, i.e. specific stances, movements, speech, gestures, actions? If I had your concern how would I act to reproduce it?

(4) *With whom* does it occur? When you have this concern, are you alone? With specific others? Does the "audience" change? How do these potential others interact with you?

(5) What are the *exceptions* to the rule of the problem? Are there times when this concern does not occur? What is different about those times/location/environment?

(6) What does the client (or clients) do differently, or what activities are prevented, *because of the problem*? In other words, in what specific ways does the concern affect their lives in terms of activities they are involved in or avoid?

(7) What does the *client show in the session* that is related to the concern? Many therapists believe that it is not possible for a client to talk about a concern without reliving it at the same time. Talking about a state recalls all the physical and mental memories associated with that state.

(8) What are the *client's explanations* and frames regarding this concern? How is it perceived from the client's unique perspective and history? This is an important check to keep your guesses and possible projections at bay.

(9) What are the client's (or other's) attempted solutions regarding the "problem"? You need to know what has already been tried so you don't fall into the trap of doing "more of the same," and also to gain some insight into the client's problem-solving approaches.

(10) How will we (and others) know when we get there? What *objective* tests and behaviors will be available so that you know the problem is resolved? Stating behaviors that others can observe concretizes the client's difficulties into a solvable problem because the outcomes are known. These outcomes must be realistic.

Identifying what, to the client's mind, has *stopped* him in the past, gives you clues to his connecting strategies. However, you should avoid dwelling on impasses, and spend more time in the search for the *exceptions* that house the seeds of solutions. Also, although it is useful to know how the problem progresses, *it is more useful to know how the problem abates*. After all, the severest migraine does wax and wane and finally abate. *How* did the latter occur, and can it occur more quickly?

It is useful to gather as much information about the concern as possible. In studying Erickson's cases, for example, it is clear that he frequently spent a very long first session in just getting acquainted with his client, in obtaining a detailed history. Experience will dictate how much information is needed before moving on. You could probably obtain most of the information implied in the ten questions listed above in fifteen to twenty minutes, if you keep the client on track.

b. Idiosyncratic background information
Everyone is unique and the more personal and idiosyncratic the information you have about the client, the more accurate the connections you can make between his concerns and the metaphors you use. Is the client a devout or a lapsed Catholic? What are the client's hobbies, talents, profession, upbringing, rural/urban/suburban background, travels, age/sex/marital status/birth order, education, and work? You wouldn't generally tell a metaphor about farming to a lifelong city dweller, and vice versa. Metaphors make connections between this and that, so you need to know the "this" in the client's experience. When dealing with children, for example, it would be important to know what is shown on children's television and what are the currently popular children's books. What are the child's favorite stories? There are some "standard" or "universal" metaphors that can be adapted to many clients, but it is better to use specifically tailored metaphors. People learn based on their experience (constructivism).

2. Building the metaphor

The Lanktons (1983) are systematic in their construction of a metaphor and start their process with an awareness of six areas in which to find evidence of change before considering treatment complete. The six areas to check for desired outcome(s) are (p. 87): (1) bonding and age-appropriate intimacy; (2) self-image enhancement; (3) attitude restructuring; (4) social-role change; (5) family-structure change; and (6) enjoyment of life. Their condensed outline (p. 92) for developing an individualized metaphor for each client is:

(1) Listen to the problem as offered.

(2) Guided by the six areas of desired outcomes, list dramatic themes that are part of the current and desired situation.

(3) Construct metaphors that parallel those themes.

(4) Design appropriate general outcomes.

(5) Arrange the outcome to create suspense or mystery.

We can envision two extremes in using metaphors with clients. On the one hand, we might have a "natural" storyteller who intuitively can create or relate highly relevant stories on the spur of the moment. There are such "naturals" out there. As an aside, we recall a childhood friend who naturally and unknowingly spoke in profundities—his utterances were made to be immortalized in needlepoint! By contrast, the other extreme is the systematic and conscious design that the Lanktons use, and with which we agree. Clients deserve your conscious concern and involvement. The starting point is the conscious development of appropriate metaphors—after much experience in their use, many of the steps and checks will become part of your automatic responses. Remember that it is almost always permissible to take a "time-out" (which you are devoting to the client's benefit) to consult with colleagues or to develop the metaphor (or other intervention) on your own. If you use a time-out, remember to "seed" relevant thinking on the part of your client.

In the following outline for the construction of a metaphor, we draw upon the steps developed by Gordon (1978) and by Lankton and Lankton (1983).

Outline for metaphor construction
a. *Gather information*—This was dealt with in some detail earlier. For the metaphor to be meaningful, it needs to have elements uniquely connected with the client's life. A sailing metaphor won't

work with someone who doesn't swim and is prone to seasickness. A city dweller may have no knowledge about growing fruits and vegetables. Knowledge of hobbies is quite useful. Who are the significant persons with whom the client is involved? What are their interrelationships? What events are characteristic of the problem? In what ways does the problem progress? Determine in *behavioral and objectively verifiable* terms what outcome(s) the client wants. It is always useful to know what has been tried in the past. Are there any particular things that "stop" the client from making the desired changes? (Reiterating some of the gathering-of-information aspects is our way of emphasizing the importance of this step.)

b. *Outcomes guide*—Using the Lanktons' six areas of desired outcomes as a guide, *list* the *dramatic* themes that are part of the current and desired situation. Stories are inherently dramatic. To be effective, the potential dramatic components need to be elucidated *and* connected to the desired outcomes.

c. *Construct/adapt the metaphor*—The metaphor needs to parallel the six areas in some way. You may wish to list the areas and the parallels with the metaphor. What is the context or setting of the metaphor? How much detail about this setting will be significant? To be too specific defeats internal searching and the client's filling in of details (radio versus TV). Who will populate the metaphor? The inhabitants need to be sufficiently isomorphic with the significant persons found in the gathering-information step. Generally, it is better to avoid the use of animals or extraterrestrials, unless they are specifically indicated. Children, for example, may better identify with animals or superheroes or fairy-tale characters than adults. The Wookie or Yoda in *Star Wars* may be perfect as a character. In general, the simpler the tale, the better. (See Chapter 6 for comments on multiple-embedded metaphors that involve a more complex construction.) Match the level of complexity to your client and, perhaps, his level of "resistance." Stories need to have beginnings, middles, and ends. Consciously design them into the metaphor. In particular, design in appropriate *general outcomes*. We deliberately indicate the plural here since you want to give your client *many choices* to select from. The choices need to be connected to the client's desired outcomes. It is worthwhile noting Talmon's observation (1990) that, when clients on follow-up were asked to identify statements that their therapist made that were particularly helpful, the therapist frequently did not recall making that statement, or in that way, or that it was particularly significant!

Creating new and unique metaphors for each client can be time-consuming and even intimidating. Hence, it makes sense (see below) to have available a set of adaptable "standard" metaphors. For example, the theme of a person or plant or animal growing up can be adapted to many situations. The construction of a house, computer program, play or novel, or organization has many parallels.

d. *Drama/ suspense/ mystery*—Good stories are dramatic, and that characteristic is bolstered by suspense and mystery. Whodunit? What will happen? and when? and to whom? and in what ways? The "tease" for these elements needs to be planted early in the metaphor. Humor, of course, can always be incorporated. The wordplay of puns, oxymorons, and homonyms is also dramatic. In Shakespeare's tragedies, the most dramatic times are invariably preceded and set up by a scene involving comic relief. A study of play and story construction would not be amiss.

e. *Reframing*—To a great extent, the value of telling a story lies in the reframing inherent in the story. Tales are told and the outcomes are *new* perspectives and choices. With this in mind, the metaphor can contain consciously designed reframes of the presenting concern.

f. *Closure*—Metaphors may be told with the client in the waking or the trance state, although the telling of a good story invariably invokes some level of trance in the listener. So the client will need to be reoriented to the present time and location at the end of the story. Where indicated, amnesia for the metaphor may be induced by direction, or by the indirection of a *non sequitur*, or distraction at the end of the metaphor. Although a story may have a verbalized "moral" or punch line, it is rarely necessary to emphasize the "point" of the story. The effectiveness of metaphors is primarily at the unconscious level of internal searches and discoveries and choices.

Once the metaphor has been constructed, and it can be written out or memorized, then it must be told. The next section discusses the factors involved in the delivery of the metaphor.

4.3 Goal-directed metaphors

The following are Lankton and Lankton's protocols for creating emotions, attitudinal, and behavior goal-directed metaphors (pp. 28–29, 71. 1989). This is a simplified outline—details and illustrations are in the source material.

1. Affect-and-emotion protocol

a. Establish a relationship between the protagonist and a person, place or thing that involves emotion or affect (e.g. tenderness, anxiety, mastery, confusion, love, longing etc.).

b. Detail movement in the relationship (e.g. moving with, moving toward, moving away, orbiting etc.).

c. Focus on some of the physiological changes that coincide with the protagonist's emotion (be sure to overlap the client's facial behavior).

2. Attitude-change protocol

a. Describe a protagonist's behavior or perception so it exemplifies the maladaptive attitude. Bias this belief to appear positive or desirable.

b. Describe another protagonist's behavior or perception so it exemplifies the adaptive attitude (the goal). Bias this belief to appear negative or undesirable.

c. Reveal the unexpected outcome achieved by both protagonists which resulted from the beliefs they held and their related actions. Be sure the payoff received by the second protagonist is of value to the client.

3. Behavior-change protocol

a. Illustrate the protagonist's observable behavior similar to the desired behavior to be acquired by the client. There is no need to mention motives. List about six specific observable behaviors.

b. Detail the protagonist's internal attention or nonobservable behavior that shows the protagonist to be congruent with his or her observable behavior.

c. Change the setting within the story so as to provide an opportunity for repeating all the behavioral descriptions several (3) times.

4.4 Themes for basic metaphors

Good storytellers have a repertoire of stories that they can slip out on any occasion, just as good comedians have a fund of jokes they can tap into for any particular audience. The story usually starts with, "That reminds me of ..." You can build your own repertoire by reading the books discussed in Chapter 1, by listening and recording good stories you have heard, or by creating your own stories. In this section seven general themes for metaphors will be given. These are general-purpose metaphors that you can adapt for a particular person by incorporating language that is meaningful to him, or use for a group. (Note that different groups would also require specifically tailored language.) The following will be provided for each theme: (1) a title; (2) the intended audience, i.e. the purpose of this particular metaphor; (3) opening—setting the stage by giving basic elements such as time, setting, ambience, characters, conditions, background, and devices; (4) development—components of the narrative in step-by-step sequence; and key words, phrases, and images; and (5) closing—morals, punch lines, special reorientation. As an exercise, you can take one or more of these themes and write out the entire script. The next section has a sampling of scripts of my own and from the literature.

1. Trip to a Guru

a. *Audience*—anyone who is stuck in making sense of his life. The guru has guidance and answers, but the art of this metaphor is that the guru does not ever say anything explicit—you imply by your language that the listener hears the guru speak within his own mind. This facilitates (much as in an ambiguous-function assignment) the client's finding his own unique answers from his own unique self. The guru provides answers and perspective to any problem, so this can be used for a general audience.

b. *Opening, setting the stage*—Posit the existence of a wise person, a guru. This can be generalized to: a guiding spirit, a saint or other religious figure, a teacher, a power animal, a shrine, or a holy object whose presence or touch conveys the needed knowledge. The guru can also impart strength, power, and healing of the mind, body, or spirit. The guru lives, typically, in a remote area, and it takes some effort and enterprise to get into his/her presence. In your language you can specify the sex of the guru, or be artfully vague about this point. An offering may be taken to the guru.

Setting the stage also involves seeding expectations of what will transpire in the interaction with the guru—what will you learn? discover about yourself? achieve? come away with? what will be forgiven? what will help you heal? how will you find peace?

c. *Development*—The listener starts out on a journey to find and visit with the guru.

Possible words to include are:

- starting out with something specific in mind
- finding your way
- searching for the path
- wisdom is sometimes hard/easy to find
- asking just the right questions
- sharing a special offering
- openly receiving this gift
- just sitting quietly, making contact
- he/she/it knows exactly what you need
- in his/her/its presence a sense of calm/peace/serenity/ understanding/healing comes over you
- and the journey may be long and hard
- you've worked for this
- this is your time, now
- finding what you wanted
- and those answers are so obvious and realistic
- facing: yourself/him/her/it/your concerns/these difficulties with simple courage

- sitting in silence together
- receiving: blessing/forgiveness/permission/understanding/ courage/joy/peace/healing/patience/inspiration/meaning
- making contact
- touching
- a sense of: self/others/nature/love/peace
- worth waiting for
- being: renewed/energized/strengthened/calmed/healed/ forgiven/restored/enspirited
- thanking him/her/it for their gift

The previous suggestions can be woven into an endless series of individual treks.

d. *Closing*—It is important to be polite and thank the guru for his/her/its time and offerings. Then the person takes his leave, and some of the following may be used:

- and having found what you came for
- you've learned some surprising things, haven't you?
- learning what you already knew
- and ready to move on now
- answers can sometimes be so simple
- it was right there all the time, wasn't it?
- it was worth the trip
- feeling ever so peaceful now
- knowing what to do
- it was within you all the time, wasn't it?
- finally making contact with: yourself/this other part of you/ your healing powers/your inner strength/those fears and knowing what to do about them/that lost part of yourself/ your parents
- feeling that the healing has already begun
- feeling your immune system growing stronger
- feeling: blessed/forgiven/at peace/inspired
- and the meaning is clear, isn't it?
- returning to this room, here and now
- what an accomplishment!

Obviously, the closing statements need to be connected to whatever you wove into the development section.

2. A Hero's Journey

a. *Audience* —The hero or heroine's journey is a rite of passage, generally a challenge that has to be successfully met to become a member of your tribe or a special group. This journey can also be undertaken as the "champion" of your group to realistically or symbolically win something for them. In modern terms these are transitions into (or out of): adolescence, manhood or womanhood, marriage, parenthood, divorce, catastrophic disease, a job, retirement, status (like promotion or demotion), grandparenthood, and death. Society and religion provide ceremonies for these transitions, yet your client may need extra help or may not have a functioning support system. So this journey is for people who find difficulties in the transitions that are an integral part of life.

b. *Opening, setting the stage*—The parameters for the hero's journey need to be established at this point. (1) Does the hero travel alone, as part of a group, or as the leader of the group? (2) What preparations are needed before the journey is begun? Equipment? Food? Maps? Communication devices (we live in the era of the cell phone and GPS!)? Training in terms of fitness? Rehearsal of the journey? Protection devices? Specific ceremonies? (3) What is the nature of the setting of the journey? Forest? Desert? Mountainous terrain? Savannah or plains? Ocean or lake or river? Climate, in terms of cold, hot, moderate? On foot, horseback, vehicle, boat? (4) How much danger is involved? All heroes' journeys involve some danger or peril. Can the hero lose his life, for example? (5) Nature of the encounters to be expected—animal, human, extraterrestrial, mythical, spiritual. (6) What kinds of personal challenges will be involved? Intellectual? Physical? Mythological? Riddles? Single combat? (7) The nature of the reward(s) attainable from this journey. Sacred object? Wisdom? Fairy princess? Handsome prince? Freedom? Surcease of some personal or tribal affliction? Manhood? Womanhood? Status like becoming a leader? Internal peace? Power? There are obviously many elements involved in setting the stage, and this leads to an enormous variety of possible combinations that will make it relatively easy to isomorphically match your clients needs.

c. *Development*—A number of possible words and phrases for use in the hero's journey follow:

- as you start out, how much will you take with you?
- having completed all your preparations, carefully
- and, going with the blessing of your tribe/people
- knowing exactly what you are seeking
- being ready for all contingencies
- being prepared
- finding your own way (there)
- being scared and yet proud
- the hardest journeys begin with that one step
- your hopes and dreams
- finding: yourself/fulfillment/your courage/your roots/what you were seeking/meaning/your goal/peace/your strength/your direction in life/the way/the magic/the healing/love/forgiveness
- overcoming: all obstacles/that trap/your inner fears/what had held you back/any qualms/any dangers/the hunger/the thirst/the deprivation/those old restrictions/those old messages
- believing in: yourself/your quest/your destiny/this way to help/your support/your God/the rightness of this journey/your inner strength/your courage/your perseverance/that the journey will be successful
- solving: the riddle/the mystery/the question/the labyrinth of your life/those old problems

d. *Closing*—The end of the hero's journey is a successful return, a triumph of some kind. In addition to a reorientation the following may be helpful:

- and having overcome those obstacles
- finally finding: yourself/meaning/love/peace/what you were looking for/the key/the clue
- bringing back: the solution/that special object/the magic/ your victory/love or your loved one/that sense of strength/ the healing power
- having accomplished your goals
- completing that heroic task
- having slain your dragons
- having become who you really are/were meant to be
- telling your story
- being proud
- ready to start your next journey/quest

3. *Constructing a Building*

a. *Audience*—This is mainly a metaphor for people whose primary representational system is kinesthetic, i.e. construction involves objects that are handled. If your client is visual or auditory, you can describe the construction process in terms of things that he *sees* or *hears*, in addition to kinesthetic descriptives. This client is stuck and needs a *foundation* and a means of building upon that foundation. The construction metaphor also uses the fact that many different components and skills need to be integrated in a conscious design. The process is systematic and organized, and at the end you have something that is quite practical. Of course, this general idea can be built upon (sic!) in the construction of anything from a tree house to a piece of furniture to a doll's house to a filing system.

b. *Opening, setting the stage*—Based on what you have learned about your client, you decide on the type of construction. Some possibilities are: skyscraper, residential home, tree house, shed, vacation cottage, doll house, add-on room, remodeling of a kitchen or bathroom, bookcases. Take into account the client's knowledge and skill levels. Are there plans available that are professionally prepared or drawn by the client? Are approvals needed from governmental agencies? What about the materials of construction— wood, brick, concrete, steel, glass, electrical, and plumbing? How is the building roofed? Is this a general description of professionals constructing the building with the client as observer, or is the client a participant? You may wish to use the Habitat for Humanity (a church-based group), where volunteers construct low-cost housing as your model. Where is the building located: urban, suburban, rural, remote? Purpose of the building?

c. *Development*—You can start with the planning stage and move on, or with the actual construction in progress. Here are some suggestions:

- building a solid foundation
- getting down to bedrock
- putting in a solid support structure
- having your plans all ready
- all the supplies are there
- with safety

- putting the first part in place
- making the connections
- so you can see out
- being protected
- walls to protect you
- with a roof over your head
- all utilities in place
- doing the finishing work
- putting the last coat on
- finding that everything fits
- integrated/coordinated/connected/together
- being supportive/finding support
- with a core of steel
- rock-solid
- cementing/cementing together/reinforcing/riveting/nailing down/screwed together
- with sturdy locks
- enclosing your world
- building/building upwards/building your dream
- vision/hopes/dreams/what you've always wanted
- doors to/open/close/lock
- fastening onto
- connected to: the earth/the sky/your surroundings
- putting down roots

d. *Closing*—Many of the suggestions in (c) would fit here. If it is a house, how would you live in it? There is pride in construction, solidity, building with your own hands. This is something to: house you, put down roots in, protect you, go home to, find fulfillment in, enjoy, grow in. And are you surprised? What have you: found, learned, experienced, accomplished? And, what have you: roofed in, roofed over, walled in, walled out, created? Then reorient.

4. Weaving Cloth

a. *Audience*—Since the concept of "weaving" is generally known as a metaphor for creating something out of separate strands, this metaphor is for those who need connections in their lives. It can also be used for finding meaning in patterns. The cloth is stronger than the thread.

b. *Opening, setting the stage*—Does the weaving involve: working with rattan as in caning or basket weaving, using a loom and fibers or threads, knitting or crocheting, knotting as in macramé and some rugs? Has your client any experience with weaving? Have you ever wondered how cloth was made?

c. *Development*—Suggested words/phrases are:

- deciding on the pattern
- finding the right: thread/yarn/cane/loom/design
- how colorful can you be?
- setting up the loom
- it's all in the design
- not starting until you are ready
- having everything in place
- choosing the right needles
- everything is matched
- shuttling back and forth
- raising the heddle appropriately
- one thread, one row at a time
- beating so your cloth is tight
- adding: color/pattern/flexibility
- hanging by a thread
- the thread of life
- and what is looming in your life?
- turning the edge/firming up the edges
- watching it grow under your guidance
- patience
- laying the foundation
- knitting together
- making cloth/clothing/a scarf/a hat
- pulling it all together
- binding/tying/fixing/constructing/weaving/knitting
- making a thing of beauty
- finding: fulfillment/a pattern to life/meaning/inner resources

d. *Closing*—Again, some of the preceding may also fit in well in this section. Making whole cloth, bringing together, finding the pattern in your life, weaving it all together, making something useful, many strands coming together, covering yourself, bringing loose ends together, weaving it well. Having deliberately put in one mistake because only God is perfect.

5. Baking Bread

a. *Audience*—This metaphor can help people connect to pleasant early-childhood memories, but, if it is used in such a manner, check first that this is true for this particular person. There are elements of careful planning and growth. The metaphor implies both growth and sustenance. This metaphor can be a pleasant but neutral experience or one fraught with special significance.

b. *Opening*—Is your client an observer or the baker? What is being baked—bread, muffins, cookies, a roast, fish, poultry? Is the baking done in: a kitchen, grandma's kitchen, mother's kitchen, in the open, in a bakery? What does your client know about baking? Is it from scratch or using a prepared mix? Can you adapt this metaphor to a bread-making machine? Who eats the baked goods?

c. *Development*—There are many possibilities here. Some suggestions:

- and how does the flour flower?
- bringing it all together
- mixing everything up
- yeasty/rising/taking the time to rise/kneading/needing/rolling it out/forming: the bread, roll, cookie/doughy/sticks to your fingers/adding ingredients/following the recipe/aroma/odor/punching it down/rolling
- just the right amounts
- baking just long enough
- the bread of life, finding sustenance
- old pleasant memories
- reassuring
- cleaning up afterwards
- greasing the pan
- adding flavor
- browning to perfection
- the staff of life

- being crusty enough, developing a protective crust, hard out-side and soft inside
- making enough dough
- giving it time to rise
- adding: raisins/honey/fruit/nuts

d. *Closing*—Reorient to present. Having baked to perfection/savor-ing those memories/enjoying each bite to the fullest/finding sus-tenance for yourself/cleaning up the mess afterwards/such a satisfying experience/being fulfilled/tasting once again/a sense of fulfillment/breaking bread with family, friends, loved ones. There is just something special about preparing food, and "baking bread" can be adapted to preparing any particular dish—such as a salad—or to entire meals. *Bon appetit!*

6. Sailing

a. *Audience*—This is a specific metaphor that would work best with someone who sails or is familiar with sailing. (Do not use with some-one who is afraid of the water or being in small boats or who gets seasick.) The general thrust is to connect the client with the open air, open spaces, "smooth sailing," freedom of movement and getting away. I have used this for smoking cessation and breathing problems.

b. *Opening*—Ascertain how familiar your client is with sailing—how much experience, in what kinds of vessels, whether active sailor or passenger. Does he own his own boat? This can connect to a remembered sailing experience or an anticipated one.

c. *Development*—Here is some possible language:

- sailing forth
- having made all the preparations
- sailing safely/wearing your life jackets/putting on sunscreen/knowing these waters
- exploring new seas
- watching the wind/reading the wind
- breathing in deeply
- weighing anchor/being aweigh/being away/making way
- filling your sails

- moving into the wind/tacking upwind
- keeping on an even keel/heeling over/balancing/trimming the weight/keeping in trim
- going downwind
- watching the clouds/reading the weather/reading the surface
- scudding along
- emptying the (your) bilge/bailing
- trailing your hand in the water
- steering your own course
- following your star
- all hands working together
- experiencing being in "irons"/the calm before the storm/ weathering all changes
- sails flapping/coming around/dropping the sails/hoisting the sails/lowering the boom
- watching the (your) telltail/charting your way/following the compass
- docking/going into dry dock
- cleaning off: the barnacles, the (your) hull, the deck
- ready for: action/lazing in the sun/staying the course/finding your way
- alone with: your boat, your thoughts, the stars, wind and wave
- enjoying the competition of a regatta
- being shipshape/everything in its place/ropes coiled/anchored
- knowing your knots/unknotting that tangle
- fishing/distant shores/on the beach/swimming

I obviously got carried away, just sailed off, with all of these possibilities. Be focused in your choices.

d. *Closing*—And having sailed home safely, finding your berth, anchoring in a safe harbor, having found your way, having sailed upwind and down, securing your vessel, all shipshape again, a satisfying sail. Some of the suggestions in (c) would also work well in closure, ratifying changes and what the person learned.

7. Growing: Corn/Tree/Flowers/Tomato

a. *Audience*—The planting and growing of flora lends itself to many variations. Is the plant for food or beauty or shade or all of these?

The growing metaphor has been used when people are stuck in their own growth and development. The listener does not need to be knowledgeable about gardening.

b. *Opening*—Decide on what kind of plant is appropriate for this time in your client's life. A slow-growing oak tree, which loses its leaves in winter, is different from a fast-growing evergreen, a flowering shrub different from a protective hedge, ground cover versus grass, vegetables versus flowers. A rose with thorns (a favorite for metaphors) is different from a begonia, perennials versus annuals.

c. *Development*—There are many ways of preparing the soil, and planting your seeds ...

- preparing the soil/sifting the soil/digging deep enough/ adding enough compost, fertilizer, mulch, peat moss/clearing the ground
- planting your seeds, the seeds, just deep enough
- tilling the soil/plowing/turning it over
- the good earth/fertile soil
- protecting your new plant/mulching/staking/spraying/feeding/watering just enough
- putting down roots/the roots anchoring/the root hairs finding water and nutrients/rooting/building that firm foundation
- watching: the growth, the new shoots, the buds forming, a flower emerging, a bud bursting
- pushing up through the ground, irresistible, finding its way to the sun
- some plants have their own built-in protection—thorns, tough skins and bark, bad taste, prickles, protective coloration, toxins (like poison ivy), odors
- and flowers cannot survive alone—they need the bees and other pollinators; a symbiotic relationship
- so many different colors and shapes and forms for even one kind of plant
- providing nourishment for us
- how does a sunflower follow the sun? fields of yellow turning together, resting when ripe, fulfilled, seeds continuing the cycle
- tomatoes going from buds to flowers to hard green to ripe red, naturally, without thinking

- in the fall, leaves falling, crunching underfoot, variegated, each tree its favorite color, some leaves very individual
- how does a tree know to be conical or pear-shaped or spreading? following its (your) instincts
- trees and people grow better when you hug them
- and the dead plants make compost for the new ones
- what does a thousand-year-old redwood think?
- and we all know how to grow, each in our own way

d. *Closing*—Finally bearing fruit, living through your own cycles, growing well, spreading your branches, flowering, blossoming, growing into the light, having found your roots, planting your garden, planting that acorn for the future, providing beauty, giving nourishment, turning a new leaf, arranging your growth, knowing. Planting seeds is like ... planting seeds.

4.5 Some basic generic metaphors

In this section a number of basic generic metaphors from several sources are given. The first is from Battino and South (1999, pp. 187–8).

1. Construction of a Building

Have you ever been a sidewalk supervisor, watching a skyscraper being built? They always dig so far down to *construct the foundation*. And isn't it interesting that you first have to *clear a site*, and then remove so much dirt and rubble *before you can begin*? What a *wonderful balance*, since there is always someone who wants clean landfill—one person's waste or excess is another person's need. As water seeks its own level, the foundation needs to be waterproof or with a way to pump out the excess fluid. I am always surprised at how deep foundations need to go—*to rise above* the level means to *build solid* and deep supporting structures. To *be grounded* applies to buildings, as well as people. To *be rooted*, to plants as well as people. The framing may be steel or reinforced concrete. Foundations must be steel or reinforced concrete. Foundations must be concrete and *solidly based*. As the skeletal frame rises, it almost seems so airy and insubstantial. Yet all the stresses and strains are calculated with *safe margins* of error—to be economical you don't want to overbuild more than is necessary *for your security* and safety. It is in the interlocking and *interconnecting* of all of the structural elements that the *strength* comes. The whole is *much more* than its parts, yet each part has a part to *play together*.

What kind of walls should this building have? Some buildings are almost transparent, some you can see out of, but not into—mirroring the outside world; some have solid substantial sealing walls, and some *have a balance*. There are so many ways to skin a building, *what is your façade like*? And that's *just the outside*. How many rooms and what shapes, and is there enough room? And you always need to provide places for storage and *ways to get in and out*. What kinds of doors? And how do you roof and cover and *protect the insides*? And all those simple but *important lines to the outside world*, with water and sewage and electricity and communications. So many details when you *build something*. And when a building is completed, that is *only the beginning of its life*. Many buildings have built-in ways to *ease remodeling, adaptability* in steel, *changing* within concrete, *expanding* rooms and vistas. And how will you build the skyscraper of your life?

Commentary: Particular phrases and words are highlighted by being italicized. Would you emphasize the same words? Where would you insert pauses, and of what lengths? Of course, this could be adapted to building a house or other structure.

The following script, in a different style from the previous one, is from Havens and Walters (1989, pp. 73–4) and is also about building a house.

2. Building a House

It can be very relaxing
to watch someone working.
Educational as well.
And I wonder
if you know
what is involved
in building a house, home,

a place to live, to be.
I don't know
everything involved,
but I remember watching,
as a child,
the way they marked it off
with stakes at each corner
on the vacant lot
and then dug the foundation,
deep in the soil,
and poured truckloads of concrete,
for the basement floor,
and the thick walls,
reinforced with steel bars,
to prevent cracking
or crumbling.
That house
was built to last.
A solid foundation
to rest upon,
to build the rest of a life upon.
And as you rest there,
continuing to relax,
your unconscious mind
can use that time
to examine closely
the foundation
of thought,
ideas,
beliefs,
values,
of experiences
defined by the blueprint,
the design,
of what is wanted
and where it is built,
already or planned.
Because someone
had to foresee
to see in the mind's eye,
what was to be,

what would be
how it would look
where it would sit,
how it would function,
that house,
sitting there,
a place to live,
a place to be,
for someone to enter,
and relax comfortably,
welcomed
and protected within,
arranged and organized,
for living within.
So if the walls
could talk
they would soothe,
and observe
a smooth, effortless flow
from one room to another,
one space to another,
a living space,
living room,
the private places,
private room,
where private events,
and private thoughts,
can occur safely,
and be kept
safe and sound.
Where a child
could go,
to explore and examine
room after room,
floor after floor,
hidden spaces,
crawl spaces,
storage places,
full of memories,
and things put away until later.
Some remembered,

some forgotten,
old toys, school papers, pictures and books
some used, some ignored,
each with a feeling,
that also was stored.
A house full of places,
empty spaces,
to be filled
and transformed
to meet the needs,
the desires,
of those who choose
to live within,
within oneself,
to weather the storms,
to work on ideas
to let the mind wander,
gazing out at the sky,
or the people walking by
or coming in, and sharing and talking.
And as I talk
that solid foundation takes form
the ground floor takes shape.
The plans that tell
where things go,
how things will be,
what and where
is the key.
A key question,
what will be done,
what are the plans
that guide and provide
a solid foundation to build upon
for the future.
All from a few stakes
that mark out the place
where they dig a hole
deep down
in the ground,
where something was once,
but is now replaced

by a new place to be,
a new space to see,
a relaxed place to be
even now as you relax even more
and drift in thoughts
about what will be
and what was found
that can be used later on.
Because I don't know,
what your unconscious mind knows,
or what it shows you,
when you wander and wonder
what you want,
what you will be
what it will take for you
to live comfortably here and there,
but you can know,
or begin to know,
now ...
[*Go to trance termination.*]

Commentary: Their scripts end with a direction to complete with a standard "trance termination" ending, since their book is about hypnotherapy scripts. This format is an interesting way to present a script as a series of phrases. Where would you put in pauses, for what duration, and what words or phrases would you mark out for emphasis in delivery? Contrast the language styles in this and the previous basic metaphor.

We continue with a Havens and Walters metaphor for test anxiety and fear of failure (1989, p. 94).

3. Fail Safe

Because everyone needs to relax at times,
even Olympic athletes
who are under a great deal of pressure to perform,
and sometimes must be perfect to win,
need some way to relax
and to put things into perspective,

to recognize that it is just a sport
and not a war between nations.
Because a war is one thing
and a game is something else entirely,
especially in this atomic age
where a war could mean the end of everything.
We really cannot afford to make
even the smallest of mistakes,
and so some people are terrified
that the fail-safe system will fail,
and that will be the end of it all,
all because of some tiny little error,
somebody doing something wrong
or saying the wrong thing at the wrong time
in the wrong way to the wrong person,
and everything goes up in flames.
Which is why they have special programs,
for the people working with those systems,
because what they have to do
is so dangerous and so terribly important
that special training and counseling is required.
The only place in the world, perhaps,
where mistakes cannot be allowed,
and it is comforting to note
that almost everyplace else,
an error is just an opportunity
to do it differently later on,
because perfection is rarely required
and perfection is seldom needed,
and even Olympic athletes,
are never perfect all the time,
and sometimes do things wrong
like the Navahos when they weave a rug,
who always leave a knot, an imperfection,
so the gods won't be angered
and think they are trying to be gods themselves.
But that is another story
about what is really important
and what is not
and how it feels to give permission
to enjoy the feeling of the freedom

to feel safe doing those things
knowing that the world won't end,
if you leave a knot someplace,
so the gods can relax
knowing you are not challenging them,
just doing the best you can,
letting it go at that.
[*Go to a direct suggestion or to trance termination.*]

Commentary: This is a nicely worked-out metaphor.

A last metaphor from Havens and Walters (1989, p. 132) is designed to increase the immune system's responses to infections.

4. Protective Ants

There is a tree in Africa
that has a special relationship
with a particular kind of ant.
The ants spend their entire lives
living on that tree.
They build their nests
out of its leaves,
they only drink
the particular kind of sap
that tree produces and secretes
or eat the special tiny berries it grows.
They never leave that tree,
because that tree provides
everything they need.
And this type of ant is the only insect
that does live on that tree.
Whenever any other insect
begins to crawl upon it
or lands on one of its leaves
the ant sentries send out an alarm,
and all the other ants come running.
They attack those foreign bodies
and either destroy them
or drive them away

and in this way
they protect that tree
from any invaders
that might attack it
or even destroy it.
They save the tree
and the tree saves them.
There are many other examples
of the same thing throughout the world,
where one tiny creature
protects a large one
from dangerous invaders.
And in each and every case
they always seem to have a way
of paying very close attention
to anything that could be harmful
so that they know immediately
if something is wrong,
and they know immediately
where something is wrong,
and they know what is wrong
and they pay close attention to it
so they can do something about it,
to eliminate it or fix it,
just the way people do
when they notice a pain in a foot
and they pay close attention
to that discomfort
so they can tell what it is
and get rid of that stone in the shoe,
as long as nothing gets in the way,
and they continue to pay close attention
to the way the body reacts
and amplify that reaction
the way they amplify the sound of an engine
to hear what's wrong
and let that body take care of itself
with the same amazing grace
that those ants take care of that tree,
automatically and continuously,
rushing to do those things needed

to heal and protect.
[*Go to a direct approach or to trance termination.*]

Commentary: Of course, you would have to know that your client was not afraid of ants and that this imagery would be appealing to him. Could this be adapted to other insects or imagery?

The Lanktons' book *Tales of Enchantment* has many metaphors for specific purposes. The next one (1989, pp. 62–3) is designed for the affect goals of satisfaction, comfort, and relief. The authors note that this metaphor was written by Nicholas G. Seferlis, M.S.

5. The Concert of the Missing Note

Karen was in the high school band. She played trombone. And as you're sitting there feeling your hand resting on your lap, maybe your unconscious makes some interpretations about a secret understanding. And she had worked exceedingly hard practicing her trombone solo that she was going to do the night of the concert. Everybody knows what it's like to work hard and people wonder what it would take to give a good performance. And each night as Karen practiced, she thought more and more about her big moment, as people will when they are appearing in front of a group. She thought about what it would be like for her to solo in front of the entire high school auditorium. She began to wonder about some of the things that might go wrong. She knew her instrument was well prepared, well oiled. Everybody knows what it's like to be well prepared and well oiled. But people wonder whether what they've planned in the future will come out well.

And your conscious mind may plan while your unconscious mind wonders or maybe your unconscious mind can plan while your unconscious mind wonders. We all know that things do turn out, sometimes successfully and sometimes even more successfully than we had planned.

The night of the big performance, Karen was backstage. She wondered what it would be like to be out there. As she looked around the room, she saw all the band members carrying their instruments and tuning up. I guess we all know what it's like to tune up and prepare for something. A little bit later on Karen walked out and took her seat with the rest of the band and they played the first two numbers. Little did Karen know that later in the evening, this concert would be remembered as "the concert of the missing note," and how this would make a dramatic turn for her.

As Karen played the first song with the band, she started again to think about her solo a little later. Then, at the end of the second song she heard the audience applaud and wondered if they would be applauding for her after her solo. Still wondering and not knowing why this would be called the concert of the missing note.

After the fifth song, Karen stood from her chair and approached the center stage. With eyes placed intently on the conductor, she waited for the band to start. As she looked out over the audience, the conductor's arms raised. Everyone knows what it's like to be prepared and getting ready to do the thing you've practiced many weeks for. Dramatically, the conductor's arms dropped, the band started up. Karen started counting her measures … 1, 2, 3, 4, 1, 2, 3, 4, … and all of a sudden she noticed that she had missed where she was supposed to come in. But immediately, she blew the note for the next beat and gave a sterling performance. At the end of the song, she looked out over the audience and saw all of her friends gazing, parents applauding. She had a feeling of satisfaction and relief. Everyone knows what it's like to feel relief when something is over. She also had a sense of comfort about doing a good job.

She was probably the only one who knew that this would be called "the concert of the missing note." And she felt more and more satisfied and relieved as the concert ended and she walked out. She sat down in the band room and just gazed for a moment into the bell of her trombone, surprised at the unexpected reflection that caught her eye.

There was her face reflecting relief and satisfaction. Of course, it was a little bent and distorted in the shape of the trombone, but the face undeniably reflected something about that satisfaction. There were the little turned-up corners on both sides of her lips and the rest of her face was quite relaxed. And she looked, gazing deeply, and noticed her breathing in and out, aware of the chair, of the comfort. And you can be pleased to discover how nice it is when you feel a relief and happiness with your conscious and your unconscious mind.

Commentary: This is a classical form of a metaphor as a story about someone whose concerns are isomorphic with those of your client. A proper introduction is needed to segue into a story like this. Perhaps something like, "One of the things you said reminded me about a high school student I'll call Karen."

The Lanktons introduce the following metaphor (1989, pp. 122–3) as being for someone who has the existing attitude of, "If everyone around me acts unpleasant, it is not my fault in any way." The goal attitude is, "People will give me what I expect of them."

6. *Searching for a New Home*

There once was an old man who each day sat and meditated on the top of a hill overlooking a small city below. One day as a traveler passed by with his bundles on his back, he asked the old man, "What kind of people live in that city, for I'm in search of a new home?" The old man immediately replied with a question, "What kind of people lived in the town where you lived before?" "They were a sorry lot," the passerby said. "Every last one of them was dishonest, rude, selfish, with not a care for anyone except themselves. They wouldn't give their own mothers the time of day. It's good to be rid of them! But what of the people that live in the city you are looking at?"

The old man listened and then said, "I'm sorry to tell you that you'd better pass right on by this city. I'm sure you will find the people here to be exactly the same as the people in the city you've left." The passerby left. And the old man continued to sit alone.

The next day, by chance, another traveler passed by with bundles of his back and asked the old man the same question, "What kind of people live in that city, for I'm in search of a new home?" Again, the old man replied with his question about the kind of people who lived in the town the traveler had left. "Oh, it grieves me to remember leaving them—they were so honest and brave and caring, generous and giving, every one of them a true friend. They would give a stranger the shirt off their back."

Having heard this description, the old man smiled and said, "Then, welcome to this city. I'm sure you will find the people here to be exactly the same as the people in the city you've left."

Commentary: This short story is almost of the form of a parable and is open to a variety of interpretations, which is what makes it a good general metaphor in the classic style.

One final metaphor from the Lanktons (1989, pp. 314–15) is connected to avoiding internalizing stress (sadness in this case) into physical symptoms. They note that this story was told as part of a multiple embedded metaphor (treated later as part of the chapter on advanced metaphor) for a woman taking steroids for bladder control problems.

7. Sadness

It's certainly true that there is a lot of sadness in the world. Children cry for dogs that have died, personal setbacks, for dreams that they won't be able to accomplish, losing sight, losing a friend, never having a child, losing innocence—there are so many more situations.

A woman who had gone to an allergist for twelve years told me that she had tried everything, and nothing worked, she was down to bread and water, it was about the only thing that she could eat without having allergic reactions. I asked her to tell me the rest of her story and it turned out that she had gotten divorced 12 years earlier. She didn't even make any conscious connection between the two events.

Her husband was a gourmet cook—it's hard to swallow, isn't it? When I finally was able to help her to cry about it, she thought this therapy was really amazing because her allergies went away. Teaching her how to substitute her emotional system for her allergic system took a bit longer. But it was very simple actually.

You can map your troubles in your allergic system, but it is a *better idea* to give them over to your *tear* system, that system has a better way of regulating and gets it over with. Some people have trouble with their parents being too aggressive and they fail to learn to use their aggression. When you overstimulate parts of their body, make cholinergic fluids going to the stomach, lungs, colon, liver, it's no wonder that organ failure happens. Other people are shamed into always being strong as children or have weak parents that they have to *take care of for fear* that they will be overcome and they never *recognize that ability that we all have to be soft and tender* and evoke nurturing. And, instead, those tense up their muscle system, stand erect, they move fast and pump adrenalin into their musculature, cardiovascular system, their skin-nervous system. Over the years a chemical imbalance eventually finds something that will go wrong, and they are the people we find with heart attacks, plus a sense of bursitis, eczema, and the heartbreak of psoriasis.

I think that you ought to use your unconscious ability to *transform old and unnecessary ways of adjusting yourself* with your environment of the past. *You seem to cry nicely, and I think you ought to consider using your tears.* You can wonder which eye will cry first. It's no fun to cry alone. Kittens are very good, I wouldn't recommend goldfish. You really ought to *learn to make contact through your emotions to responsive mammals*, like a child learning to do it with kittens and puppies. You will have the foundation that you need to *do it with human beings*. I don't know whether you are amused to know which eye was going to tear first.

Commentary: How would you generalize a story like this to deal with psychosomatic ailments?

Since I particularly like the metaphor I wrote about growing corn (Battino and South, 1999, pp. 309–10), it follows.

8. *Growing Corn*

One of my son's favorite books was about a kernel of corn. We had read that story so many times that he knew if I made the slightest mistake in reading—children have *such good memories* for *pleasant* things, and *know so much more* than you give them credit for. Corn is so good to eat, and did you know that each kernel carries within it the *seed to grow* a whole stalk? We started out with two kernels of corn, each in its own jelly glass full of potting soil. Sometimes a kernel will not grow, and we can be sad about that one and rejoice with the other one—*you need to be prepared for life*. The potting soil was broken up and dribbled into the glass so it would provide such a soft, *receptive* bed for the kernel. We enjoy the *soft*, moistness of the soil.

Now it is time to *plant your seed* and wonder just how soon the *roots will descend* and the stem *rise*. Gently make a hole with a finger, about one inch deep; put in the kernel pointy end up, and cover it with loose soil. Add the *right amount* of water. And, in a few days, *knowing how* we do not *know how* it knows what it knows, the *kernel opens* and a small tendril *reaches out, ready for growth*. And did you know that it grows down and around as much as it *grows up*? The roots start spreading and reaching out to *build a strong* foundation. The higher you grow, the stronger your roots must be. One day, one day that magic moment comes when the stem first bulges the soil, then *breaks through to the light*, ready to *assert itself, ready to grow, ready to rise* to its natural height, *reaching for the sun* and the moon and the stars. We watch and watch while it grows, seeing some of the roots against the side of the glass while the stem *stretches itself upward*.

When it has outgrown the glass, we transfer it to a larger pot with *more nourishing* soil and *so much more room to grow*. At each stage of its growth, the corn from the kernel needs *just the right amount* of room and nourishment and light. The sun *shines its light of energy* on the green-growing plant. And carbon dioxide from the air and water in the soil and nutrients in the soil combine together in the light to *make more growth*. Just the right amount of *each* nutrient is used so unknowingly and so accurately *to balance and grow*. In its thankfulness, the plant gives us oxygen.

We *prepare a sunny spot* in the garden. *Always be prepared*, and transfer the growing plant so it can now be on its own and *sink its roots* even deeper, *find stronger foundations, reach even higher, differentiate* and *grow* new kernels of corn, *new ears*, what does an ear of corn hear? And each new kernel in this sturdy, tall, being proud of *growing on its own* plant, has a tassel that *awaits fertilization* from another

113

plant. So, the corn *depends on its neighbors*, friends, and relatives to *become fully mature*, to be able to *bear its own fruit*. The corn *enjoy the sun*, is washed and nourished by the rain, *feels its roots* firm in the ground, sways to a passing breeze, *realizes itself.*

The time comes to pick the corn which the plant *lovingly gives us* so that we may *be nourished*, too, and *continue the cycle*, the endless cycles of growth, nourishment, death, and rebirth when we save some seeds for next year, *looking ahead*, preparing for more kernels of corn, and *more growth*. The corn bears fruit by giving and sharing to *continue itself* in whatever new ways are available in the endlessly interesting variety of life. Who would have thought a kernel of corn knew so much?

Commentary: The growing of any plant provides many opportunities for interspersing and embedding messages—the ones in the preceding metaphor are italicized. Some other possibilities are: (1) a sunflower that follows the sun and hangs its head and brightens a field and reseeds itself and feeds birds and stands tall; (2) a tomato is firm and round and red, a "love apple" that was once green; (3) a rose has its beauty and fragrance and its thorns for protection; and (4) potatoes, carrots, beets, and radishes do their growing underground in a protected environment until they are sufficiently mature to be harvested and nourishing. Match the plant to your client.

Since I also am fond of the weaving metaphor (Battino and South, 1999, pp. 312–15), here it is.

9. Weaving

A number of years ago I received a small loom and a book about weaving as a birthday gift. Before that gift I had not thought much about cloth and how it was made. Now, I started to inspect the clothing I wore with an eye to how the cloth was made. How were all those individual threads *woven together* to *cover, comfort*, and *protect* me? What *surprises* and wonderment were in store for me! How the ordinary can *be so magical* when you *really look at it*, when you see and touch and feel and smell it! I know that some cloth is printed, but that is another whole story—about mordants and dyes and chemicals and patterns, ways of imprinting and *making fast.* Some things you have to *wait to learn* about, leave for another time, when they become really important.

Since I could see only so much with the naked eye, I got out my magnifying glass. With that I could *see the individual threads* that made up the whole, just moving through each other in such regular arrays. With a stronger lens I noticed that there were little irregularities that were not visible to just my ordinary eyes—but, how wonderful the overall effect was; one I *didn't notice*; one I *could live with.* Sometimes, *you can look too closely* at what is in front of you and miss the importance of *the bigger pattern*, the designs of life, if you will. That is so, is it not? (I even remembered getting excessively annoyed over some minor thing my wife did today—it was really trivial.)

I was particularly interested in examining the corduroy pants I was wearing. To a person as naive as I was, weaving a flat cloth was simple, but how do you weave something with bumps and ridges, ups and downs, and have it *stay together*? Well, I studied and studied that corduroy cloth and never did figure it out until I made a small swatch myself—*some things you just have to do for yourself*—I still have that swatch around to remind me how the *threads of life can be woven into such interesting patterns*, ridges and valleys *into a sturdy fabric.*

So, I learned about weaving. And, I soon discovered that the most important part was the planning, the preparation, the setup. *You really need to know what you are doing in advance. Pick the pattern,* study it, *dress the loom* with the warp, the long threads bound to their beam, the *foundation* for all of the rest, *getting the threads of your life in order and tied down so you can create.* And the warp or ends move through the heddles with their eyes held securely in their harness. Depending on how complicated the pattern, you may need several harnesses, almost like harnessing up several horses to pull a heavier load.

And the shuttle carries the weft or woof of filling—there are sometimes *so many ways to describe the same thing*, are there not?—through the shed, that *parting of the threads* to let the shuttle pass. And, after each pass, the beater *firms up* the weft against its fellow threads, sometimes firmly, sometimes loosely, *depending on your purpose*. And *how tightly* do you pull to make the edges of the fabric, the selvedge? For every filling thread *turns around in its own special way*, leaving smaller or larger gaps around its edges, *all under your control*, so many choices, so many ways to *weave that fabric of your life*—tighter or more open, ragged or even, firmer or looser, ribbed or flat, complicated or simple, colorful or plain—knowing that *you can vary the pattern* section by section, patch by patch, even minute by minute to suit your needs.

And *it's all connected* even though sometimes a thread breaks. If you knot the ends together or add a new thread, *the break can be mended*. And you can even make that knot, that mending, *part of the pattern*. Persian rugs and mosaics always have one deliberate mistake that the artist incorporates since only Allah is perfect and *we are ever so human* and mortal. *That mistake may not be visible* to a casual observer, but the creator of that rug or mosaic knows it is there and that is sufficient. The knowledge of *one deliberate flaw can mask so many natural ones*, and that is right, isn't it?

The last task is *tying off* or ending the weaving in such a way that *it will not unravel*, sealing the edges so the fabric is *secure within its own boundaries*. And, the fabric may be an end in itself to hang on a wall or cover a table. Or, it may be used to cut to another pattern to sew together an article of clothing, *something useful made out of whole cloth*.

Looking at and feeling and listening to the movement of a piece of cloth, a weaving of threads and color and texture and pattern to create something that is *more than the original parts*, to make a whole around the holes between the threads, you can *continue to wonder* and marvel at the *changing patterns* in the fabric of your own life— what looms in *your future*?

Commentary: The weaving metaphor can be extended to any artistic or utilitarian process that involves a step-by-step creation of the whole from parts. These variants can be: sculpture in any medium, painting or drawing, collages, pottery, woodworking, origami, sewing, building models, needlework, basketry, and nest building. The storyteller needs some familiarity with the details and special language for each of these variants.

116

Milton Erickson was renowned for his storytelling and his uncanny ability to match *stories* to his clients. The plural of story is deliberately used here since Erickson wanted his clients to have many opportunities to discover solutions for themselves. Rosen's collection (1982) contains many of Erickson's favorite "teaching" tales. Two of these tales from Rosen are given here as a sample.

10. Being Six Years Old

I received a letter from my daughter-in-law last week in which she told me about her daughter's sixth birthday. The next day she did something for which her mother reprimanded her, and she told her mother, "It's awfully hard to be six years old. I've only had one day's experience." [p. 162.]

11. Whistleberries

One day a college girl passed flatus loudly in the classroom while writing on the blackboard. And she turned and ran out and went to her apartment, drew the blinds, and ordered her groceries over the telephone and collected them long after dark. And, I got a letter from her saying, "Will you accept me as a patient?"

I noticed the Phoenix address that she gave and I wrote back, "Yes, I would." And she wrote back, "Are you really *sure* you *want me* as a patient?" I wondered about it—and I wrote back, "Yes, I *would* like you."

It took her about three months, and then she wrote me and said, "I would like an appointment with you after dark. And I don't want anybody to see me. Now, please don't have anybody around when I come to your office."

I gave her a ten-thirty appointment, and she told me about passing flatus loudly in the classroom and running out of the room and confining herself to her cabin. She also told me that she was a converted Catholic. Now, converted Catholics are always so ardent; and I questioned her, "Are you *really* a good Catholic?" And she assured me she was. And I spent a couple of hours with her, questioning her about her goodness as a Catholic.

And then in the next interview, I said, "You say you are a good Catholic. Then why do you insult the Lord; why do you make a mockery of him? Because you are. You ought to be ashamed of yourself—making a mockery of God and calling yourself a good Catholic!" She tried to defend herself.

I said, "I can *prove* that you have little respect for God." I hauled out my anatomy book, an atlas, showing all the illustrations of the body. I showed her a cross section of the rectum and anal sphincter.

I said, "Now, man is very skilled at building things. But, can you imagine a man being sufficiently skillful to build a valve that contains solid matter, liquid matter, and air—and emits downward only the *air*?" I said, "God did. Why don't you *respect* God?"

Then I told her, "Now, I want you to demonstrate earnest, honest respect for God. I want you to bake some beans. They are called whistleberries by the navy. Flavor them with onions and garlic. And get in the nude and prance and dance around your apartment, emitting loud ones, soft ones, big ones, little ones ... and enjoy God's work."

And she did that. A year later she was married and I made a house call to check up on her. She had a baby. And while I was visiting her, she said, "It's time to nurse the baby." She opened her blouse, exposing her breast, and fed the baby and chatted casually with me. A complete change of reference. [pp. 151–2]

4.6 Summary

This chapter has presented the ideas involved in the construction of basic metaphor, along with a number of illustrations. These are in the classic tradition of the use of metaphors for psychotherapy and healing—that is, the stories are created and told by the therapist to the client with specific purposes in mind. In that sense, these are therapist-generated rather than client-generated. A good therapist, of course, follows the lead of the client with respect to content and themes. The discussion in Chapter 7 of Richard Kopp's work goes into much detail on client-generated metaphors. For the moment, though, let me tell you a story ...

Chapter 5

Analysis of Published Metaphors

5.1 Introduction

There are many published metaphors designed for psychotherapy and healing. The literature on guided imagery also contains much metaphoric material—some sample guided imagery scripts were analyzed in the author's 2000 book, so this chapter will concentrate on the "metaphor" literature. My concern is with the careful use of language within the metaphor. This, then is primarily a linguistic analysis based on the author's bias toward hypnotic language forms (Battino and South, 1999).

How do you use language effectively in storytelling? There must be a balance between sufficient detail to create the setting(s), and the "vague" language that permits the listener to do internal searches and create her own unique stories. It is these latter personalized stories that contain the power of metaphor-inspired change. The listener knows herself and her background and what is important to her in ways at which we can only guess. Of course, a *guided* metaphor in which you incorporate the listener's own imagery and story is even more effective. There is no substitute for initially collecting adequate information before launching a metaphor. At any rate, the careful analysis of what others have done lets us build on their strengths while avoiding potential pitfalls.

Selections from different authors will be treated separately in the following sections.

5.2 *Berman and Brown (2000, pp. 65–8)*

Berman and Brown's book is about guided journeys and story-telling from a shamanic perspective. Many of the "guided visual-izations" are prefaced by a story from a particular culture. The following excerpts are taken from the story entitled, *The Book of Life*. Commentary in italics are suggested word changes.

Excerpt	Commentary
Make yourself comfortable and close your eyes.	Eye closure is not necessary.
Take a few deep breaths to help you relax.	*Notice your breathing, and let each breath relax you more.*
Feel the tension disappear stage by stage from the top of your head to the tips of your toes.	To follow this instruction you first have to **"feel** the tension." Only then can it disappear. *And, continue to relax … from the top of your head … to your torso … to your legs … to the tips of your toes.* Talk directly about relaxation and *not* the absence or loss of tension.
Let your surroundings fade away as you gradually sink backwards through time and actuality and pass through the gateway of reality into the dreamtime.	First, this is written for a specific audience that will understand: actuality, gateway of reality, and dreamtime. Most listeners would not connect to these words. Also, I am not sure I would want to "sink backwards through time" or "pass through the gateway of reality."
Today's a very special day for you because you're being given an opportunity to look into your future, an opportunity most people will never have so make sure you don't waste it.	This statement is too much of a sermon and could put the listener on the defensive; "… make sure you don't waste it." Also, negation in a message is frequently ignored, and the listener will hear, "… waste it." Instead, you might say, *"This is an interesting opportunity for you, and I wonder how much you will learn from it."*

Excerpt

You're standing at the foot of a mountain with a winding path ahead of you leading to the top. The weather's hot and sticky and the climb is steep but you're determined and refuse to be deterred. Eventually you reach the summit where you find a palace cut out of crystal glittering in the sunlight. You have a minute of clock time, equal to all of the time you need, to take a breather and to appreciate the building now facing you ...

[After entering the palace you find an altar stone with a book with your name ...] and a forecast for the next five years of your life. You have a minute of clock time, equal to all the time you need, to study what it says ... ... you have the right to add a sentence of your own to the forecast, something you long for and hope will come true. You have a minute of clock time, equal to all the time you need, to add your dream to the page ...

Remember you have the power to dance this this dream awake and all you need is faith.

Commentary

Transition to being at the foot of a mountain is very fast. Why make the weather "hot and sticky?" "Refuse" to whom or what? How high is this mountain whose summit you "eventually" reach? There should be some comments about being able to do this safely, even though the trek is arduous. Why a "crystal" palace rather than a "palace," and let the listener fill in the details? The time distortion is helpful here. *Taking just a minute or so, resting, and wondering what this special palace holds for you ...*

Why not a table rather than an altar stone? Or a chest within which is this "book of life." *And, within this chest, your chest, is a book in which your future was written—a future you may change. Taking whatever time you need, knowing just how fast the mind can work, study what had been written, and change it so that your future is full of your hopes and dreams, knowing what is realistically possible and, yet, what can happen when dreams come true. Sensing and savoring that future reality, your life.*

"... dance this dream awake ..." implies a certain kind of shamanic awareness. "... you have the power ..."—*and having written in the book of your life, it has changed already, hasn't it?* "... all you need is faith ..." is a major presupposition. Why not imply that the *act* of writing in the book of your life has already altered it?

Despite the detailed critiquing above, this is a reasonable metaphor for the authors' stated purpose of learning "... how to take control of our lives." This kind of metaphor works best with more permissive and suggestive language, and allowing much time for the listener to create her own palace of possible futures. Also, a *direct* statement like "... and change it so that ..." is more enabling than

"… all you need is faith." Please notice the way that grammatical tense is used in the suggested alternate statements.

5.3 Lee Wallas's stories

In Lee Wallas's first book (1985) there are relatively long stories, each designed for a particular disorder or condition. This is evident in the descriptions: "A Story for an Avoidant Personality Disorder," or "A Story for a Client with Passive-Aggressive Personality Disorder Who Plays Schlemiel," or "A Story for the Treatment of Phobia." She writes from an Ericksonian perspective. An example would be "The Seedling" (pp. 117–23), which is a story for a client who had been abused as a child. The basic metaphor is about a boy rescuing a plant and caring for it. Some excerpts follow.

Excerpt	Commentary
Once upon a time in a faraway place, there stood a very beautiful greenhouse. It was all shining glass and it was enormous. Inside the greenhouse the muted sunlight filtered. The air was wet and warm … [This is followed by much detail about the greenhouse.]	Her stories typically start with the "once upon a time …" format. Depending on the listener this can be helpful or annoying. The descriptive details belong to traditional storytelling. More open-ended commentary lets the listener fill in his own personalized details.
[The tale of tending this "saved" plant ends with …] the young boy watched it and tended it carefully, taking delight each day as he saw each new leaf appear until at last the buds began to swell. And with room at last to spread its roots, and with room to spread its stem and leaves, the little plant flowered into the most beautiful plant of all because its root system was so strong.	The author matches the client's early trauma with the isomorphous plant. The ending has the embedded messages that the story was designed to deliver.

Wallas's stories are, by and large, well designed, and the language usage around the punch lines or messages is good, but they all tend to be overlong, overinvolved, and have too much detail.

However, trimmed down, the basic stories can be readily adapted to more clients than the specific ones she lists.

Her second book (1991) specifically contains stories for the reparenting of adult children of dysfunctional families via the use of hypnotic stories in psychotherapy. The stories are moderately long and often involve dialogue. Excerpts follow:

Excerpt	Commentary
[From "First Date."] This story is about a young adolescent girl. She is sprawled on the floor with her head resting against the side of her bed. In her lap is a telephone and she holds the receiver between her shoulder, the mattress and her ear. She's set for a long leisurely conversation with one of her girlfriends. There are lots of giggles and "Oh, you don't mean it! … No kidding!" [After some phone dialogue her mother comes in and they talk about dating. After much adult to daughter talk, the mother ends in part with …] I'm very glad that you came and asked me about it, because I know how hard it is for a young person, just beginning to take her first steps into adulthood, to tell her mom or her dad about this kind of thing. I just want you to know, darling, that I think that you are a very intelligent and very wise young person. … At the same time I am aware that you must take your steps out into your own world, getting ready to be a grown-up.	*Something you said about your past reminded me of this teenage client I had. Her name was Mary—she was a typical teenager struggling with emerging sexuality and all the social things in high school. One day, and they were both surprised, she actually had a long and open heart-to-heart talk with her mother. And, you can just imagine, how, with what you've learned since you were a teenager, what you would have told Mary in a caring and sharing and equal way. Take some time now to talk with Mary within your own mind. As you do that, you may share some of those thoughts with me. … there are many ways to learn, and you don't really know how much you know even when you're wise enough to know when to say no along the way to knowledge, or is it no-ledge? That Mary learned many things, some the hard way. Maybe what you told her helped.*

These are two completely different styles. Wallas's is more direct, more detailed, and much more preachy. The language is almost archaic, and the mother's advice has the flavor of coming straight out of some teenage advice manual. By contrast, my suggested (and much briefer story/intervention) is open-ended and designed to have the client teach this teenager out of her own experience. The process allows her to teach herself and to ratify her own development. Again, it is important to match the story style, its length, and the amount of detail to the client. Generally, I prefer shorter open-ended stories.

5.4 *Mills and Crowley's* Therapeutic Metaphors for Children

This book (1986) is an excellent introduction and practical manual for the use of therapeutic metaphors for children, and includes material on artistic and cartoon metaphors. On pp. 58–61 they tell the story of a pink elephant that is designed to help "different" children fit into groups. On p. 140 they take one section and italicize the interspersed suggestions, and on pp. 142–3 they boldface the interwoven sensory predicates that can expand the listener's awareness. In the analysis here the opening section will be reproduced, and then the separate section illustrating special language usage.

Excerpt

Just imagine yourself going on an incredible, marvelously relaxing journey … a journey where you can just close your eyes and imagine all kinds of wonderful, exciting, beautiful things to see, feel, taste, smell and touch. That's right. And you can begin this journey by getting in a very comfortable position and allowing yourself all the room you need … and take a nice, slow, deep breath in through your nose and exhale slowly out through your mouth. That's right. And continue breathing easily, comfortably, as the journey begins so easily for you now.

Commentary

This is an excellent use of language for starting people out—suggestions for being relaxed, closing eyes, using imagination, and being aware in all senses are in the opening sentence, but gently permissive. The use of "and" and "while" connects and implies and furthers the involvement. The slow deep breath is generally less obtrusive if in-and-out through the nose, or without any direction other than to sense the inhale and exhale.

Excerpt

While you are on this journey you can imagine a wonderful place you'd like to be. Perhaps you'd like to float high above the clouds. I don't know where you would like to go, but with your wonderful imagination you can create whatever kind of place you would like to be in. And while you are floating and drifting and feeling comfortable, I'd like to tell you a story—a story about a little elephant who lived in a zoo. A little elephant who was somewhat different from the other elephants, you see, because he was pink.

[In the following segment multi-level communication is indicated by the authors by italicized *interspersed suggestions*, and the **interwoven sensory predicates** in boldface.] At that moment a **twinkle** appeared in the little elephant's eyes. He realized there was a time, there is a time, when *it is so important to be different*—when *being different can even be wonderful.* The older, wiser elephant **nudged** him **gently** and said, "That's right. There are many, many times when *being different is such a wonderful ability, like all the abilities you have now.* And I wonder if you are able to *teach some of those abilities*, to *share some of those abilities with the other ones* who may not understand."

Commentary

This starts with an open-ended imagining of a "wonderful place," but continues with a too specific floating high above the clouds, and this is reinforced later with "while you are floating and drifting." The "perhaps" sentence could be deleted, and later the "floating and drifting" replaced by: *and while you are enjoying being in your wonderful place, and feeling ever so comfortable …* The segue into the little pink elephant's story is graceful.

The authors have chosen particular phrases and words to mark out and emphasize in their delivery. In reading through these excerpts you should consider their choices and whether you would mark out other words. These excerpts are presented here as a straight narrative—where would you put in pauses, and of what duration? The listeners need time to process what they hear, put their own interpretations and imagery to the suggestions, and incorporate them into their own lives in ways that make sense to them. These authors are masters of the language of metaphor, so these excerpts are examples more to emulate and study rather than critically re-write.

Excerpt

The little pink elephant **thought**
and **thought** and **thought** with
that same twinkle and said,
"Yes, I certainly could."

He went back to where the
other elephants **played** and he
began to *show them three other
abilities* that he had. He wanted
to *share those three abilities* so that
they could *experience them in a
new and different way*. He
showed them how many things
he could do by being pink. And
they were **amazed**. They
realized that being pink could
be quite **exciting** and different,
and they really tried **hard** to
become pink.

5.5 D. Corydon Hammond's edited Handbook of Hypnotic Suggestions and Metaphors

Hammond's edited volume (1990) is a superb resource for hypnotic suggestions and metaphors in many categories. It is encyclopedic and has contributions from a rich assemblage of experienced hypnotists and psychotherapists. There are scripts that can be used directly or adapted for the enormous range of conditions discussed. Each major section has a brief introduction written by Hammond, which is in the nature of a review of the literature on that subject, as well as commentary on the individual contributions. The first metaphor examined (pp. 535–6) (see opposite) is one that is for sickness, but is also adaptable to various traumas such as incest, grief, and divorce. (The italics were in the original.)

Excerpt

Remember a time when you got the flu, and how completely *miserable* you can feel. Remember how your *stomach* feels, when you're sick like that, and how your *head* feels. [Pause] And there's the *nausea* and sometimes the congestion. And when you're *so sick* like that, it *drags on*, seeming *endless. And you wonder if it will ever be over.* [Pause]

And you feel so *exhausted*, worn out, and *depressed*. And you may recall how miserable the *high fever* is, how hot you feel. And with high fevers, sometimes our *perceptions become so altered, distorted* …

But as really miserable and bad as that was, *you got over it. It ended.* And it really wasn't very long before, *you began forgetting* how bad it was. You were so completely miserable. It *seemed* endless, and like torture but *you lived through it*, and before long, *forget how bad it was.* … And with *this* pain, that you've been through, even though it was much worse than the misery of the flu, it also, will seem this way. And later, it will be hard to remember, how bad it was.

Commentary

This is a particular style of hypnotic metaphoric intervention that paces the client's misery by mentioning all of their bad feelings and then develops positive outcomes like, "you got over it," "it ended," "you began forgetting," and the direct statement of "forget how bad it was." Another school would say that the continuing mention of miserable states accesses them, reinforces those bad feelings, and that the "forget" injunctions may not be sufficiently powerful to replace the bad feelings. A brief alternative script is: *There are many times that things have happened to you that you would like to, and can forget. And how do you remember to forget those times and remember to remember just how fast they went, and how you got over them, and the comfort that you feel now at being a survivor? There are these good times, these comfortable times, knowing how far in the past that is, remembering to remember that you lived through all of that then and are now feeling so much better, so much better about yourself. You did, and you do, do you not?*

The suggested alternate statement in the commentary is more positive and does not dwell on or recall the past misery/discomfort in detail. Yet Hammond's formulation may work very well with certain clients. The next excerpts come from Hammond's metaphor around an injury, scab formation, and healing (pp. 536–7). He states about this metaphor (p. 536), "This is a trauma metaphor that is valuable in working with incest, rape or trauma victims, as well as with patients struggling to work through divorce. It consists of truisms about a virtually universal experience, tending to facilitate acceptance by the patient."

Excerpt

We've all had the experience of scraping a knee, or an arm, or an elbow. And after we're injured like that, *when it's first beginning to scab over*, it's still soft, and kind of bloody, and many people don't like to look at it, and kind of wince when they see it. And that may even make us feel self-conscious. *And when it's still raw and painful*, we don't want people to touch it, because the wound is still too painful and fresh. But it can be nice when there are people who show care, and who are nurturing and show us the tender loving care we need, without touching the hurt directly.

[There is then a section about the scab hardening to protect the person. The metaphor continues with …]

Sometimes, when we're young and don't know better, we're tempted to keep picking at it and bothering it, which only reopens and exposes the wound too soon, so that it takes even longer to heal, and leaves a scar. So you don't want to take off that protective scab *right away*. You want to allow a certain amount of time that's necessary, for natural healing to occur. …

But *most of us* in the process of growing up get some scars, that later, may be little reminders that something happened a long time ago, but which doesn't have to mean much later on. And after a while, we hardly even have to notice it …

And with this pain that *you've* been through, I think you'll find that your healing process is really very similar to what happens with your body.

Commentary

This metaphor is, again, a direct pacing of a trauma via the universal and isomorphic scraping of skin, scab formation, and healing of the wound. Most of the language usage is masterful, yet from my perspective there is too much inadvertent reinforcing of the injury. The interweaving of scar formation and getting over scars is useful. The statement, "So you don't want to take off that protective scab right away." can also be heard as, "Take off that scab right away" since people tend *not* to hear negation. Instead say, "*Just leave that protective scab on until it has completed its healing work.*

An alternative way of utilizing this general idea in a gentler way would be: *And we've all had the experience of cutting a finger or scraping a knuckle. It hurts right then, and can even hurt for a while afterwards. Yet, the mind and the body have remarkable healing mechanisms, automatic and routine ways of healing. A few hours later you're no longer aware of that finger or knuckle. If you bang it into something by accident, the hurt returns for a short time. And, before you know it, you even forget which finger or knuckle that was. Hurts just naturally go away and are forgotten. You don't even need to remember to forget. And, the body is just so marvelous that it even reproduces a fingerprint exactly, or those wrinkles on a knuckle. A scar may remind you of what you've already forgotten, something that's only a fading memory now that you are all healed. That's right, isn't it?*

5.6 Concluding comments

Although the format of this chapter has been that of analyzing, critiquing, and offering alternative phrasings, as a way of illustrating the better use of language for constructing metaphors, the format has been potentially unfair to the authors of the excerpts. The full metaphors are generally well constructed and serve the intentions of the authors. These cited metaphors were meant to be used and judged in their entirety. With that proviso, they have served the purpose of illustrating different styles, *and* that is the essence of preparing a practical metaphor—it needs to be for a particular audience and for a particular purpose. Given the creativity of storytellers, there are many stories that can work. Also, the *art* of any story is as much in its delivery as it is in its content.

Chapter 6
Advanced Metaphor

6.1 Introduction

Advanced metaphor is really just a more complex structure of a metaphor. Rather than tell just a "simple" and straightforward story, advanced metaphor involves what the Lanktons (1983, pp. 247–311), call " multiple embedded metaphor." (Art therapies as metaphors may be considered to be part of advanced metaphor, and are treated later in Chapter 15.) The development here is based heavily on the Lanktons' work (op. cit.), and also on Battino and South (1999, pp. 325–40). In this chapter the structure and related characteristics of a multiple embedded metaphor are discussed first. This is followed by an example for psychotherapeutic work, and another example for healing work. Finally, some examples of more complex metaphors from the literature are given.

From the perspective of hypnotic usage, a multiple embedded metaphor may be classified as a confusion technique or an overload technique. The basic process is to tell stories within one or more other stories. For example, a character in the lead story tells a story about a character in a second story who tells a story (in addition to his own) about a person in a third story. Or, several characters in the lead story tell other stories. Or you may say that the story you are telling reminds you of another one, and then something in that story reminds you of ... The level of complexity is adjusted to the client's needs. Each story can also make multiple "points" in that the listener finds many potential solutions to his concerns, and many different perspectives (reframes) of his life's situations. This complex structure is one way of dealing with several problems at one time. A metaphor triggers unconscious and conscious inner searches. When a multiple embedded metaphor is used, owing to its complexity, it tends to create states of amnesia for many of the areas explored. This is useful, for it keeps the conscious mind from sabotaging the solutions generated in the inner explorations. Such amnesia or forgetting can be seeded as part of the storyline. "He remembered to forget what it was he forgot so he could remember what it was important to not forget that is so useful to him."

It is relatively easy to keep track of the different stories. You can help yourself by using notes or your fingers as anchors to let you know which story you are on. It is, of course, OK to take a "time-out" to design a multiple metaphor. There is nothing unprofessional about using notes in your client's presence; in fact, you should have already seeded in his mind that the notes are a simple aid for you to *help him* more effectively. Listening to a story involves going into some level of trance, which usually involves a natural eye closure or defocusing. Then, consulting notes is not a problem. Also, I invariably take notes during a session (after asking the client's permission to do so).

Some superb storytellers, such as Milton Erickson, do not appear to have a systematic way of telling stories. Erickson simply told a multitude of stories, from his vast repertoire, that were carefully and consciously chosen to connect with the client's concerns. He preferred to provide many choices. Lankton and Lankton have done a systematic analysis of the structure of a metaphor and give a logical explanation (1983, p. 311) for the development of therapeutic metaphors for use while the listener is in a hypnotic trance. Their use of metaphor is from a hypnotherapeutic perspective, and they offer the following steps for developing and implementing multiple embedded metaphors:

1. Engage the conscious and unconscious attention of the client.

2. Retrieve and help build the necessary experiential resources.

3. Direct hypnotic work at the core of the neurotic bind.

4. Link the resources to the immediate social and practical concerns in the client's world.

5. Facilitate generative change by associating the changes to perceptions and images which the client will encounter in the next stage of social development beyond that in which s/he is currently engaged.

This is a useful model for working with metaphors, which also pays careful attention to outcomes and actually implementing what has been learned.

The Lanktons (1983, pp. 247–311) use a seven-step model for metaphoric work. The seven steps are: (1) induction; (2) matching metaphor; (3) metaphors to retrieve resources; (4) direct work on the core issue; (5) linking resources to social networks; (6) ending the matching metaphor; and (7) reorienting to the waking state. Information gathering must precede these seven steps. They give several case examples along with transcripts and commentary illustrating their approach. This chapter in their book is well worth studying. Their approach involves the conscious design and construction of a metaphor for a particular purpose. This development may be done between sessions.

Based on the Lanktons' work is the following structure for a multiple embedded metaphor using three linked stories (A, B, C):

1. *Induction*—This can be a formal induction or a conversational one, or the induction can be incorporated as part of the first story.

2. *First story begins (A)*—This follows the basic metaphor formula and matches the client's problem in some isomorphic way(s). Pacing and leading are involved as the metaphor parallels the client's concerns and background.

3. *Second story begins (B)*—The second story grows out of the first story in some way, e.g. a character in story one tells a story. The purpose of the second story is to stimulate, access, and retrieve resources within the client that are pertinent to solving his/her problem.

4. *Third story complete (C)*—Again, the third story grows out of the second story in some way. You can parallel the development of the second story or use a new approach. The purpose of the third story, which is told to its completion, is to work directly on the problem. This "direct" work involves hints and ideas and actions within the story that would stimulate new or different feelings, thinking, and behaviors. Indirectly, the story shows how to solve the problem. The story may emphasize support systems, imagery, words and phrases, and interesting new actions or behaviors.

5. *Second story ends (B)*—Connection is made back to the second story, whose ending links the ideas and resources from the third story to the desired outcome. Also, the resources earlier elicited in the second story are reiterated and connected to outcomes. Future associations and actions are connected to resources. The second story can end with a punch line or reinforcer.

6. *First story ends (A)*—Connection is made back to the first story. The continuation of the first story reiterates earlier themes with an attempt to consolidate and continue (future-pace) gains. The desired outcome may be modeled in some fashion. The ending can be logical or have a surprise. A closing memorable, profound, or wise statement can add weight to the story. It can also have an amnesic effect. The ending provides closure for the collection of stories.

7. *Reorientation*—The client is reoriented to the present in a way that is consciously chosen to induce amnesia for one or more stories, or with positive injunctions to remember and continue the work of change that is already in progress.

There is much conscious effort on the therapist's part to construct and interweave the stories. The pattern suggested above is A-B-C-B-A as indicated by the letters. Depending on your skill, more stories can be added or you can crosscut among the three stories for added effect. (A related skill to the multiple embedded metaphor is writing a computer program with the use of a flow chart to indicate the interconnections and dependencies of the parts.) Listening to the client and taking notes is important since you want to weave in words and phrases that he uses. If you write out your metaphor, be sure to indicate where you put in pauses, of what length, and which words or phrases you wish to emphasize in the delivery.

6.2 A multiple embedded metaphor for psychotherapy

This is a metaphor that was specifically designed for a client named Lenny. There are three linked stories in the A-B-C-B-A format. First, some background information is given about Lenny and his particular concerns. Then the metaphor is presented in its seven parts. Deliberately, pauses, length of pauses, and words and phrases to mark out for special emphasis are omitted. It is left as an exercise for the reader to decide on the specifics of the delivery of this metaphor. This is something you can experiment with by taping the metaphor and listening to yourself.

Background information

Lenny at age 66 is a retired professor of sociology. He taught at a middle tier university in the Midwest, and opted for early retirement at age 62. He has a modest reputation in the field with two books and a reasonable number of research papers and presentations. In retirement, he has taken up seriously playing piano, something he began at an early age, but with several fallow periods. He is good enough to give several public solo concerts each year for friends and other guests, with the encouragement of his piano teacher.

In addition to piano, Lenny's other hobbies include biking, hiking, reading, traveling, and listening to music at home or at concerts. He has been married for forty years. He and his wife, Mary, have two grown, married children and two grandchildren. Mary is a retired public school teacher of English.

Lenny has three presenting concerns: (1) he has performance anxiety about playing the piano at his recitals (this is partly about the actual playing, and partly feeling tongue-tied in introducing and commenting on each piece); (2) he is concerned about getting old and slowing down, and the creaks and aches of aging; and (3) there is also a concern about his being able to continue both physical and communicative intimacy with Mary in their retired life.

Lenny

1. *Opening*—As you know, Lenny, I like to tell stories from time to time. As you listen to what I am going to tell you today, you may wish to just lean back into a comfortable position, perhaps close your eyes, and breathe comfortably and easily. It is always so much easier to listen when you are relaxed, you learn more, and you

might even imagine that you are reclining in your favorite chair. That's right, just softly and easily. And, you know, I'm always amazed at how interesting and useful new ideas just seem to pop into my head when I'm relaxed, when I'm daydreaming.

2. *Story A*—Not too long ago I had lunch with my friend Harry. He's a chem. prof. at the university and teaches those big freshmen classes. For some reason or other he got to reminiscing about lecturing, and how he went from a scared assistant prof. hiding behind the lecture desk, to his present ease where he can talk comfortably to literally hundreds of people. He's really comfortable now, talking to large audiences. Harry almost got into a trance, a reverie, talking about talking.

He recalled his first seminar when he was a senior, talking about his senior research. He was really nervous then, and it certainly was OK to be nervous at that time. Now it is all different, for he is an experienced and seasoned lecturer.

Harry had to specifically tell me about an experience in graduate school. He was away at a research lab and learned a cutting edge analytical method there. His adviser talked Harry into giving a special seminar. People came from universities as far as one hundred miles away. Harry was worried until his adviser told him, "Not to worry, Harry, you are the expert on this topic, and you can play it any way you want. Nobody out there knows as much about this as you do." Keeping this special knowledge in mind, and knowing how much he had practiced the method, Harry just sailed through. He was the expert.

3. *Story B*—Learning how he got to be such a smooth lecturer, got me to thinking about how I taught my son George to drive a stick-shift car. First, we made him wait until he was seventeen. Some people just need that extra time as a transition—you do need to be mature enough to do certain things. He understood that. Do you remember what it was like to drive a stick-shift car? There are all those things to keep in mind—three different pedals and two feet, and which do you use on which? Then there is the steering wheel and the stick shift and two hands. And where do you look? Straight ahead? Which of the three mirrors and when? And there are all those things on the dashboard to read. We won't even

mention the turn signal and the lights and the windshield wiper. So many things to do at once, and you just note them and do them in some pattern, even being able to do several at the same time. George learned quickly, and then there were so many things he could do smoothly and automatically when he was in charge of his own driving.

4. *Story C*—So many different ways to learn, so many things to talk about. My mind seems to be wandering today, maybe wondering, about talking and communicating. Harry told me his story, and George and I certainly talked. I don't know if you've ever seen Thornton Wilder's play *Our Town*. All about ordinary lives in an ordinary small town, yet all lives are really extraordinary, aren't they? There's a particular scene in *Our Town* that sticks out in my mind now. Dr Gibbs and his wife were chatting quietly one evening. Mrs Gibbs got to thinking about a particular worry she had before they got married. Sure, they had plenty to talk about then—they were starting on an adventure, a new life together, lots to learn and explore about each other. But what would they talk about later, when they were old together? Would they run out of conversation? She was so relieved to discover that they still had things to talk about, meaningful things to talk about. And they were still learning about, and from, each other. When you love someone, there is no end to that love, and those discoveries. Keep talking, keep exploring, keep widening horizons, so much to learn by and from and with. Each day is new, each touch, each word, just being there.

That wonderful short scene of such ordinariness was and is extraordinary, and remembering Mrs Gibbs's words continues to help me. So many ways of being with someone, and what else is new?

5. *Back to Story B*—Cars were a novelty in Wilder's small town of Grover's Corner. George would have learned to drive himself in a different way then. Times change and we change with them. Before he knew it, George was driving that stick-shift car automatically, feet on the correct pedals with just the right amount of pressure, and in the right order, all coordinated smoothly. And he learned to use his hands, too, and his eyes: just when to look up, and when to look down, or straight ahead, or right or left. So automatic, each

step noted in the right place, with the correct emphasis. George knew he was a good driver, a good performer, if you will, when he could comfortably and safely talk and drive at the same time. Of course, when it was important, all of his attention was on his driving, his driving performance. And we've all had that experience, have we not? It's all so simple now, and practice is always important.

6. *Back to Story A*—My friend Harry told me that when he first lectured he actually memorized the content of his lecture notes. Now, as an experienced lecturer, the notes are there more as reminders. He feels free now to play around with those notes, sometimes improvising on their content, so that he can present their essence as he knows it in that moment. In fact, Harry talks about his lectures as being performances where he plays around particular themes. And he's able to talk easily and freely, since he knows his subject so well—he's had so much practice—and it almost flows as if the students, his audience, was not even there. Yet he knows when he talks as if to one person that it all happens so much easier, a smooth flow from him to them, through his fingers almost performing the magic of transformation from his mind to writing on the overhead projector. All so easy and simple now. And he does wonder sometimes about those early days and how he got to be so easily sure of his abilities to lecture, to perform. He even admitted that there were occasional doubts that arose, only to be put in their place by all of his experience of being in front of people. I enjoyed listening to Harry, and found much of myself in his story.

7. *Reorientation*—Remembering, and remembering to remember so much of that earlier turmoil which is well worth forgetting. There is just so much pleasure in having been through that and knowing what we know now, isn't there? So much is so much easier now, talking, being, communicating, playing.

Thanks, Lenny, for listening to these stories. Lots of shared experiences to ponder and wonder about. When you are ready, taking whatever time you need to assimilate what you've learned, just come back here and now. We can talk about some of this now, or you may wish to just let it simmer for a while. OK?

6.3 A Multiple embedded metaphor for healing

This is Elaine's story. She survived breast cancer by being in remission for that disease for ten years, only to succumb to a leukemia when she was 71 years old. This healing metaphor (or meditation or guided-imagery session—it is difficult to decide on labels sometimes) was designed to bring her comfort after she decided *not* to undergo a second round of chemo for her leukemia. Her oncologist had told her before the first round that it had a 33 percent chance of really helping her. Being the optimist and battler she was, Elaine leaped at the opportunity. There were many uncomfortable side effects, and the chemo only slowed down the leukemia for a short time. That is when, in consultation with her husband and family, she decided to forego any additional treatment. The following was made into a tape to which she often listened. She frequently used the tape as a kind of sleeping pill. (In fact, as an aside, most of the people for whom I have made tapes use them as a sleeping aid. In principle, the tapes are supposed to be *listened to*, but, if they bring my friends comfort, then that is a bonus.)

Elaine had been retired for some time. She was primarily a homemaker, but did various clerical jobs over the years. Her hobbies included sewing, reading, church, family, friends, and some traveling. She had been married for 48 years, had three children, and four grandchildren. Elaine's husband is a retired engineer. She had been a member of the support group I co-facilitate. Until the leukemia appeared, Elaine attended the meetings to provide support for *other* members.

Basically, what Elaine wanted from the tape was an aid to being comfortable and to dying with dignity in her own style. Three "stories" were used in the A-B-C-B-A format with A involving the Holy Spirit, B healing light and music, and C love. Elaine was a devout Christian and these were her choices. She was also familiar with the healing meditations we do at the end of our support group meetings. As I re-create her tape (unfortunately, I have no copy), I can sense this wonderful friend's presence.

Elaine

1. *Opening*—Elaine, here is the special tape we talked about. It repeats on the second side. Please be sure that you are in a comfortable position, and feel free to move at any time to become even more comfortable. This is your time now, a peaceful, calm, and healing time. With nothing to bother or concern you, your special healing time. And we can start with paying attention to your breathing, calmly and easily, noticing each breath as it comes in, belly and chest softly rising, and each exhale, muscles relaxing. Just one breath at a time. And, if a stray thought wanders through, notice it, thank it for being there, and go back to noticing your breathing, simply, easily, automatically, in and out, ever so softly. Your time, now, breathing easily.

2. *Story A*—And, within your mind, now, you can drift off to your sanctuary, your special healing place—a holy healing place. There are so many special places like that—I don't know which one you will choose this time. Just being there, be there sensing the space around you, looking around, noticing, smelling, listening, touching, being particularly aware of the light.

In this holy place can you now sense the presence of the Holy Spirit, here, now, to spend some time with you? Is there a change in the air? the light? some music? Knowing that presence, and with it a sense of awe and light and love. And, most important, a sense of understanding, being understood and accepted for simply being who you are, for just being Elaine. Your time, your healing time, such a relief, such a lightness of being, a calm understanding and acceptance, having done so much, a full life with all its memories and events, your life, lived moment by moment in that special grace granted by the Holy Spirit—a lightening of the heart.

3. *Story B*—And the Holy Spirit brings with it its own special healing light and music. A soft light, a gentle light, just the right colors, shifting, changing, entrancing, bathing you with its healing power, illuminating inside and outside, perhaps a gentle pulsating glow, moving over and through you, shining, shining on and within you. Your light, your healing light, your time, now.

With music, always with music, filling you and fulfilling you, carrying you away to there, and bringing peace here. Listening, fully, completely, the sound sounding soundly, resonating, your special music, perhaps a choir, or a soloist, or an orchestra, or one instrument. Calm, peace, soothing, knowing, and just being in this moment with that note, that chord, and the next. Music, musing on the music.

4. *Story C*—With the music and the light a sense of love, enduring, lasting, eternal love just fills your heart and radiates throughout your whole body, cell by cell, tissue by tissue, bone by bone, nerve by nerve, being bathed in this universal love. And, as you know, you can never receive love without giving it, touch without being touched, give gifts without receiving gifts. And love is the key, is it not? Loving and being loved, such richness, such light, such peace.

So many have benefited from your love—your husband, your children, their spouses, your grandchildren, family, and friends, and all those whose lives you've touched and enriched. To love and be loved, what a legacy! Calm, peace, your time to be, just be.

5. *Story B*—The music, and the light, healing, helping you along on your journey, smoothing the way, one note, one shining ray at a time. Easing, smoothing, transporting, transcending. A calmness, a peace, a fulfillment. Your time, now, simply enjoying and accepting the music and the light. Easily, simply. Perhaps a manifestation of the Holy Spirit itself.

6. *Story A*—In its presence, with you, that sense of total acceptance, understanding, as only the Holy Spirit can accept and understand. Peace, quiet, calm, knowing that it is OK. Everything in its time, in its season. Having participated in your life, the memories, the light, the music, the love. And, in that spirit, knowing an inner peace, an inner strength. Your time.

7. *Reorientation*—Continuing to breathe calmly and easily. One breath and then another. Your healing time. Peace.

Thank you, Elaine, for being my friend and letting me spend this time with you.

When you are ready, just take a deep breath or two, stretch, blink your eyes, and return to this room.

Thank you.

6.4 Henry T. Close's "The Slimy Green Monster"

The following is a metaphor with the author's commentary taken in its entirety from Close (1998, pp. 36–9). It is a story addressing children's phobias, and can be considered to be an example of a well-written advanced metaphor.

The Slimy Green Monster

Children's stories can be wonderful opportunities for pediatric psychotherapy. As a pastoral counselor, I sometimes lead worship services and always enjoy including a sermon for the children.

On one occasion, I wanted to address their phobias—specifically their fear of monsters. These fears are distressing not only to the kids, but also to their parents, who are often unable to reassure the kids.

I think this kind of fear often results from an inner aggression that is disowned and then projected onto someone else. Therapy helps the child to reclaim the aggression and to incorporate it into his or her own psyche. But the child must feel that it is safe to do so. So I told the following story as part of a worship service.

Sitting on the floor with the kids, I leaned toward them, and spoke in a slow, deep, scary voice. "Once upon a time, there was a great … big … terrible … horrible … slimy green monster who liked to scare little children."

The five-year-old girl sitting next to me was obviously alarmed. She put her hands over her ears and said, "Oh no!"

Advanced Metaphor

I continued in the same slow menacing voice. "And do you know what that great big … terrible … horrible monster's name was?"

"No."

I paused a moment, sat up straight, smiled playfully and said cheerfully, "It was Jimmy, Jimmy J. Monster!"

They all giggled. I continued playfully.

"Sometimes Jimmy J. Monster would crawl under the children's bed at night. Then when they were fast asleep, he would crawl out and make terrible scary sounds. He would get right up next to their ears and would roar in their ears. But he said it very softly, like, 'roar.'

"Do you know why he whispered it so softly? One time he yelled out real loud and scary, 'ROAR!' But he said it so loud that he scared himself! He ran all the way home to his mommy and got up in her lap.

"She put her arms around him to tell him it was all right. She would protect him from that big bad noise. He was still her little baby—even though everybody else thought he was a great big, terrible monster. So he never said 'roar' again very loud, because he didn't want to scare himself again.

"You see, his mommy did not know that her little Jimmy went around at night trying to scare little children. She thought he was a very nice monster. When he went out at night, she thought he was just playing with his other monster friends, the slimy blue monster, and the slimy pink monster, and the slimy purple monster. That's what his mommy thought. She did not know that he was actually out trying to scare little children!

"One night, Jimmy came to a house in a big city, hoping to scare all of the children: the youngest one first, then the middle child, then the oldest. All three of them the very same night! That Jimmy J. Monster was really a mean monster.

"But do you know what happened? When Jimmy Monster crawled under the littlest boy's bed, his lollipop fell out of his pocket. It was a great big green lollipop, all wrapped up in pink paper. When the littlest boy climbed into bed, he saw the lollipop lying on the floor and knew exactly what it meant. He knew there was a slimy green monster under his bed.

"So he called his mommy, 'Mommy, there's a slimy green monster under my bed, that's going to try to scare me tonight.'

"Mommy came into the room and saw the green lollipop on the floor. She lifted up the edge of the covers and yelled at the monster. 'You listen to me, you big, slimy green monster. You're a bad monster to try to scare my children. If you ever come here again, I'm going to tell your mommy on you. You'll be in big trouble then. She won't let you watch cartoons for a whole week! So don't you ever come back here again, or you'll be in really big trouble!'

"Jimmy J. Monster didn't like that. He didn't like to be yelled at—monsters never like it when people yell at them. And he certainly didn't want his mommy to know that he had been trying to scare little children.

"He crawled out from under that bed just as fast as he could. He told the littlest boy's mommy, 'Oh please don't tell my mommy on me. I promise I'll never come here again. I'll do anything you want if only you won't tell my mommy on me.' With that, the littlest boy himself yelled at Jimmy J. Monster. 'You get out of here, you slimy green monster, and don't you ever come back.'"

At this point I asked the kids if they could demonstrate how they might yell at a monster, and I heartily approved of their performance before continuing.

"Well, Jimmy Monster ran away from there just as fast as he could, all the way home. He ran into his bedroom, closed the door, crawled into bed and pulled the covers over his head. He did not want anybody ever to yell at him again. And he sure didn't want to miss out on a whole week of watching cartoons.

"He thought and thought and thought for a long time. Finally he said to himself, 'I've got to figure out some other ways to have fun at night. What can I do when my friends are asleep, and I want to go out and have some fun?' Then he had an idea. He could go out at night and have a wonderful time *protecting* the little children.

"So whenever a little boy or a little girl thinks there is a great big, slimy green monster behind a tree at night, they can be very glad to know that the monster is there to protect them.

"Now, there is one more thing I haven't told you yet. It's about the lollipop that fell out of Jimmy J. Monster's pocket. The next morning, when the littlest boy woke up, he found the lollipop lying there, on the floor. The monster hadn't even unwrapped it yet. So he took the lollipop and put it on his dresser, on a little stand. Whenever he looked at it, he would laugh and laugh and laugh.

"And that is the story of the slimy, green monster and the littlest boy and the lollipop."

I then asked the kids, "So, do you know what to do if you ever think there's a monster in your room, trying to scare you?"

The little girl who had been so alarmed at the beginning mumbled something.

"What?" I asked.

"Kick his butt."

"Kick his butt! That's a great idea. You could kick his butt, or you could yell at him, or you could get Mommy and Daddy to yell at him too. Because no monster ever wants to be yelled at, and no monster ever wants to get in trouble with his mommy."

*****

There are three important principles implicit in this story. First, I needed to establish rapport. I knew all the kids, at least slightly, and liked them. I sat on the floor with them. To make contact with their fears, I started talking in a very scary voice.

Then I quickly reframed the whole situation. My tone of voice changed. I gave the monster a harmless sounding name and described him as non-dangerous. It is rather hard to be terrified of a monster who still sits in his mommy's lap so she can protect him. Or a monster who is terrified of being yelled at, who watches cartoons, and eats lollipops.

This was all expressed metaphorically, with the metaphor's inherent power to draw people into its world view. The effectiveness of this process was dramatically demonstrated by the little girl who had been so alarmed at the beginning. After hearing the story, she could envision herself displaying enough aggression to "kick his butt!"

6.5 *Carol and Stephen Lankton's* Tales of Enchantment

Earlier we commented that the Lanktons have contributed much to the conscious design of therapeutic metaphors. Their 1989 book is an excellent collection of annotated "tales" for many purposes. Here, we reproduce their metaphor "Just an Ordinary Joe" as a companion piece to the one in the previous section. This is for a child. The Lanktons (p. 380) quote a school psychologist named Nick Seferlis as follows for a framework for telling therapeutic metaphors to children in his school system:

1. Make sure to be age-appropriate or grade-appropriate with vocabulary selection.

2. Attention span is shorter with younger children and stories need to be shorter and contain less verbal drama and detail.

3. The child will show greater identification with children or people as opposed to inanimate objects. Therefore, the greater the base of reality in the story, as opposed to fantasy, the better. It seems that the child is able to identify quicker with real people as opposed to fantasized and made-up things.

4. Use story voices as dramatic devices. The use of rudimentary tonal emphasis, dropping tone or raising it to portray characters, is

adequate for most children. Children become engrossed at the tone of the story, whereas adults often prefer that drama be regulated with syntactical (word selection) devices.

5. When children hear a story being told, they are more likely to respond with experiential participation if there is a slow delivery done with great emphasis.

This is a useful set of guidelines.

The following Lanktons' cited metaphor (which they indicate was contributed by Marianne Trottier, M.S.) is for an existing attitude of, "If I don't do something better than someone else, I am not special." The goal of the metaphor is, "I am special." Here is the story from Lankton and Lankton (1989, pp. 397–99):

Just an Ordinary Joe

Joe was a boy I used to know at another school I was at, and Joe always wanted to be special. And he was in the second grade because that was the class I used to have. His best friend was named Randolph, and Randolph was big and strong and tall, and Joe really wished he was more like Randolph because when Randolph got up to bat, he could really slug that baseball and he could also throw a football real far, because he was so tall and he could see above all the other boys.

Maybe you've wondered at times about being taller or maybe even stronger and maybe you've thought of ways you would like to be. But Joe always wished he could be a little more like Randolph.

As he sat in his class, he thought maybe he would also like to be like Eric, who was smart and always seemed to know the answer. Every time the teacher asked a question, Eric would raise his hand and would always be right. And Joe would sit there and sometimes he knew the answer but other times he didn't want to volunteer and kind of hid, hoping the teacher wouldn't call on him. As you're sitting here, maybe you think about what that's like for you when the teacher asks a question.

147

And when he was out on the playground, he also noticed how fast Deborah could run. She was the fastest runner in class. And he thought how wonderful it would be if he could have a special talent or if he could do something that was really outstanding.

And Janny, she was very tiny and he wondered what it would be like to be so small and have everybody cater to you because you were so little and small.

But he was just a regular Joe, an ordinary Joe, and he wondered how could he be different or unique. And the teacher told him that everybody has a special talent, everybody is special in some way and you need to stop and think how you're special. That's what she said. But then he received his report card and he had average grades, just those regular grades, nothing super duper and nothing really terrible.

Well, the class was getting ready for spring concert. And as he was getting ready for spring concert, he noticed that Janny was put in front of the class and Mike, who had a big loud voice, was given a speaking part. And Randolph, who was so big and tall, was able to stand in the very back of the row and he was going to carry a flag because everybody would be able to see him. And Stacy and Jeff were going to sing a duet together because they had nice singing voices.

But ordinary Joe was just going to be part of the group. He wasn't given anything special to do. And as he was standing there, he noticed that Marcus had ears that stuck out just a little bit, and Marcus could actually wiggle those ears.

He thought, "Wouldn't it be great to have ears like that?" And he noticed as he was standing there in the group getting ready to practice that Phil had all these great freckles. He had so many that you couldn't really see his skin. It was all freckly. And he thought how wonderful it would be to have a face like that. Maybe you've thought of some ways that you would like to be special, just like ordinary Joe did. And then something happened.

He was reading a book that his uncle had given him a long time ago called *The Phantom Tollbooth* by Norton Jester. And as he was reading this story which is about a young boy named Mylo who receives a magical tollbooth as a gift. And as he drives through the tollbooth, he finds himself in the land beyond. And throughout his travels in this enchanted land, he is joined by Humbug and a watchdog named Toc. And in one of the chapters Mylo finds that he's lost. And as he wanders with Humbug and Toc, they come to a small house.

And on one of the doors to the small house, is a sign that reads "the giant." Mylo says, "Wow, a giant. I wonder if that giant can tell us if we're lost." So they knock on the door and a man opens the door but he's not a giant. He's sort of an ordinary-sized man. Mylo says: "Are you a giant?" And the man says, "Yes, I'm the smallest giant in the world." And Mylo said, "Are we lost?" The giant says, "Well, I think you ought to go to the next door and ask the midget."

So Mylo went to the next door and knocked on the door. A man came to that door who looked very much like the giant looked. It looked like the same man. They could be twins. Mylo asked, "Are you the midget?" And the man said, "Yes, I'm the tallest midget in the world." So Mylo said, "Are we lost?" The midget said he didn't know the answer to that question and suggested that Mylo ask the fat man at the next door. So they went to the next door of the same house and they knocked on the door. The same man answered the door.

Mylo asked, "Are you the fat man?" "Yes," answered the man, "I'm the thinnest fat man in the world." "Are we lost?" Mylo asked again. "I don't know," said the fat man, "maybe you should go around back and ask the thin man." So he goes around to the next door of the same house and he knocks on the door marked "the thin man." Well, guess what, the same man answered the door. Mylo said, "Are you the thin man?" The man said, "Yes, I'm the fattest thin man in the world." Mylo said to him, "I think you're all the same man." The man said, "Well, I always thought of myself as an ordinary man, and I like to feel special. So I can be the fattest thin man or the thinnest fat man or the tallest midget or the shortest giant. It's all the way you imagine yourself to be."

As Joe read that story, he thought about it and somehow it stayed with him for quite a while. He remembered that story and on the night of the spring concert, when everyone was running around in costume and Jeff and Stacy were practicing for their duet and Debra was running around in her costume and Janny was getting prepared to be the tiniest one in the concert. As he walked through the hallway, he heard some sobbing, sort of like moans. And he stopped to take a peek and over in the darkest corner was Randolph, who he always wanted to be like. And he asked, "Randolph, what's wrong?"

You've probably been with friends who are crying and wondered how you could help and that's what happened to Joe. So Randolph was crying and he said, "I wish I wasn't as big as I am. I wish I could be like you, Joe. I wish I could be your size. Sometimes it's hard to be the biggest kid in class." Joe said, "Hey, Randolph, you can be the tallest short boy in class." And Randolph put a little smile on. Joe said, "Come on, you've got to get that flag." Randolph said, "Yea, okay." And they went down to the spring concert. And after that, Joe thought of himself not as an ordinary Joe, but as an extraordinary Joe, someone who could take a different look at himself and feel extraordinary.

6.6 Concluding comments

The division between basic and advanced metaphor is arbitrary since there is a continuum between simple and complex stories. Advanced metaphors provide more opportunities for the listener to fill in details and to make choices. The starting point is always sufficient information from your client as to his background, needs, and goals. The metaphor needs to be consciously designed or adapted for this particular unique person. There are also general-purpose metaphors, which function much like a master key that can open many locks. Yet, artfully constructed and told, with that "precise use of vague language," most metaphors can be considered to have a universal quality—certainly, the best folk tales have this quality.

It is always useful to have in mind a repertoire of many tales. It is particularly useful to have available a number of tales that can be readily adapted to changing clientele. Consulting collections of metaphors, such as those in Close's and the Lanktons' books, is a good beginning.

Chapter 7

Richard R. Kopp's Metaphor Therapy

7.1 Introduction

The process by which I learned how to be a psychotherapist was "quantized" in the sense of discovering and then learning how to use a succession of psychotherapeutic approaches. I was, of course, influenced by reading much of Freud's works when I was young. Freud was the single most important investigator and influence on the development of psychotherapy in the twentieth century—a true pioneer. After an unsatisfactory personal experience with psychoanalysis, which stretched out over seven years, my personal involvement started with training in Gestalt Therapy with Howard H. Fink, Ph.D., and Bob Timms, Ph.D., in the Southwestern Institute of Gestalt Therapy of Ohio. This training opened me up to the work of G. Frederick (Fritz) Perls and other Gestalt therapists. There was clever use of language, wonderful exercises and interventions, and the continuing emphasis on staying in the present. This was fascinating and exciting therapy, as compared with the rigid formalisms of psychoanalysis, for example.

Then I was introduced to Alexander Lowen's work (1975) in bioenergetic analysis, and spent three years in training groups in this area. Lowen connected mind with body in a series of body postures and exercises. What a rush to find that just a thought can effect bodily processes (as, for example, in psychosomatic illnesses or in locked musculature), and that working with the body can effect changes in thought patterns. Releasing the tension in neck and shoulder muscles also opened up pathways to freeing the mind of psychological tensions and impasses. About this time I was "Rolfed," which is a deep muscle massage that breaks up frozen muscular patterns by loosening the fascia between muscles.

The resulting realignment of the body was a release and a relief. Body and mind were connected.

Also about this time I read Bandler and Grinder's two books (1975, 1976) on the *structure* of magic. This "structure" is connected to the transformational grammar of linguistics. In essence, they attempted by linguistic analysis to answer the question, "How do you know what to say when your client says X?" By analyzing the words and the grammar in their connections, it was possible to know just how to respond: i.e., the analysis led to the therapist's response as statements or questions. Responses were not made on the "gut" level, but via an understanding of language. This approach, called NLP or neuro-linguistic programming, appealed to the scientist in me—the client said "X," and the proper answer to move the client along was the linguistically determined "Y." No guessing games or relying on intuitions or theories like psycho-analysis. This *meta model* of language usage changed my way of thinking.

The work of Carl Rogers was more of an influence on my ideas of teaching (1994) than on my practice of psychotherapy. Rogers's "unconditional positive regard" was and is the foundation for respectful and effective interactions with clients.

In their study of linguistics Bandler and Grinder devoted two books (1975, 1977) to the way that Milton H. Erickson, M.D., used language. Their analysis of Erickson's hypnotic language forms opened up an entirely new area for me—hypnotherapy. This was reinforced by the excitement of reading about Erickson's work in Jay Haley's *Uncommon Therapy* (1986). It took me years of study to develop an appreciation and understanding of Erickson's use of language, and of the many pioneering ways he developed to do effective psychotherapy. Erickson was a pragmatist who was more interested in *changing* a client's behavior than in theories (he had little use for psychoanalysis). Yet Erickson wrote many research papers, and trained several generations of hypnotists. He almost single-handedly moved the field away from its obsession with "why" to focus on the pragmatism of "how."

Each of the above-mentioned approaches caused me to radically change the ways I thought about and did therapy. The next major shift in my thinking came from studying Steve de Shazer's work in solution-oriented or, as it is now called, "solution-focused brief therapy" (SFBT) (1994). The shift in thinking about working on "problems" that clients presented and lovingly talked about, to focusing on *solutions* or the things they were doing well was one of those "light bulb" experiences, actually more like a flashbulb going off. It was a paradigm shift of 180 degrees.

It connected with what I knew from behavioral approaches in that positive reinforcement is more effective than negative reinforcement. Focus on what the client is doing well, her successful ways of coping, the times during the day or week when she was free of her "problem" or was able to keep her troubling demons at bay. Wow! This was great material, and, when coupled with the *miracle question* and the ways that de Shazer and his colleagues conducted sessions, a satisfying way was found to do therapy, and incorporate into my own style.

Reading Bernie Siegel's *Love, Medicine & Miracles* (1986) was another milestone in my journey. Bernie, his books and tapes and talks and life, served as a model that changed the direction of my life in terms of getting involved as a volunteer working with people who have life-challenging diseases and their caregivers. (If you are interested, you can read about this work in my book on guided imagery and other approaches to healing (2000).)

The next shift in my thinking came from studying the narrative-therapy work of Michael White and David Epston (1990). Bill O'Hanlon (1994) considers their work to be the beginnings of the "third wave" of doing therapy—the first was psychoanalysis, and the second was all the problem-focused therapies like Gestalt therapy, NLP, behavioral therapy, cognitive etc. The client's *story* about her own life is central to this approach. That is, it is the *narrative* of her life as she describes it to herself and others. White and Epston have developed effective ways of working with these personal narratives as the vehicle for change. It will become evident in this chapter that there is a close connection between their work and Kopp's. There will be a detailed discussion of narrative therapy in Chapter 14.

Another major influence on my work has been the work of Ernest L. Rossi in exploring the foundations of hypnosis and hypnotherapy. His book *The Symptom Path to Enlightenment* (1996) attempts to explore the roots of hypnosis in nonlinear dynamics or chaos theory. The second half of this book is on therapeutic applications of the theoretical part. In particular, Rossi's four-step streamlined model of doing therapy is germane to Kopp's work. Rossi's four steps are:

1. Establish that the client is willing to work on a particular concern at this time.

2. Survey all *relevant* factors related to this concern, going as far back in time as needed.

3. Explore present-day realistic solutions for this concern.

4. Ratify that the client is willing to use these solutions at the present time.

There will be more on how this four-step model connects to Kopp's work later.

The key books on metaphor are the groundbreaking one by Gordon (1978) and the two Lankton and Lankton books (1983, 1989), particularly their 1989 book. These three books opened my eyes to the systematic and conscious design of metaphors for therapeutic work. (These contributions were discussed earlier.)

I had already prepared a detailed outline of the current book and started writing it when I came across R. R. Kopp's *Metaphor Therapy* (1995). Kopp presented a major paradigm shift from the "traditional" ways of using metaphor, and I almost abandoned this book until I realized that it would be possible to build on Kopp's innovative work and connect it to other approaches. This chapter will summarize Kopp's work, and comment on what he has done. However, it will not be possible to reproduce the rich case studies that illuminate his approach—read his book for the full impact of his work.

7.2 What is Metaphor Therapy?

In his introduction to the book, Kopp writes a number of things about Metaphor Therapy. Some of these are quoted below with the page numbers in brackets. With respect to types of metaphoric intervention Kopp states:

> Two broad categories are identified: *client*-generated metaphors and *therapist*-generated metaphors. Two types of client-generated metaphoric interventions are introduced in this book: (1) exploring and transforming the client's metaphoric language, and (2) exploring and transforming the client's early memory metaphors. [p. xvi]

> The theory of Metaphor Therapy rests on the proposition that individuals, families, social groups, cultures, and humanity as a whole structure reality metaphorically. It is proposed that, at an individual level, the metaphoric structure of reality is comprised of six substructures (called metaphorms) representing self, others, life, and the relations among these elements, i.e., self in relation to self, self in relation to others, and self in relation to life. At a family level, the metaphoric structure of reality involves the metaphoric structure of the family system and subsystems, and the metaphoric structure of family communication and behavior interaction patterns. At a sociocultural and transcultural level, the metaphoric structure of social and transcultural reality is revealed in language and myths, respectively. [pp. xvi–xvii]

> The theory of Metaphor Therapy also proposes a neuropsychological explanation of the brain mechanisms that mediate mental (linguistic and cognitive-affective) metaphoric structures and processes. [p. xvii]

> * Metaphor Therapy advances the view that metaphor is central to the process of change in psychotherapy and is not related to any single approach or method. [p. xvii]

> Metaphors are mirrors reflecting our inner images of self, life, and others. [p. xiii]

> It is suggested that Metaphor Therapy integrates the view that cultural myths are the narrations by which our society is unified and

the view that personal myths revealed in one's earliest childhood memories are the guiding fictions that unify an individual's personality. [p. xxii]

In Part II of his book Kopp reinforces his comment (asterisked above) that his approach is not related to any single approach or method by showing how it is integrated or part of: psychoanalytic psychotherapy, Jung's analytic psychotherapy, Ericksonian hypnotherapy, cognitive-behavior therapy, Adler's individual psychology, family-systems therapy, and individual and family therapy.

Also in Part II, Kopp ends on some, "speculations of the neuropsychology of Metaphor Therapy and therapeutic change." This is followed by an epilogue that, "… presents Gregory Bateson's (1979) view that mind and the evolution of all living organisms in nature are unified within a single principle, "the pattern that connects," and that the pattern that connects is metaphor." (p. xxiv)

We will first present a summary from his Chapter 1 (pp. 3–16) on his systematic approach to doing Metaphor Therapy via six steps and four phases.

7.3 Outline for doing Metaphor Therapy— Current Metaphors

The following is a summary of Kopp's instructions (pp. 3–16) of how to do Metaphor Therapy for current metaphors. This summary uses his format of six steps in four phases.

A. Phase 1. Through the Looking Glass—Entering the Client's Metaphoric Imagination
Step 1—Notice metaphors, i.e. be sensitive to your client's speech in terms of *listening* for metaphors or metaphoric language. You can also guide the client on an inner exploration of the metaphoric image via the following steps.

Step 2A—You can invite the client to explore the metaphoric image saying, "When you say or think the metaphor what image or picture comes to your mind?" "Please describe that image." (Kopp uses *visual* language here, but you should use permissive language that invites other experiences.) The client's "image" ("memory" might be better here) is what is important. You need to listen carefully, and even take notes, to accurately record the client's specific language in describing or depicting her metaphor. The therapist *guides* the process by following the client as he creates a narrative of her own image or images or memories.

Step 2B—Since "the therapist knows that the client has shifted to the domain of creative metaphoric imagination when the client creates a unique inner image using the language of sensory-affective imagery" (p. 7), she may need help if the response in Step 2A is essentially about the current life situation. For example, the therapist might say, "If I were seeing it [*the metaphoric image*] the way you see it (in your mind's eye), what would I see?" (p. 6) The therapist might even say something like, "May I tell you the image that occurs to me when I hear you say [the metaphor]?" (p. 6) In Step 2B the goal is to be sure the client has a clear/sound/solid inner image of her metaphor.

B. Phase 2. Curious-er and Curious-er—Exploring the Client's Metaphoric Imagination

Step 3—In this step the client is invited to explore the metaphor as a *sensory image* along the following dimensions: (a) setting—description of setting—what does she see there; (b) action/interaction—what else is going on within the metaphor and what are other people within the metaphor saying or thinking; (3) within the metaphor in terms of other sensory modalities, what does she hear, smell, taste, touch; and (4) with respect to *time*, what led to this metaphoric situation, and/or what was happening just before, and/or what happens next? Kopp indicates that in his experience, only a few of these "explorations" will be followed in any given single metaphoric intervention. This step is intended to provide more substance to the client's metaphor.

Step 4—"Once the exploration of the imagery is complete, the therapist invites the client to describe his/her feelings and experiences associated with the metaphoric image. For example, the therapist can ask, 'What's it like to be [*the metaphoric image*]?' or, 'What's your experience of (*the metaphoric image*)?' or, 'What are you feeling as you (*the metaphoric image*)?'

"The therapist guides the client through this process, using non-leading questions, i.e. *the therapist leads the client's inner search of the metaphoric image, but meticulously avoids introducing any new content to the image.* By not intruding into the client's metaphoric imagery, the therapist allows the client to be free to create and explore the client's own image. This is crucial because questions that introduce content into the client's metaphoric image can interfere with, rather than foster, the client's inner exploration." (p. 8)

This step is reminiscent of Step 2 in Rossi's *moving hands* technique. Step 1 of Rossi's approach involves holding your hands about 8–10 inches apart and imagining some kind of force (magnetic, electrical …) between them. Then the client is given the instruction, "Will you find those hands moving towards each other, almost by themselves, if you are ready at this time to work on a specific concern?" Typically, the hands move slowly toward each other and then touch. At this point you give the Step 2 direction, "And, now, will you find one of those hands moving downward all by itself as you carry out an internal review of all of the relevant factors surrounding this concern? … Your hand will rest gently on your lap when you've completed this review." Rossi's *moving hands* is a "secret therapy" approach since the client does all of the work in his own head. Kopp's approach involves the client's *telling* the therapist about the metaphoric image. (In Section 7.7 is my version of how to do Metaphor Therapy based on my experience in Ericksonian hypnosis and psychotherapy, and in guided imagery.)

Now, to continue with Kopp's systematics.

C. Phase 3. Looking Differently—Inviting a Transformation of the Client's Metaphoric Image
At this point the therapist *invites* a transformation in the client's metaphor in one of two ways: (a) directly invite the client to change the metaphoric image; and (b) *invite* the client to consider a change suggested by the therapist. (As an aside, I italicized "invite" above because I especially like the *respectful* way in which Kopp phrases his suggestions and requests.)

Step 5A—To accomplish (a) above, the therapist can say, "If you could change the image in any way, how would you change it?" This step has a number of parallels in other approaches. It is related to the NLP techniques of "Changing Personal History" and "Time-Line Therapy." In David Cheek's ideomotor work he will say after assisting the client to find the origins of her particular concern, "Would it be okay now to give up those old feelings [or ways of behavior] now that those experiences are twenty years in your past and you know so much more and are such a different person now?" This is a direct suggestion to change/transform the metaphoric image or memory that initiated the unwanted behavior. Kopp's Step 5A is also related to Rossi's Step 3, in which the therapist states, "Now that you've completed that internal review, will you find that other hand moving slowly downwards all by itself as you consider alternative realistic ways of resolving your concerns? ... And, that hand will touch your lap when you've found some practical alternates." Kopp's question is an elegantly phrased *presupposition* that the client will be able to (a) change the image and (b) change it to her benefit.

Step 5B—If the client has trouble transforming her metaphoric image on her own, then the therapist may assist her by saying, "What if the [*the part of the metaphor to be changed*] were a [*the suggested change*]?" These suggested changes should be rooted in what you know about the client, and in her metaphoric imagery. The suggested change needs to be proffered tentatively with more emphasis on the "what if" than the change itself. An alternative way of accomplishing Step 5B would be by saying, "What changes in your [metaphor to be changed] would a person who knows you quite well (or some very wise and knowledgeable person) suggest?" This formulation allows the client to externalize (within her own mind!) suggested changes.

D. Phase 4. Back to the Tea Party—Connecting Metaphoric Patterns and Life Problems

After exploring the client's metaphoric imagery and possible transformations, it is necessary to connect the client back to the real-life concern.

Step 6—"The therapist invites the client to "bridge back" to the original situation, asking, "What parallels do you see between your image of [*the metaphoric image*] and [*the original situation*]?" Once the similarities between the explored metaphoric image and the current situation have been discussed, the therapist asks, "How might the way you changed the image apply to your current situation?" (p. 11) This is rather verbal and almost analytical. Another more open-ended formulation might be, "Just take some time now to explore within yourself how the changes you have already made to your [metaphoric image] change your life at this time in ways that are useful and beneficial to you. You may be surprised at what you find. Consider what you will be doing differently." This formulation has many presuppositions built in.

Rossi's last Step (4), which occurs after the second hand is resting on a lap, goes, "And, now, will you find your head nodding 'yes' all by itself to let you know that you will be using one of these new ways of caring for yourself? Good. Thank you." This is a kinesthetic anchor to the change process.

One general concern about the language that Kopp uses is in order—it is highly visual, and some allowance needs to be made for clients whose primary representational system is auditory or kinesthetic. On the other hand, Kopp's case illustrations are well chosen, informative, and good examples of Metaphor Therapy. His emphasis is on working permissively with the client's own metaphor(s) about her concerns. This is a radical shift from the "standard" use of metaphor in therapy.

E. The Therapist Listens with the Third EYE
If you have a client who does not easily generate her own metaphor, then you may wish to use Kopp's "Third EYE" approach as illustrated in the following quote (p. 15):

> To "listen with Third EYE," the therapist attends to his or her own internal images and then describes the inner metaphoric image to the client. The therapist might say, "When you were talking about _____ just now, I got an image of [*the therapist's image*]. Does that fit your experience of the situation you were talking about?" This phrasing is extremely important, because (1) it shows that the

therapist does not presume to know the contents of the client's inner world of metaphoric imagery, and (2) it encourages the client to use his or her own metaphoric imagination by modeling using the content of discussion as a stimulus for evoking an internal image. The phrasing also leaves the client free to reject the image, and replace it with one of the client's own.

Obviously, this procedure of tentatively suggesting a metaphor out of your experience can be useful.

This section has outlined Kopp's work on exploring and transforming current metaphors. The next section does the same for *early memory metaphors*.

7.4 Outline for doing Metaphor Therapy— early-memory metaphors

The background for this work lies in the observation that early recollections (ER) and early-memory metaphors can play a considerable role on current difficulties. In a way, these "early memory metaphors" (to use Kopp's term) can control current behavior. Kopp's Chapter 3 (pp. 35–63) presents an eight-step model for doing this work, along with commentary and case illustrations. His eight-step model is summarized in what follows, after we first discuss early recollections and autobiographical memory.

An " autobiographical memory" is a memory about one's own life. Brewer (1986) identifies three forms of autobiographical memory: (1) *personal memory* refers to a mental image that corresponds to a particular episode in one's life; (2) an *autobiographical fact* is the recollection of a fact from one's past; and (3) a *generic personal memory* refers to a *general* mental image. An *early recollection* (ER) is a specific *one-time* incident or episode that one remembers from one's childhood, and can "picture" in the mind's eye. *Reports* are general descriptions of childhood experiences that have happened many times, and they tend to lack specific details. Although *personal memories* meet the criteria of an ER, both *autobiographical fact* and *generic personal memory* are to be considered reports. ERs are related to a specific incident.

With respect to early recollections as metaphors, Kopp writes (p. 39):

> Like spoken metaphors, ERs can function as metaphors for some-thing else, e.g., a life situation, a problem, etc. Early recollections differ from linguistic metaphors in one important aspect, however. A spoken metaphor uses an image as a means of conveying the meaning of the situation to which it refers. Thus, spoken metaphors are always metaphors whereas ERs must meet certain criteria to be metaphors. *To be complete metaphors early recollections must do what metaphors do, namely, carry meaning over from the domain of imagery (in this case, a recollected image from early childhood) to a relevant situation in one's current life.*

> Whether or not an ER is a metaphor depends primarily on timing, i.e., when the ER is recalled. *An early recollection that is recalled at the moment when the client is experiencing strong feelings (or symptoms) in relation to a problem or issue he or she is describing is likely to be a metaphor for that problem, issue, feeling, or symptom.*

> One need not wait for ERs to occur spontaneously, however. Therapists can actively elicit the recall of an early recollection metaphor at key moments in a therapy session.

Steps for working with early recollections

Step 1—The therapist asks the client, "Where in all of this are you most stuck?" or, "In what way is this a problem for you?" or, "Which part of this is the biggest problem for you?" (p. 39) Step 2 follows after the client describes the part where he is most stuck.

Step 2—The therapist then asks, "Can you remember a recent time when you felt this way? Form an image in your mind of the situation so that you begin to get the same feelings you had then—so that you actually begin to feel those feelings now in your body the same way you felt then. Use as many of your sensory modalities as you can—try to remember what you heard, saw, smelled, touched, or tasted." Allow time for the client to form the memory image and to re-experience the feelings (p. 40). The emphasis on sensory lan-guage and the sensory experience in the body shifts from a verbal description to an imaginal one. At this point the therapist is ready to elicit an ER because it will most certainly be a metaphor for the current problem. This is done when the client reports experiencing in the session the same bodily feelings that were experienced when the actual situation occurred. (There are two cautions that I (RB) will add here: the first is to be careful about the appearance of abre-actions in Step 2; and the second has to do with the word "try," since this word implies failure.)

Step 3A—Now the therapist can ask, "What is the first early child-hood memory that comes to mind right now? Something specific that happened only once, preferably before the age of seven or eight years old." (p. 41, also see Mosak, 1958.) Kopp indicates that the phrasing in the preceding question is important for "… it is the first early memory image that comes to mind when the client is experiencing the bodily feeling associated with the problem situa-tion that will be a metaphor for the current situation." (p. 41) You do not directly ask for a *linked* memory, but rather let it surface on its own. If a *report* is offered rather than an ER, go to the questions in the next step.

Step 3B—"Could you tell me one time that this occurred?" or "Can you remember a specific example of this?" (p. 42) If this does not elicit anything from childhood, go to Step 3C.

Step 3C—"Take your time. Something will come." (p. 42) Wait. If no response then say, "It's okay if you remember something from later in your childhood, say about 10 or 11 years old or so." (p. 42) Wait. Finally, if nothing is recalled you can reassure the client by saying, "That's okay, some people have difficulty remembering things from their childhood at first …" (p. 42) Then, you suggest that something might pop up later that the client can tell about at the next session.

Step 4—"It is important to write down the memory image, using exactly the same words the person uses. The therapist inquires about the details of the memory, asking, 'What happened next?' 'What did you (he/she) say/do then?' 'Describe it as if you were watching a play and describing what you see,' until the memory is complete …" (p. 42) Go on when the client can recall no more details.

Step 5—"Once the client has described a complete memory image/episode, the therapist asks, 'What stands out most vividly in that memory? If you had a snapshot of the memory, what instant stands out most clearly in your mind's eye?' Write down what stands out most for the person, using the person's own words. This identifies the core memory image ..." (p. 43)

Frequently, this is the part of the ER that most clearly represents the metaphoric meaning of the current problem or situation.

Step 6A—"The therapist asks, 'How did you feel at that moment (the moment that stands out most)?' " (p. 43)

Step 6B—"The therapist asks, 'Why did you feel that way?' or 'Why did you have that reaction?' " (p. 43) (I personally have trouble with the "why" questions in this step since there is too much room for digression and creation of responses simply to please the therapist. "Why" questions can be distracting—just go with the experience.)

Step 7—This is where the transformation of early memory metaphors occurs (p. 44):

> "If you could change the memory in any way, how would you change it?" Often, clients will respond by saying that the bad thing that happened in the original memory wouldn't have happened. In such cases the therapist asks the client to "Describe what you would have liked to have happened instead. The beginning of the memory can start out the same way, but tell the rest of it as if it actually were a memory that happened the way you would have liked it to."

Record the changed memory using the client's exact words. With resistance to the above, use (p. 45):

> Occasionally, a client will resist changing an unpleasant ER, saying, "I can't change the past. It happened that way and that's it." In such cases it can be helpful to encourage the client by saying, "True, you can't change what happened. What I'd like you to do is to create something new—a new memory. If this childhood memory were to begin the way it did originally, but you could create a

new image of the way you'd like to be, how would you change it so that it would turn out the way you would like it to?"

If the client still declines to change the memory, the therapist should accept this and move on.

If the ER is a *positive* memory, the client may not be able to think of any way to improve it, and this is fine. The final work is in Steps 8A and 8B where the connections between the current situation and the early memory metaphor are explored.

Step 8A—"The therapist reads the ER and the changed ER aloud and then asks the client, 'What parallels do you see between the memory and/or the changed memory and the current situation you focused on earlier (see Steps 1 and 2)?' The therapist empathically reflects the client's ideas.

"At this point the therapist may offer additional ideas and suggestions." (p. 45)

Step 8B—"The therapist might say, 'I'd like to tell you the connections I see. Let me know which ones seem to fit you.' " (p. 46) In some ways Step 8 is not really needed since the client has already done the significant change work in Step 7. A client who is interested in "why" would probably find some closure in Step 8.

In the outlines of Kopp's two major interventions in Sections 7.3 and 7.4 there was much verbatim quoting directly from his book so that the reader could get an appreciation of Kopp's careful use of language and the thoughtfulness of his work.

7.5 Kopp's Metaphor Therapy and the metaphoric structure of reality

Kopp presents in his Chapter 5 (pp. 91–111), Chapter 13 (pp. 157–69), and his Epilogue (pp. 170–3) some speculations and literature information relative to the "metaphoric structure of reality" and possible neurophysiological connections. His ideas along these lines will be summarized, mainly using his own words (for the full flavor of his thinking, read the original in its entirety).

Under the section heading of "Does Metaphor make Sense or Nonsense: Two Philosophical Traditions" Kopp writes (also see the references cited within these quotes) (p. 92):

> Aristotle held that to "metamorphize" well is a sign of genius in the poet and, in poetry "the greatest thing by far is to be the master of the metaphor" (quoted in Ricoeur, 1984, p. 23). In Aristotle's view, metaphor involves giving a thing a name that belongs to something else. Ricoeur (1979) points out that, according to Aristotle, making good metaphors involves the capacity to contemplate similarities. Moreover, good metaphors are vivid because they can "set before the eyes" the sense that they display. It is through this "picturing function" that metaphoric meaning is conveyed (Ricoeur, 1979) …

> In contrast, philosophers following a positivist tradition that emphasizes objectivity, fact, and logic have maintained that metaphors are frivolous and inessential, if not dangerous and logically perverse. From the perspective of positivism, metaphors do not contain or transmit knowledge, have no direct connection with facts, and convey no genuine meaning (Cohen, 1979).

Kopp continues (p. 94):

> In her landmark book, *Philosophy in a New Key* (1942/1979), Langer presents a persuasive argument for the central role of metaphor in the evolution of language and symbolic thought in homo sapiens … Langer suggests that *metaphor is the principle through which literal language develops* and that our literal language is the repository of "faded metaphors" (p. 140).

> Where a precise word is lacking, a speaker resorts to the powers of *logical analogy* (i.e., metaphor) to designate novelty by using a word denoting something else that is a symbol for the thing the speaker means (Langer, 1942/1979) …

> Thus, *just as metaphor is the source of novelty and change in language, exploring and transforming a person's metaphoric imagery can be a source of novelty and change in psychotherapy* …

We have seen that linguistic metaphors are typically *word-pictures* that create a resemblance between an image and a referent situation. *The metaphor-maker paints a picture with words, combining, and, in fact, integrating non-linear/imaginal communication with linear/verbal communication.* Langer's concept of logical analogy describes that quality of metaphor that integrates the logic of words and the "analogic" of imagery. Lackoff and Johnson (1980) echo Langer's view, maintaining that metaphor is imaginative rationality uniting reason and imagination.

Kopp reinforces these ideas with the statement, "Indeed, *metaphoric cognition appears to integrate both imaginal and propositional/syllogistic cognition.*" (p. 95) McNeill (1992) is cited as concluding that speech and gesture are elements of a single integrated process, and that metaphor can be considered as *gesture expressed as words.* A few more relevant Kopp quotations follow (page numbers in brackets):

> ... imaginal cognition is essential to the creation of new ways of looking at things. [p. 96]

> ... *because imaginal cognition also plays a central role in metaphoric language and metaphoric cognition, metaphoric interventions are especially well-suited to the therapeutic task of creating new patterns and connections.* [p. 97]

> These findings suggest that when clients are encouraged to stay within *their own* metaphors and expand and elaborate them, the meaning and insight clients gain can be more profound than if the metaphor is talked about or analyzed. [p. 97]

Kopp likes Bateson's idea that metaphor is the "pattern that connects." (See Bateson (1979) and Capra (1988).) Kopp states (p. 171) that "Bateson maintains that *metaphor is the pattern that connects—a pattern that characterizes the evolution of all living organisms.*" Additional quotations from Kopp regarding Bateson's ideas are:

> Bateson suggests that linear correspondence describes correspondence of discrete items characterized by linear, logical, cause-and-effect relations (Capra, 1988). In contrast, nonlinear

correspondence describes correspondence of pattern and organization characterized by nonlinear causal chains. [p. 98]

Bateson's concept of "the pattern that connects": metaphoric structure identifies the pattern that connects two different things. [p. 99]

The two things compared in a metaphor *can* be both different *and*
similar because their difference and similarity involve different
levels of comparison. [p. 99]

Kopp concludes his Epilogue on Bateson's ideas, and his book,
with the following two paragraphs (pp. 172–3):

It is clear from this analysis that Metaphor Therapy and the
metaphoric structure of reality also rest on the principle of
metaphor as the pattern that connects. This is consistent with
Bateson's view that metaphor is the pattern that connects in the
domain of mind and in the domain of nature. In fact, mind and
nature are unified under this single principle.

It appears that long before humans spoke or thought in metaphor,
and long before metaphor was the source of novelty in language
and thought, nature spoke its own language of metaphor—the pattern that connects. Indeed, the metaphoric structure of reality in
individuals, families, and within and across cultures may be seen
as the expression in humankind of the metaphoric structure underlying the biological evolution of all living things.

Back in Chapter 5, Kopp states (p. 102), "... *an individual's
metaphoric language reflects that individual's metaphoric cognition.*"
and "... *metaphors ... represent internal metaphoric-cognitive structures
that structure our personal beliefs, thoughts, feelings, behaviors, and relationships in the life situations they represent.*"

On page 103, Kopp states in a footnote, "The term ' metaphorm'
was coined by Todd Siler (1987, 1990) who used it to refer to the
process of relating 'information from one discipline to another,
connecting potentially all sources and forms of information.
Metaphorms are expressions of nature's unity.' " Kopp considers
there to be three elemental metaphorms (p. 103): metaphorms for
"self," metaphorms for an "other" or "others," and metaphorms

for "life"; and three relational metaphorms: metaphorms for self-in-relation-to-self, metaphorms for self-in-relation-to-others, and metaphorms for self-in-relation-to-life. This is an interesting formalism and may find some use.

The summary and conclusion of Kopp's speculations about the neuropsychology of Metaphor Therapy and therapeutic change is in Chapter 13 (pp. 157–69) and this summary is quoted in its entirety (p. 169).

> It appears that the creation of spontaneous spoken metaphors and early memory metaphors evokes sensory images that may engage neurological holographic processes that are distributed over large areas of the brain. A metaphoric image may create a resemblance, not merely between the image and the external referent situation, but between holographically encoded representations and the external situation (as perceived by the individual). These representations, in turn, may relate to primary memory patterns holographically recorded early in life. The power of metaphorical interventions may lie in the fact that metaphorical images are distributed throughout the brain in a holographic manner. If so, then exploring linguistic metaphors and early memory metaphors may activate this expansive network, and transforming metaphors may reverberate throughout the entire range of distribution of the image and/or memory.

See Pribram's work (1971, 1978, 1985, 1990, 1991) for more information on the brain's storage of information in a holographic pattern. This completes our direct summary of Kopp's book (1995).

7.6 Commentary on Kopp's Metaphor Therapy

The previous sections have quoted extensively from Kopp's book to give you a reasonably accurate description in his words about Metaphor Therapy. His switch from therapist-generated to client-generated metaphors for psychotherapy is a major contribution to the field. Rather than imposing the therapist's ideas and implied goals, Kopp has developed a structure that lets the client lead and decide the direction of the therapy from her own unique perspective and personal story.

In the previous sections there are some implied criticisms about how Kopp's system works—these arise from my training in Ericksonian hypnosis and psychotherapy, my other trainings and experience, and also from my work in guided imagery for healing and therapy. There would appear to be, for example, much overlap between the systematics of Metaphor Therapy and guided imagery, particularly in terms of eliciting from the client what "image" (really a metaphor) would work best for her. In the case of guided-imagery work (see Battino, 2000) the image/metaphor is *directly* elicited by simply asking the client what works for her. Thus, in the next section I will present my pared-down model for Metaphor Therapy for working both with early recollections and current metaphors.

It should also be pointed out here that there are similarities with Metaphor Therapy in the NLP approaches of Time-Line Therapy (James and Woodsmall, 1988) and Changing Personal History (see, e.g. Bodenhamer and Hall, 1999, pp. 271–3), Rossi's "moving hands" approach (Rossi, 1996, pp. 191–6), and Cheek's ideodynamic approach (Rossi and Cheek (1988); Cheek (1994)). It would be instructive to compare these people's work with Kopp's. In the second part of Kopp's book he does write about connections to Metaphor Therapy with: psychoanalytic psychotherapy, Jung's analytic psychology, Ericksonian hypnotherapy, cognitive-behavior therapy, Adler's individual psychology, and family-systems therapy, as well as with psychotherapy in general.

Earlier it was mentioned briefly that I inferred from Kopp's writing style and the content of his stepwise approaches that his primary representational system is probably visual. It seems to me that it is restricting to write and work mostly with visual images relating to metaphors. The next section suggests a more general approach. However, I am very much aware that what I am doing in the next section is building upon Kopp's pioneering and innovative work.

7.7 *Alternative ways of doing Metaphor Therapy*

In this section we will present our adaptation of Metaphor Therapy for working with (a) client-generated metaphors for immediate or present-day concerns and (b) client-generated metaphors based on early recollections (ERs).

A. Client-generated metaphors for immediate concerns

1. Discovering the metaphor

Discovering, or perhaps uncovering, your client's metaphor about how she perceives herself as existing in the world can be done in two ways. The first is just by careful *listening* for life metaphors. This is somewhat similar to learning about the existence of representational systems, in which it is assumed that each person has a preferred sensory way of perceiving/interacting with the world, i.e. visual, kinesthetic, or auditory. Once you are *aware* of this linguistic distinction, then you readily find it in people's speech and writing. Similarly, once you are aware of life/circumstance metaphors, then you become sensitive to your client's spontaneous uttering of such a metaphor.

On the other hand, in a programmatic way you can elicit this life/circumstance metaphor by one of the following:

- Please *describe* what it is *like* for you at this moment to be in your present situation.
- If I were to be in your shoes now, what would that be *like*?
- Supposing you could *describe* what your life is *like* now *as* a story or a fairy tale or a myth, what comes to mind?
- Here is an experiment (that has been quite helpful)—complete the following sentence, "Right now I feel *like* a ..." What comes to mind?

These are all *direct* elicitations of a present-day life/circumstance metaphor, and can be used at an appropriate time, hopefully early, in a session. The presupposition is that we all have stories/descriptions that we have already developed to explain our lives to ourselves—i.e. how we have arrived at the present circumstance (impasse). There seems to be an inherent need for such self-explanations.

Here are four (named) examples:

- Mary: My life is like a closed room.
- Sam: It's always been uphill for me.
- Charles: I'm slowly dying.
- Gloria: Right now I feel like a seed that's never been watered.

2. Enlarging the metaphor

The *dimensions* of the metaphor can then be explored, but in a limited way, to elicit a sufficient amount of description so that the metaphor takes on more form and substance. If too much elaboration is elicited, then the client can get so involved in "problem" talk and "woe is me" talk that the focus shifts to these things and away from the story itself. Some caution is needed here. Enlargement can proceed via some of the following, which are keyed to the people in the previous section:

- Mary: What is that closed room like? What goes on in there? What is happening in there now? Please describe what it is like to live in that closed room. What would I notice if I were in there (with you)?
- Sam: Describe what going uphill is like. Is it steep? A city street or country road or path? What is going on on that slope: are there other people around? What do you sense (see/feel/hear/smell/touch) on that slope? What is happening there now? What would I notice if I were there (with you)?
- Charles: Describe what dying feels like to you. What is going on around you while you are dying? What would I notice if I were dying with you?
- Gloria: Describe what it is like to be an unwatered seed. What are your surroundings? What do you sense as that seed? If I were a seed like you, what would I notice?

Key elicitations are: Describe what is going on; describe what that feels like; what is going on around you?; what would I notice if I were there with you? Again, the concern is to control this enlargement to obtain sufficient elaboration to make the metaphor more real, more substantial.

3. Transforming the metaphor
"Suppose you could change in some simple and easy and realistic way so as to be more comfortable with yourself—that closed room, that uphill slope, dying, that seed—how would you change that? What would be different?" or "Suppose that right now a miracle occurs and you can change [the metaphor]—what changes would occur?" or "If a miracle occurred right now, how would you change [the metaphor] to get what you want?" And, "What are the things that would be different in your life after [the metaphor] was changed?"

- Mary: If you could change that closed room in any way, how would you change it and what would be different in your life?
- Sam: Supposing you could change that uphill road—how would you change it? Describe what would be different.
- Charles: If you could change that sense of dying, how would you change it? What would happen?
- Gloria: Suppose you could change how that seed were treated—how would it be treated differently? What other changes would occur?

This "transformation" is actually a variant of the de Shazer (et al.) *miracle question*—some of the above formulations make this explicit. In the miracle-question sense it would be useful at this point to ask for sensory-based descriptions of how this transformation will have changed the client's life. This way of working *moots* Kopp's Step 6, which connects the changed metaphor to the client's current situation by reifying the changes via the details of the transformative changes.

4. Ratification of changed metaphor
After the metaphor-transformation step, it is useful to ratify the changes in the metaphor to consolidate those changes.

- Mary: Now that the room has opened up/you've found the key to the door, how will your life continue with its new possibilities?
- Sam: Now that you've found that your life has level paths and even easy downhill paths, what will you be doing differently?

173

- Charles: Now that you know that you are always alive until that single last moment when we all die, how has that already changed what you are doing now?
- Gloria: Being watered and nurtured and cared for, how will you now grow and blossom?

Commentary

This is a simplified form of Kopp's approach, which avoids the emphasis on "images" and "imagery." The four "case" studies provide language that can be adapted to others.

B. Transforming early-memory metaphors

Kopp's distinction between "reports" and genuine, one-time-incident, early-memory recollections is a useful one. It is generally accepted that these single incidents can have a profound (almost like "imprinting") effect on a person's behavior and character later in life. As mentioned earlier, there are NLP techniques designed for this kind of change work. Also, there are hypnotherapeutic methods that work through a regression to a significant incident and then assist the client to resolve/put in perspective that event so that it no longer impacts on present-day behavior. Cheek's ideomotor method (1994; Rossi and Cheek, 1998; Battino and South, 1999) is a rapid way to access and resolve such early decisive events. This section is an adaptation of Kopp's approach based on Cheek's work but as a content-free secret-therapy process. That is, the client is guided in doing all the necessary work within herself.

1. Accessing the early-memory metaphor

"About this concern that has been troubling you, and thinking just to yourself, where in it are you most stuck or experiencing the most difficulty? [*Pause.*] When you have enough of a sense of that to experience in a mild form some of the connected feelings and bodily sensations, just let your mind drift back to your earliest childhood memory, staying connected with those bodily sensations and feelings. This is something specific that only happened once, most probably before you were seven or eight years old. When you have that memory firmly and clearly in mind, please let me know by saying 'yes' or nodding your head yes. [If it is at another age, that's fine.] Thank you."

[If no early memory comes to mind, i.e. head nodding no, or saying no, or not saying yes, then say, "The origins may be at a later time in your life. Nod, yes, if that is the case." If there is no "yes" here, then say, "Sometimes that earliest memory may at first appear a bit fuzzy. Stay with those sensations and allow that memory to form. [*Pause.*] When it does, please nod or say 'yes.'" If there is still difficulty, say, "You can explore for that earliest memory some other time. Perhaps it will just pop into your head before our next session."]

2. Experiencing that early-memory metaphor
"Now, experience that earliest memory just enough to let you know that it is really connected to your present concerns. Let me know when you have done that by nodding or saying 'yes.' Thank you."

3. Transforming that early-memory metaphor
"Since that earliest memory contains in some way the roots of your present concerns, would it be OK to just change that memory to what you would have liked to have happened instead? The memory can start out the same way, yet adjust it and let it change so that the ending is what you prefer, especially looking back. Please nod or say 'yes' when you have changed that memory to your satisfaction. Thank you."

4. Returning to present with changes
"That's fine. Please return to the present, noting how having changed the ending of that earliest memory has changed other memories and how you feel about them along the way to the present. Take your time, noting with interest specific other changes. Let me know when you are in present time by saying or nodding your head 'yes.' Thank you."

Commentary
The preceding is a rather different version of Kopp's approach to working with early-memory metaphors and is based on Cheek's and Rossi's approaches to rapid change. The emphasis on "secret" therapy is quite different from Kopp's open verbal interactions with his clients. Yet I feel that this will accomplish the same changes based on early-memory metaphors. Of course, if the client wishes to divulge verbally what is going on in her head at each step, then the therapist should be receptive to this and listen attentively, and make appropriate comments. This approach obviously builds on Kopp's work.

7.8 Concluding comments

Kopp's paradigm shifting work via his Metaphor Therapy needs to be carefully studied and used by anyone interested in doing metaphoric therapy. It is an elegant way to do this work. Notwithstanding his methods, alternative methods of applying his work are also presented. In a later chapter, the application of Metaphor Therapy and variants based on it for healing will be presented in some detail. Thank you, Professor Kopp.

Chapter 8

Guided Metaphor

8.1 Introduction

"Guided metaphor" is a made-up term, just like the title of this book, *Metaphoria*. This is a new approach that was devised to combine Kopp's *Metaphor Therapy* (Kopp, 1995) with the author's work on guided imagery (Battino, 2000), and also with elements of traditional approaches for the use of metaphor. In thinking through the systematics of Kopp's pioneering work described in the previous chapter, it made sense to combine his idea of client-generated metaphors with the formalism of guided-imagery work. After all, the best way to use guided imagery is to structure a session around the client's own "image" of what will work for him. That "image" is actually the client's own metaphor for healing work. At a recent workshop that the author gave he was asked if guided imagery as he taught it would also be useful for psychotherapeutic interventions. This was indeed a new idea, for up until that question the author was stuck in the traditional use of guided imagery for healing. Could this be used for psychotherapy? If the answer is "yes," then how would this kind of guided-imagery session differ from the traditional one? One name for this new approach could have been "metaphor-guided therapy," but "guided metaphor" is more inclusive since it can be used for both healing and psychotherapy.

This chapter presents a way to use guided metaphor for psychotherapeutic purposes, since guided imagery for healing and improving health has been treated elsewhere (Achterberg, 1985; Achterberg, Dossey, and Kolkmeier, 1994; Battino, 2000). The next section is a step-by-step description of guided metaphor with commentary. Then there are examples, and this is followed by a workbook using the approach of what is called "distance writing" or "structured writing." This approach connects with and builds on other approaches.

8.2 Step-by-step guided metaphor

The following is an outline of a five-step process for using guided metaphor for psychotherapy. This is followed by a detailed exposition of each step.

1. *Opening*—Introduction and explanation of importance of everyone's having his own life story, i.e. the story he tells himself (and others) about how he got to the present time. Life stories have beginnings, middles, ends, themes, and key episodes.

2. *Elicitation of client's story*—Ask for the client to tell his life story in a one-page summary, one sentence, and finally as a word or phrase.

3. *Elicit how he would change his story for personal benefit*—From the perspective of the present, how would the client change his life story, assuming he could as if by a miracle, so that his present and future life would be comfortable and free of old constraints.

4. *Delivery of client's personal life metaphor*—In the style of a guided-imagery session retell the client his life story, how he would change it, and provide him with the opportunity to think through how this changed life history would have affected various parts of his life up to the present, and into his future.

5. *Ratification and reorientation*—Ratify by an ideomotor signal (such as head nodding) that he has indeed experienced these changes in his story and the effects of those changes on his life at this time. Then compliment him on the courage to do this work, and reorient him to the present.

A. Opening

"Everyone's life is a story, one that you may tell to others, or one that you tell yourself about how you got to this point of your life. You are the hero of that story, of all the things that have happened to you and that you have done. There are many remarkable things you have done, like learning how to walk and talk and read and write. There were difficulties and triumphs, illnesses and healing.

And all sorts of relationships. There are so many parts to a good story—beginning, middle, and end, and all the transitions from one phase to another. The time sequence of a life is: birth, development, childhood, teenage, young adult, adult, midlife, present, and a sense of the future. There are so many roles that we try on and also live—hero, heroine, mother, father, husband, wife, child, victim, oppressor, active or passive participant or observer, doer or person done to, creator, active designer, student, teacher, learner, and so many others that are unique to you.

"Most lives have a central theme or role, that which gives meaning to your life. There is usually a punch line or bottom line or moral or message or purpose. Even a one-actor play has many other characters in his story—all those people who have had some impact on his life. They may not be on the stage, but they are nevertheless there. Who are they? What are they like? How much has each influenced your story? When you look back over your life, or recall a play or a novel, you can identify key incidents that were particularly important in molding your life, setting direction, shaping your story. Individual lives are so endlessly interesting, and everyone has a story."

The previous opening statement in some form, adapted to your client, is the entrée into eliciting his story. The statement sets out the parameters, the framework, for the story. It goes on for a while so that the client can have time to do his own inner search for the elements of his story. As such, the opening should incorporate appropriate pauses while the client reflects and recalls. Just listening to this opening narrative starts the therapeutic process—it presupposes that: the client has a story; the story has structure; the client will be able to tell his story; and that his story is unique and valued—it will be listened to.

B. Elicitation of the client's story

"Now, just imagine that you were asked to write one of those jacket blurbs for a novel. You know, just a few short paragraphs that both summarize the content of the book, and whet the reader's appetite to find out more. If you were to write—by telling me—the jacket blurb of your life's story, what would be in those few short

179

paragraphs?" (After the client does this ...) "Thank you. That was a great summary. Now, could you boil those paragraphs down to just one sentence? Good. Go ahead." (After the client has done this ...) "I wonder if at this time you could describe yourself in one word—or several different single words—that accurately describe yourself to yourself. For example, are you brave/scared/anxious/ happy/depressed/energetic/lazy/fat/thin/intelligent/arty/ slow, or whatever? Just say whatever comes to mind. Thank you."

This elicitation is a critical part of the guided-metaphor process. In a brief narrative form (the jacket blurb, or other appropriate idea such as an abstract or the brief biography put in school yearbooks) the client reveals his life story. That is, what he *believes* to be his life story, since this is *his interpretation* of how he got to his present age and circumstances. It may be appropriate from time to time to say, "Please tell me a bit more about that [some specific element of his story]," but only after letting him tell his story without interruptions.

The next part of the elicitation is to narrow the client's focus to describing himself/his story in one sentence. This would be the theme of his life. You might hear things like:

- John is a dreamer who never gets anywhere.
- Mary is a supermom who lost herself.
- Harry is a successful X, but he has no feelings.
- Gloria is trapped inside her fat body.
- Max lives only in his head.
- Jayne is an overachiever.
- Ben is a selfish no-goodnik.
- Harriet is a depressed clam.
- George is a frustrated teacher.
- Marilyn lives in her own world.
- Patrick can't stay away from drink.
- Ellie wants love and can't find it.

These are vivid self-descriptions. They are also, of course, "forced" choices. The client needs to sense that the choices will lead somewhere. But there is also benefit, almost an "Aha!" experience, in being able to explicitly come up with this précis of his life—"I never consciously thought of myself in that way."

The last request is in effect to ask for the one-word nominalization that he feels fits him. Examples are:

- depressed
- anxious
- happy
- dependent
- unlovable
- victim
- overachiever
- crazy
- superlogical
- too giving
- sinful
- phobic
- desperate
- stupid
- indecisive
- overcontrolling
- suicidal
- Pollyanna-ish
- rigid
- pushover
- fat elephant
- bulimic
- lost

The list is as endless as a volume of the DSM, *but* these are all *self-diagnoses* and are therefore more significant than authority-generated diagnoses. How a person describes himself is actually who he is since he *acts as if* he were that nominalization. (I once had a client who said she was a depressive because that was the label a psychiatrist pasted on her. She did not and would not believe or hear my observation that she was one of the more energetic and active people I knew. She didn't act depressed. With the label she interpreted all of her behavior as manifestations of being depressed.) These labels are self-perpetuating. I think it was Bill O'Hanlon who said, "Every time I get a hypothesis about a client, I lie down until it goes away." He was referring, of course, to therapist-generated labels and therapist-guessed-at causes.

These self-descriptions, in any of the three forms discussed here, are *believed* by the client to be true. Please note that the self-descriptions/metaphors/stories are *directly* asked for. You do not need to wait for your client to blurt out accidentally this information—just ask for it. Otherwise, you are playing guessing games. "This is an interesting way of getting what you want. OK?"

When you have the client's story, what do you do with it?

C. How would you change your story?

One of the central tools in solution-focused brief therapy (SFBT; e.g. de Shazer, 1994; Miller and Berg, 1995; Berg and Dolan, 2001) is the *miracle question*. "What if, while you were asleep tonight, a miracle occurred whose result was that in the morning the difficulties you came to see me about, were resolved (realistically) to your satisfaction?" This is a wonderful and effective intervention. Guided metaphor makes use of this idea *and* the knowledge that memory is malleable.

"In the story of your life there are a number of places where you got stuck (or were sidetracked, or were fixated, or were deciding events for you). Imagine that, as an editor, you could go back to that particularly decisive event, and change it so that you were now free of that old thing. How would you now rewrite the story of your life to get a happy ending?" (*Listen.*)

"Assuming you could rewrite or change your life, so that your life now is what you want it to be, what changes would you make?" (*Listen.*)

"Would it be OK now that you know how you would have changed your life, to just go ahead and rearrange your past and how you think and feel about it? Great. Just take some time to do that. [*Pause.*] Now, move forward from that time to the present, noting how those changes have already affected subsequent events and your feelings about those events. [*Pause.*] Do some crystal-ball gazing and notice how these changes will affect your future life. [*Pause.*] Thank you."

"Please summarize your new life story in a few paragraphs. Thank you. Now distill your new story to one sentence. Thank you. Now summarize all of that in a word or two, or a phrase. Thank you."

The information you have elicited in Parts B and C are what you need to structure the guided metaphor that is the next step. For some people (much as in Time-Line Therapy) the completion of Step C will be sufficient. For others, the guided metaphor that incorporates all of this client-generated information serves to reinforce and ratify and instill the changes the client has introduced. The guided metaphor then objectifies the changes as retold by a caring listener.

D. The guided metaphor

Three examples of guided metaphors are given here. The reader can infer the clients' stories and their solutions from the narrative.

1. Harriet is a depressed clam—depressed

Harriet, I want to thank you for sharing your life story with me. Fascinating, just fascinating. It's a wonder how you've managed to raise two kids who are pretty reasonable, and how long your marriage has lasted. Quite a story. I didn't realize how much a clam could do from within its shell. Still, that must have been confining. With what you've told me, it's no wonder that you felt all closed in for all of those years, just venturing out from time to time.

As you listen to me go over your story and the changes you have envisioned, you might wish to close your eyes, relax, and adjust your position so that you are even more comfortable. Just listen to your story. And, if I don't get it just right, you can correct what I say within your head. Your story, the story of a good little girl who got trapped, hemmed in by life. Continuing to relax. Your story. And, there were some good times in there, too, weren't there? Some times when you happily bubbled forth.

It must have been hard growing up with an older sister who seemed so perfect, and a father who was either at work or buried in his reading, and a mother who was so demanding, so strict, so many standards. So you became a good little girl, and a good teenager, and a good wife, and a good mother. It was easy to do that from within your protective shell, keeping mum, being quiet, being passive, hiding in that dull depression down in the seabed. Safe, secure, humdrum. An "OK" life.

But, that wasn't enough, was it? Being repressed and confined. There was so much more to you—even clams can hope and dream and imagine. You did escape from that shell a few times—what freedom! A bit scary at first. Yet you survived and endured. There are some advantages to having a hard shell.

And, thinking back over your life, you wrote a new story, a transformative one, one straight out of the myths and legends of old. What can move a clam? A storm! A powerful storm came and swept you ashore. Knocking against some rocks, the clam opened and you floated up on shore just like that goddess in the painting. Free and open and radiant and bursting with energy and inner beauty. Magic. A myth come true. And, stepping ashore, you left that shell that had served its purpose in protecting you in the past.

Thanking that shell, within your mind, it was and is now time to move on, exploring the world freely. Tasting, smelling, experiencing, feeling, exploring, doing. And you told me about how coming ashore, stepping forth, has been a kind of rebirth, letting loose your hopes and dreams, to flower and blossom and grow. Noticing how that release from the shell has modified and changed not only how you think about yourself, but who you are. Even memories have changed now that you are out of the deeps and in the open air. How could that have happened? When? So different.

Sometimes it takes a storm to open a clam and wash away and open up. A new story.

2. Patrick can't stay away from drink—desperate

Thank you for telling me your story, Patrick. A fascinating one, with all of those ups and downs and adventures. Yet the desperation, the stuckness, the sense of doom was always there. It was a classic tragedy in some ways—you know, the hero with that tragic flaw. And how many heroes have overcome their difficult childhoods? For many, that was the spur that drove them into a different life, a happier and less driven one. Somehow, somehow, despite all of the odds against you, you have managed to survive and make a reasonable life for yourself most of the time. There is that sense of desperation, of time running out, through the story of your life.

When you were small you couldn't protect your mother or your sister or your brother from your father's wild and erratic drunken episodes. You all coped somehow. His tragic death when you were thirteen was both a relief and a burden. In those circumstances, all kids would have wished their father to die or to go away. He died, you were not responsible, but could not avoid the guilt of your wishing him dead. Looking back, that was natural. It was also natural, in some ways, that you would become an alcoholic, too. That was one way to get close to the father who was so erratic and remote. The difference was that in your desperation you kept fighting that drive to drink. And you were successful many times. If your life story is that of a man who can't stay away from drink, it is also a story riddled with exceptions. You told me that somehow you were able to be sober for an entire two years in there. That was heroic, and that hero is here in this room.

We also talked about how you were able to change your story for those two years. You remember that and how you felt then. And you came up out of your desperation with a new story for your life, a new way of picturing yourself. Let me go over that now while you listen comfortably, eyes perhaps closed, to your own new story. And, if I don't get it exactly right, edit it and change it again so that this is your life, your history, your story.

Remember you said, and you chuckled about it at the time, that it was a new spirit that came over you. This pure distilled inner being that took over and cleaned your mind and your body, washing away, dissolving all of that old desperate junk you had stored in that dark basement. A real cleaning out, not a garage sale, but straight to the rubbish heap. The spirit, your new spirit, had a magic broom. And the two of you wielded it together, sweeping away, eliminating, throwing out, cleaning that old rubbish. That childish guilt trip was buried deep, and went out with the rest. Plastic bag after plastic bag of garbage. And, after that, those old feelings of desperation that used to drive you got swept away, too. Free at last. An inner peace. The freedom to be who you always were inside. A new spirit. A free spirit. A story retold. Patrick reborn. What a story. What an ending!

Patrick, thank you for letting me share in your story.

3. *Mary Supermom—lost*

With many stories it is hard to tell just how the person got to be who they are when they tell their story. You know, you can never be other than who you are at this time. You are always you. Yet, the stories we tell ourselves, our dreams and hopes and internal picture of who we are may not match the reality we live in. Those dreams, those stories we told ourselves of who we were going to be later in life, and what we were going to be doing then, those stories live inside us and are a kind of mirror we look at now and again.

So, you are here, now, being a supermom, and, from what you tell me, doing a pretty good job of it. Raising three active kids is quite an accomplishment. Your story of how you got here is pretty traditional, although you are a unique woman and have done it your own special way. You were the oldest of four kids, your mother relied on you to help bring up the others, and you lost out on a lot of kid, irresponsible fun time. You were good at taking care of them, even proud of how they turned out. You are good at taking care of your children and your husband. Who takes care of Mary? You were always too busy to find time for yourself. Although, you did manage to become quite good at piano and singing. You even managed to sing in a high school musical—not that your mother didn't lay a guilt trip on you about the time you spent on rehearsals. That Mary, the singing and playing Mary, is still here. Your children all play piano and are involved in school music programs. What have you lost? When did you lose your way? Living music through your kids does not have the same magic as making music yourself.

So, here you are—fulfilling dreams for others, and just all frustrated and lost. You can, maybe, blame it all on Responsibility, that unrelentingly demanding ogre. The big R trapped you when you were young, trapped you in marriage, and has held you bondage as a mother. Not that you haven't escaped from R from time to time, and found some space for yourself.

You've talked about keys, and there are many meanings to key. What is the key to unlocking the door of your life? To finding that you who was always there? To singing your own unique song? With a full accompaniment? What is the key in which you will play your life? Will you be cutting cords by playing the right chords, the underscore of the main theme? What will be noteworthy in the space opened by that key, your keys? And you told me that you could easily key up to being, doing, playing, exploring, enjoying, finding that new/old melody. The interesting thing you said was that by opening doors, by finding the keys, by putting R in its place, that would let you continue to be a mom and a wife and a lover, but in even freer ways. The Real you, and that is a different big R in Real, already knows how to play that music.

As you listen, now, feeling those keys in your hand, opening doors, locking away that old troublesome R in that old box, sensing the keys turning, opening, playing, noting them on the score, hearing and feeling your music, you just know inside, in that inner self, that, in some interesting way, all of this has already changed, hasn't it? A new story, growing out of the old one, building to a crescendo in your life. And, once you've turned those keys, played your new song, that melody, your melody, will be you, is you, is who you are.

Thank you, Mary, for sharing your story with me, and telling me about the new developments in it. You might even say that I've become "attuned" to your inner music. Play on …

* * *

The "guided" metaphor as illustrated above has much of a standard guided imagery session in it. The therapist basically retells the client's story, using their language, and then guides them through a new story using the client's own metaphor for change. Mary Supermom's session also had some elements of narrative therapy interwoven. The retelling of the story and its resolution/new story by another person has the effect of making it more real, and ratifying the new story. If the therapist can describe the new story, then it must be real—i.e. I can believe in it, in me, too.

8.3 Workbook for guided metaphor

The following "workbook" is an example of what is called *structured writing* or *distance writing*. This is quite different from keeping a diary or a journal of your feelings and activities. The participant is asked to *answer in writing* specific questions, or to write about particular topics—these items are "structured" to help the writer resolve a particular concern, deal with a specific condition, or to create a dialogue with himself in writing. There is an extensive and growing literature in this area, most of it centered on the use of workbooks for psychotherapy. Some general references follow (principal researchers are J. W. Pennebaker and L. L'Abate): Esterling, L'Abate, Murray and Pennebaker, 1999; L'Abate, 1992; L'Abate, 1997; Pennebaker, 1997. Many studies have shown that the act of writing about traumatic events or emotional concerns helps the writer resolve and/or minimize the impact of these things on his life. There is an old observation about crying alone and laughing together. Sharing pain and discomfort and unease is beneficial—therefore it is not too surprising that "sharing" with yourself via the medium of structured writing can be helpful.

In this section, a workbook building on the ideas involved in guided metaphor is presented. There are instructions for its use. This workbook may be freely copied and used—the author would appreciate feedback on its effectiveness and how to improve it. Depending on the particular concern, the user of the workbook may wish to keep its contents private, share with a trusted individual, or consult with a psychotherapist about the process and content and changes. In fact, a psychotherapist may wish to use this workbook as one component of a treatment plan.

Workbook for guided metaphor

The questions in this workbook have been designed to help you work through a particular personal concern or problem. Please find a quiet time and place to do this writing over a period of successive days. What you write is personal—you may wish to keep it private or share all of it or parts of it with your therapist, or with someone you trust. There is no room in this workbook to write your responses—please write them out separately (but numbered appropriately) on other pieces of paper. You may wish to directly type your responses into a computer file. There are no "correct" responses—whatever comes to mind for each item is the right thing for you. Take whatever time you need to respond. You should know that a number of research studies have shown that the very act of writing responses to the kinds of questions and requests in this workbook have been beneficial for both mental and physical health. This process is most helpful when you write from "your inner self."

1. Suppose that you were asked to write a one-page story of your life. This is not a brief biography, but rather a *story* as you might tell it to someone. This story would contain the significant events that molded your life. That is, what were the key elements, those parts of your life that would be highlighted if this were a short story, or a novel, or a drama? It may be helpful to outline your life's story before writing it. Please write that one-page story now.

2. After rereading your one-page life story, think about what you have written, and then summarize it in *one* sentence. This might be something like, "Mary is someone who always took life too seriously, and never made any time to enjoy herself" or "John was always so wrapped up in himself and becoming a success that he never learned about love." A one-sentence summary, please.

3. As you think about your responses to (1) and (2), what word or words or phrases come to mind that would accurately describe your life? Some examples are: happy, sad, frustrated, lonely, overachiever, successful, supermom, worker, scientist, teacher, depressed, humdrum, desperate.

4. Think about the self-description you came up with in (3). This may be a good time to expand on what that means and has meant to you.

5. After rereading your life story in (1), what is the central theme in your life?

6. Stories have beginnings, middles (the development part), and ends (where you are now or what you anticipate for the rest of your life). What are they for your life's story?

7. If your life's story were like a fable, what would be the *moral* at the end?

8. Assume you were an editor with the power to rewrite your story the way that you would like it to be—what parts would you change, and how? The more specific you are about these changes, the better. Write your new story in a page or less.

9. Summarize the *new* story of your life in one sentence.

10. Summarize the new story of your life in a single word or a phrase.

11. How has thinking of your life in terms of your new story already changed your present life, how you think and feel about yourself and your future? As you contemplate your new life's story, and your new life, what specific things come to mind?

12. This is a place to summarize what has happened for you by responding to the items in this workbook.

Thank you.

8.4 Concluding comments

The idea of the guided metaphor builds upon Kopp's Metaphor Therapy and the field of guided imagery. It is an attempt to utilize the formalism of guided imagery for psychotherapy. This chapter has presented a systematic way of using guided metaphor. It also contains a *workbook* for guided metaphor that incorporates this approach for people to use on their own. It is the author's hope that the workbook will prove to be useful both by itself and as an adjunct to working with a therapist.

The remainder of this book connects metaphoric work with a number of disciplines and approaches.

Chapter 9

Reframing as Metaphor

9.1 Introduction

The way that you perceive a particular photograph or painting is influenced by the frame in which it is set, the lighting, and the surroundings. You can immediately sense how different a painting would look framed or unframed, alone on a wall, surrounded by many other paintings on the same wall, or on an easel in an open meadow or under shade trees. The surroundings affect our perception. This, of course, was well understood by Gestalt psychologists in their many experiments on figure–ground relationships. Changing the framing or the background or the surroundings changes the way that we perceive a given "figure."

A simple example that Bernie Siegel likes to use is in Figure 9.1. On an 8½ × 11-inch piece of white paper, he has a black dot of perhaps ¼-inch diameter, centered. He shows this to an audience and asks what they see. Most respond that they see a black dot. The white area is about 2,000 times the area of the black dot. (If you use a

Figure 9.1 The black dot on the white paper

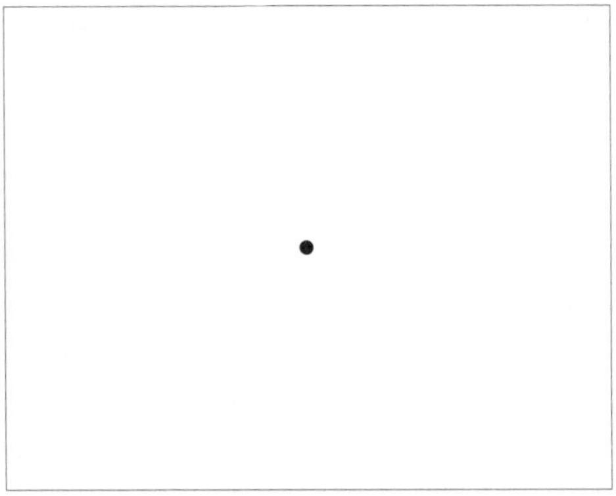

black dot of ½-inch diameter, the ratio of white to black is about 500.) Siegel then points out that this is how most people who are confronted with a diagnosis of a life-challenging disease perceive the rest of their lives—they see the black dot and not the much greater white area surrounding it. This is one exercise in the art of reframing. It deals with where you focus your attention, and that affects your thinking and feeling and associated memories. The object itself—in this case the white paper with the black dot—does not change; what changes is your perception. The fascinating thing about the human mind is that once your way of perceiving an object or an event changes, it is almost impossible to return to the earlier perception.

Figure 9.2 Opportunity …

```
OPPORTUNITY
ISNOWHERE
```

Let us examine another "trick," which I learned from John Graham-Pole, M.D., a pediatric oncologist. (You may be interested in his book, *Illness and the Art of Creative Self-Expression* (2000).) You are shown a card (Figure 9.2) on which two sequences of letters are printed. You can interpret this in two ways: OPPORTUNITY IS NOWHERE or OPPORTUNITY IS NOW HERE. Which did you choose? Knowing about the alternate readings, which one do you prefer? Is this a word game, or does it tell you about how you perceive the world? Where do you go with this latter information?

A good picture-framing shop can provide you with a number of choices for reframing the framed art work you brought in, or for your unframed work. You go to an experienced framer when your choices are limited; you go to a psychotherapist for effectively the same reason. When you are stuck in a particular behavior pattern or ideation, you expect the therapist to help you find new choices—new ways of behaving or thinking. Your personal situation and past are the reality fixed in the picture, the story, of your life up until that point. That past, that story, may be unalterable, but how you *perceive* it, how you think about it, and how you feel about it can all be reframed. The perspective can change, the frame can be replaced.

What is the connection between reframing and metaphor? The answer is the subject of this chapter. Simply, if listening to a story changes your perspective on your life, on yourself, then that has already changed you. The guided metaphor discussed in the previous chapter is one way of obtaining this therapeutic reframing. Before discussing more about this subject, the nature of change is taken up in the next section.

9.2 *First- and second-order change*

One of the most important books in the history of psychotherapy was published in 1974—*Change. Principles of Problem Formation and Problem Resolution*. Its authors were Watzlawick, Weakland, and Fisch of the Mental Research Institute (MRI), Palo Alto. In the Foreword (pp. ix–x), Milton H. Erickson has the following to say:

> There have been multitudes of books and theories on how to change people, but at long last, the authors in this book have looked seriously at the subject of change itself—both how change occurs spontaneously, and how change can be promoted ... I have viewed much of what I have done as expediting the currents of change already seething within the person and the family—but currents that need the "unexpected," the "illogical," and the "sudden" move to lead them to tangible fruition.

> It is this phenomenon of change with which this book is concerned, the actual nature and kinds of change so long overlooked by the formulation of theories about how to change people. Watzlawick, Weakland, and Fisch have, in this extremely important book, looked at this phenomenon and put it into a conceptual framework—illuminated by examples from a variety of areas—which opens up new pathways to the further understanding of how people become enmeshed in problems with each other, and new pathways to expediting the resolution of such human impasses. The relevance of this new framework extends far beyond the sphere of "psychological" problems from which it grew. This work is

fascinating. I think it is a noteworthy contribution—a damn good book—and a must for anyone seeking to understand the many aspects of group behavior.

What was it about *Change* that so impressed Erickson? This book provides a coherent theory about the process of change based upon the theory of logical types. To simplify, Watzlawick et al. consider change to be of two types: first-order change, which occurs *within* a system, and second-order change, which is *meta* to, or external to, the system. These two types of change, and ways of bringing them about, are elaborated upon in what follows. To quote (p. 10, 1974), "There are two different types of change: one that occurs within a given system which itself remains unchanged, and one whose occurrence changes the system itself."

The main characteristic of attempts to solve problems using first-order change is *doing more of the same.* This works within the framework of the existing system, and is the most common solution used by institutions—parents, schools, governments, industries, and the military. In school or at home if Johnny misbehaves, there is a particular penalty or punishment or deprivation. If Johnny continues to misbehave, then the penalty is increased, i.e. more of the same. In this sense, the solution becomes the problem because, short of draconian measures, increasing penalties tends to be counterproductive. The most glaring example of this in the United States is the "war" on drugs—as of this writing I believe the U.S. is into its eighth such war. The solution continues to be the same: more interdiction, more law enforcement, stiffer penalties (higher fines, mandatory sentences, longer sentences), and growing militarization. These are all solutions that are *within* the system and that just escalate what hasn't worked. Watzlawick, et al. (p. 39) indicate that there are basically three ways in which mishandling occurs through which the problem is essentially maintained (italics in original):

A. A solution is attempted by denying that a problem is a problem; action *is necessary, but is not taken.*

B. Change is attempted regarding a difficulty which for all practical purposes is either unchangeable ... or nonexistent: *action is taken when it should not be.*

C. An error in logical typing is committed and a game without end established ... *action is taken at the wrong level.*

Note that a logical-typing error occurs when a second-order change is incorrectly applied to a first-order problem, and vice versa.

There are problems where first-order solutions are effective. Giving impoverished people more money and food and housing works up to a point. The draconian rules on drinking and driving that are enforced in Japan and those on illegal drugs in Singapore are effective. Yet, with most presenting problems that a psychotherapist encounters, a first step is to find out what solutions have already been tried. Then you know what hasn't worked, and what to avoid doing more of.

Second-order change can be considered to be *change of change*. It is external to and outside of the existing system. It implies changes in the system itself. Some quotes from Watzlawick, et al. are in order (page citation at end of quote).

> ... second-order change is always in the nature of a discontinuity or a logical jump ... [p. 12]

> Second-order change is applied to what in the first-order change perspective, appears to be a solution, because in the second-order change perspective this "solution" reveals itself as the keystone of the problem whose solution is attempted. [p. 82]

> ... second-order change usually appears weird, unexpected, and uncommonsensical; there is a puzzling, paradoxical element in the process of change. [p. 83]

> Applying second-order change techniques to the "solution" means that the situation is dealt with in the here and now. These techniques deal with effects and not with their presumed causes; the crucial question is *what?* and not *why?* [p. 83]

> The use of second-order change techniques lifts the situation out of the paradox-engendering trap created by the self-reflexiveness of the attempted solution and places it in a different frame ... [p. 83]

... the theme of the puzzling, uncommonsensical solution is an archetypical one, reflected in folklore, fairy tales, humor, and many dreams ... [p. xiii]

Everyday, not just clinical, experience shows not only that there can be change without insight, but that very few behavioral or social changes are accompanied, let alone preceded, by insight into the vicissitudes of their genesis. ... the search for the causes in the past is just one such self-defeating "solution." [pp. 86–7]

9.3 Reframing

The previous section contains many quotes and interesting observations, but what do they have to do with reframing and metaphor? Chapter 8 in Watzlawick et al. (pp. 92–109) is entitled, "The Gentle Art of Reframing." For these authors, reframing is the central and most accessible way of doing second-order-change work. A reframe of necessity changes one's perspective, one's understanding, and one's belief about the problem. A reframe creates a new story, a new metaphor, about the client's life. In effect, to do a reframe you ask the client to step *outside* the picture of her life and to put it into a new frame or context. Paradox is at work here, since, although it is the same picture that is in its new frame, the very act of reframing the picture also changes the picture—not the picture itself, but the *way that we perceive it*. And that changed perception becomes the reality of how we experience the picture. In a similar fashion, a verbal reframe paradoxically changes the experience by altering our impression and understanding of the experience. Our memories and our experiences do not exist in a vacuum: they exist in a context within our minds, and they exist with attached meanings. So, if you help your client to alter the context and/or the meaning of an experience, you have changed her life via a reframing. In fact, it is the author's contention (even conviction) that the central factor of almost all effective change work is reframing. It is also his contention that effective reframing is metaphoric in nature.

Watzlawick et al. (pp. 92–3, 1974) cite Tom Sawyer's getting his friends to whitewash a fence as a classic example of a reframe—Tom converted work into play. Some quotes:

To reframe, then, means to change the conceptual and/or emotional setting or viewpoint in relation to which a situation is experienced and to place it in another frame which fits the "facts" of the same concrete situation equally well or even better, and thereby changes its entire meaning ... The philosopher Epictetus expressed it as early as the first century A.D., "It is not the things themselves which trouble us, but the opinions that we have about these things." The word *about* in this quotation reminds us that any opinion ... is *meta* to the object of this opinion or view, and therefore of the next higher logical level. [p. 95]

Reframing operates on the level of *meta* reality, where, as we have tried to point out, change can take place even if the objective circumstances of a situation are quite beyond human control. [p. 97]

... reframing means changing the emphasis from one class membership of an object to another, equally valid class membership, or, especially, introducing such a new class membership into the conceptualization of all concerned. [p. 98]

Watzlawick, et al. describe three aspects of reframing (pp. 98–9):

1. Our experience of the world is based on the categorization of the objects of our perceptions into classes. These classes are mental constructs and therefore of a totally different order of reality then the objects themselves ...

2. Once an object is conceptualized as the member of a given class, it is extremely difficult to see it as belonging also to another class. This class membership of an object is called its "reality" ...

3. What makes reframing such an effective tool of change is that once we do perceive the alternative class membership(s) we cannot so easily go back to the trap and anguish of a former view of "reality."

The classic reframe, which has many variants, is to tell your client sometime during the first session, "I want to congratulate you on the courage you have shown in: coming to see me/acknowledging your problems/making the time to work on this/being so open/ talking freely/acknowledging that you need some help in this/just being here/overcoming your resistance to ask for help/trusting me with all this information/letting go/being forthright/telling it like it is/showing your vulnerability/answering my questions/ seriously considering change/just being yourself/bringing your spouse with you/bringing your family with you/having survived so long under very difficult circumstances/having borne so much, but still being hopeful/retaining your dreams/making a reasonable life under such trying circumstances/going the extra step/keeping your faith/holding your job/staying in school/not drinking for that time/not giving up on yourself. These are all simple statements building on what the client has said, but also putting a positive interpretation on, for example, simply coming to see you. Her act, her life, has been reframed in the judgment of an "expert." There is now value in what might have been an overlooked action. Of course, for a given client, you may have the opportunity to use many of the above reframes in subsequent sessions.

In constructing a reframe, you ask yourself, "In what other context can this experience occur that would be beneficial to this client?" or "What other meaning can be assigned to this experience that would make it beneficial?" Reframes are concerned with both context and meaning (interpretation). Keep the possibility of alternate frames always in mind.

Another way of reframing is to use *scaling questions* in the style of solution-focused brief therapy (e.g. de Shazer, 1994; Miller & Berg, 1995). Some examples follow:

- On a scale of zero to ten where zero is not at all, and ten is being completely stuck, how stuck are you now?
- On a scale of zero to ten where zero means not at all, and ten is highly motivated, how motivated are you to actually carrying out this change?
- On a scale of zero to ten where zero is being completely and totally relaxed, and ten is the highest anxiety you can imagine, where are you now?
- On a scale of one to ten where ten means that you are completely in control of your drinking, and one means that you are helpless about drinking, what number are you at now?

These scales are metaphors for where the person is for that particular trait or problem. It is the client's scaling of herself that is important—this is her judgment of where she is at that point in time. The concern has been reframed to a scale. The typical intervention would then be, "What would it take to move that up (or down) by half a point? or even a tenth of a point?" Ask for *small* changes since what brings about significant change is *one* small step, *and then* another, *and then* …

It would be improper to leave *Change* and not mention the authors' favorite intervention. To wit (p. 114), "Symptom prescription—or, in the wider, nonclinical sense, second-order change through paradox—is undoubtedly the most powerful and most elegant form of problem resolution known to us." By *prescribing* that the client do the symptom characteristic of her problem (overeating, excessive hand washing, verbal fighting with spouse, procrastination about studying, etc.) you are asking the client to convert, via this paradox, what she had heretofore considered to be an involuntary response or behavior to a voluntary one. Her lack of control has been paradoxically reframed, and she now has a different "picture" of herself. (There is a similarity to logotherapy's " paradoxical intention" intervention.)

9.4 Some examples of reframing

Tom Sawyer was mentioned earlier—here is that entire reframe as presented in Watzlawick, et al. (1974, pp. 92–3). Tom was faced by the intolerable task of whitewashing thirty yards of board fence nine feet high. Then a boy shows up whose ridicule he had been most dreading.

"Hello, old chap, you got to work, hey?"

"Why, it's you, Ben! I warn't noticing."

"Say—I'm going a-swimming, *I* am. Don't you wish you could? But of course you'd druther *work*—wouldn't you? Course you would!"

Tom contemplated the boy a bit, and said:

"What do you call work?"

"Why, ain't *that* work?"

Tom resumed his whitewashing and answered carelessly:

"Well, maybe it is, and maybe it ain't. All I know, is, it suits Tom Sawyer."

"Oh come, now, you don't mean to let on that you *like* it?"

The brush continued to move.

"Like it? Well, I don't see why I oughtn't to like it. Does a boy get a chance to whitewash a fence every day?"

That put the thing in a new light. Ben stopped nibbling his apple. Tom swept his brush daintily back and forth—stepped back to note the effect—added a touch here and there—criticized the effect again— Ben watching every move and getting more and more interested, more and more absorbed.

Presently he said:

"Say, Tom, let *me* whitewash a little."

That last line is a gem, but it is Tom's genius "that put the thing in a new light."

Perhaps my favorite Erickson reframe is a story entitled "Vicious Pleasure" (Rosen, 1982, pp. 36–7):

Vicious Pleasure
A woman in her thirties arrived and said, "I don't suppose you want to see me." I said, "That's your supposition, would you like to hear mine?"

"Well," she said, "I am not deserving of your attention. When I was six years old my father molested me sexually and from the age of six until seventeen he used me as a sexual object, regularly, several times a week. And every time he did it I was in a state of fear. I was frozen with terror. I felt dirty, inferior, inadequate, ashamed."

"I thought, at seventeen, I had enough strength to break away from him and I worked my way through the rest of high school, hoping that that would give me a feeling of self-respect, and it didn't. Then I thought maybe a bachelor-of-arts degree would give me a feeling of self-respect. I worked my way through college. I felt ashamed, inferior, indecent. It was a terrible feeling of disappointment. I thought maybe a master's degree would give me self-respect, but it didn't. And all through college and graduate school I was propositioned. And that proved I didn't deserve self-respect. And I thought I would enroll for a doctorate degree, and men kept propositioning me. I just gave up and became a common prostitute. But that's not very nice. And some man offered to let me live with him. Well, a girl needs to have food and shelter so I agreed to it.

"Sex was a horrible experience. A penis is so hard and looks so threatening. I just became fear stricken and passive. And it was a painful, horrible experience. This man got tired of me and I began living with another man. The same thing over and over, and now I come to you. I feel like filth. An erect penis just terrifies me and I just get helpless, and weak, and passive. I am so glad when a man finishes.

"But I still have to live. I have to have clothes. I have to have shelter; and essentially I am not worth anything else."

I said, "That's an unhappy story; and the really unhappy part is—you're stupid! You tell me that you are afraid of a bold, erect, hard penis—and that's stupid! *You* know you have a vagina; *I* know it. A vagina can take the biggest, boldest, most assertive penis and turn it into a dangling, helpless object."

"And your vagina can *take a vicious pleasure in reducing it to a helpless dangling object.*"

The change on her face was wonderful. She said, "I am going to go back to Los Angeles, and can I see you in a month's time?" And I said, "Certainly." She came back in a month's time and said, "You're right! I went to bed with a man and I took a vicious pleasure in reducing him to helplessness. It didn't take long, and

I enjoyed it. And I tried another man. The same thing. And another man. And it's pleasurable! Now I am going to get my Ph.D. and go into counseling, and I am going to wait until I see a man I want to live with."

I called her stupid. I *really* got her attention. And then I said, "Vicious pleasure." And she *did* resent men. I also said "pleasure."

This story has shock and surprise and a clever reframe that built upon the woman's own story, and met her within her own frame of reference. The facts of her life did not change, but the way she perceived them did. Erickson's reframe led her to, in effect, create a new life for herself.

Here is another reframe by Erickson (1958) as summarized by Gilligan (1987, pp. 330–1):

An Awful Lot of Blood

Erickson (1958) described an incident in which his son Robert, then three years old, fell down the back stairs. Erickson did not try immediately to move the screaming boy, who lay sprawled in agony on pavement spattered with blood from his profusely bleeding mouth. Instead, he waited for the boy to take the fresh breath he needed to scream anew and then acknowledged in a simple and sympathetic fashion the "awful" and "terrible" pain Robert was experiencing. By demonstrating this understanding of the situation, Erickson secured rapport and attention, which he then consolidated by commenting that it would keep right on hurting. He paced further by voicing aloud the boy's desire to have the pain ease, then led by raising the *possibility* (*not* the certainty) of the pain diminishing within several minutes. He next distracted Robert by closely examining with his wife the "awful lot" of blood on the pavement before announcing that it was "good, red, strong blood" and suggesting that the blood could be better examined against the white background of the bathroom sink. By this time, absorption and interest in the quality of his blood had replaced Robert's pain and crying. This was utilized to demonstrate repeatedly to the boy that his blood was so strong and red that it could make "pink" the water being poured over his face. Questions of whether the mouth was bleeding and swelling properly were then raised and, after close examination, answered affirmatively.

The potentially negative response to the next step of stitching was paced before Erickson "regretfully" informed Robert that he probably couldn't have as many stitches as he could count or as many as several older siblings. This focusing of Robert's attention on counting the number of stitches served indirectly to secure freedom from pain. Robert was disappointed when he received "only" seven stitches, but cheered some when the surgeon pointed out that the stitches were of better quality than those given his siblings and that they probably would leave a W-shaped scar similar to the letter of his Daddy's college.

This case report about Erickson's son's accident contains several reframes, as well as being an excellent example of pacing and leading. (See Rosen's book (1982) and Erickson's publications for more examples.)

9.5 Concluding comments

Reframing is the simplest and easiest way to do second-order-change work. Becoming adept at its use takes practice, but almost all effective therapeutic work involves some level of reframing. Reframing as practiced by NLP practitioners (see, e.g., Bandler and Grinder (1982)) utilizes both the verbal reframing of context and content as described in this chapter, and a six- (or seven-) step process whose goal is to provide choice for a client.

For some readers it may be a stretch to consider reframing as a form of metaphor. Yet anything that changes a person's view, story, or picture of herself is essentially metaphoric in nature.

Chapter 10

Metaphoric Psychotherapy and Hypnotherapy

Psychotherapy is a discipline whose aim is to ease conflicts, unease, imbalance, turmoil, confusion, anxiety, tension, concerns and difficulties that trouble the mind or spirit. In Native American and other traditions, these mental and spiritual difficulties are considered to arise from being "out of harmony" with nature. The psychotherapist typically uses "talking" therapies in contrast to drugs and other medicaments or physical interventions. The arts, as in art, music, and dance, also have their place in psychotherapy. But, primarily, *words* are used. In behavioral approaches, for example, carefully chosen words are used to guide the client into various activities.

An early question when meeting a new client is, "How will you know when you've gotten what you want out of your time with me?" This "how" question is a central one since it deals with acknowledging at the outset what it is that will let the client know he is attaining his goals, and having his needs met. Insight may be a goal, but behavioral changes are more measurable. *What* will be different can be observed. Presumably, the client comes to see you for assistance in changing. In this regard, it is useful to think about clients as being of three types as formulated by solution-focused brief therapy (SFBT) practitioners:

- *Worker*—Someone who has come to *work* with you on a particular concern, and is ready, willing, and able to do whatever is necessary to resolve that concern.
- *Complainant*—This is a client who is unsure about whether he is really interested in changing. Complaining about a concern is safe, and the venting eases some of the inner turmoil. Complainants can convert to workers, but there is only about a 50:50 chance that this will occur, despite the therapist's best efforts.

- *Visitor*—Visitors are just that—they are in your office because they have to be, and are just putting in time. The session may be court-ordered, or it may be to get a nagging relative off their back. At best, you have a friendly visit, and invite them to return. But, do not expect any serious commitment to work toward a change.

Clients have different needs and expectations. It is always important to work (whenever possible) within their belief systems. Sometimes, just being with a concerned and attentive listener is all that they want. The client's agenda always has primacy, and not your idea of what he should be like or should be doing. Carl Rogers found that the "mere" act of being a good listener, a concerned listener, can have profound effects. In working with people who have life-challenging diseases, the single most important thing you can do is listen.

The use of metaphor in doing psychotherapy is one of the subjects of this book. In this brief chapter a few related ideas are presented. Certainly, one needs to listen carefully, especially if one is going to use Kopp's Metaphor Therapy or the author's guided-metaphor approach. Working with and through the client's own metaphor means that on some level he has found or created his own isomorphism with his metaphor, i.e. he *knows* internally what the connection is between the metaphor and his life. Of course, you can always inquire directly about these connections and what the client senses will work for him. (This is better than divination or mind-reading!)

Metaphors provide choice. Figure 10.1 represents a simplified model related to choice. A client comes to see you because he is "stuck" in some way. This means that some stimulus in his environment always results in the same response—there seems to be no other way to respond.

Figure 10.1

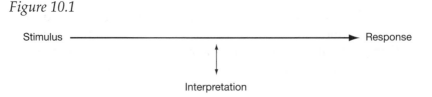

Generally, before the response, the stimulus triggers memories, and these memories admit of only *one* interpretation. It is this singular interpretation that results in a singular response. The gentle art of reframing, which was discussed in the previous chapter, leads to more than one interpretation. This, of course, leads to other connected responses. In one sense, psychotherapy's effectiveness lies in helping the client to discover many choices, and many responses. With a fixed cause–effect or stimulus–response, the client's behavior is involuntary. That is, he feels he has no choice as to how to respond, he feels compelled and constrained to respond always in that same old way. Choices lead to *voluntary* behavior, and options as to how to respond to a given situation. Milton Erickson told many stories, within which the client was able to discover (aha!) new ways of responding. The art in metaphoric work is knowing which stories to use, how general to make them, and how precisely vaguely to convey this to the client. Metaphors provide choice.

How is hypnotherapy different from psychotherapy? Hypnotherapy utilizes the observation that people appear to be more suggestible, i.e. more receptive to suggestions, when they are in a hypnotic trance. Some practitioners consider that it is possible to communicate more directly to the unconscious or inner mind or "hidden observer" when the client is in trance. So the enhanced suggestibility in trance states is connected to communicating with this "core" part of the person. There is, of course, continuing controversy about the existence of the unconscious mind. The therapist can just assume that it exists and operate under that assumption. Behaving "as if" your clients have an unconscious mind creates what amounts to a reality in the therapist–client interaction. "I don't know if the unconscious mind exists, but let's assume it does, and that it can hear and process to your benefit what we are doing this afternoon."

Telling stories to a client who is in trance sharply focuses his attention on the stories. He is more concentrated on your voice and the story since other stimuli are minimized while he is in trance. You can use hypnotic language to further focus the client's attention by blocking out other stimuli, and ensuring he hears only your voice. Yet the reality of listening to a story, whether in or out of trance, is that the mind fixates on some element of the story—a word, an image, a phrase—and then spends time thinking, wondering about, and following that aspect. This results in a kind of natural amnesia for your following words. The typical experience of someone in trance is to hear episodically what you have said. That is, he goes into and out of his own deeper trance states during the session. And afterwards his recollections of what you said will reflect this episodic character of listening. (You need to assure clients that this is a normal and natural response.) The therapist *trusts* that the client's unconscious mind will pick out of the many details of the metaphor just those aspects that will be beneficial to him. These will be unique, individual, and realistically connected to the client's personal history and situation. This is why it is so important to provide many opportunities, many choices, many possibilities, within the metaphor. The precise use of vague language enhances the possibility of the client's discovering just the right solution for himself. Hypnosis enhances this likelihood.

On the other hand, any time you tell a good story (or listen to one!), the audience will go into some level of trance—you have fixated their attention on the story. For example, how many good movies or plays have you seen where the time just disappeared? You look at your watch on the way out and suddenly realize that two to three hours have passed. A similar experience occurs in concerts, or when you are wrapped up in a good book, or in browsing the web. So "ordinary" storytelling is not much different from doing this in a formally induced trance state. Hypnotherapists are just more overt about "entrancing" their clients.

The content of the story and its delivery are more important than the formal induction of trance. The artistry is in the storytelling, and that tells the story, doesn't it?

Chapter 11

Ambiguous-Function Assignment as Metaphor

11.1 Introduction

An *ambiguous-function assignment* (AFA) or *ambiguous task* is a sec-ond-order-change technique that gets the client to carry out a task in a particularly intriguing and open-ended way—the therapist implies directly or indirectly that the client will learn something of special importance from this ambiguous activity. It is second-order change in that the special activity is outside of the client's normal behavior. It is "secret therapy" in the sense that the client does the significant discovery work on her own. It is metaphorical since the client carries out this ambiguous activity as a way of living and experiencing in a new way, thus creating a new story for herself.

Many of Erickson's clients were given such assignments. One, in particular, the climbing of Squaw Peak in Phoenix, Arizona, was assigned to many clients with instructions that were developed for each individually. This is not a strenuous climb, although it is steadily uphill, and can be done in about 45 minutes by a person in reasonable health. The views from the top are quite spectacular, and do give a 360-degree perspective. Clients were told to climb it for sunrise or sunset, or times in between. The constant factor was the *implication* that the client would learn something special about herself on the way up, at the top, on the way down, or afterwards in thinking about the experience. It is a feature of the International Ericksonian Congresses held in Phoenix to organize such a climb for attendees. In December 2001, in honor of Erickson's 100th birth-day, a bench was dedicated to him about halfway up. Erickson had an abiding interest in having the client *do* something, and the more different and ambiguous the activity, the better. He may not have thought in the NLP terms of kinesthetic anchors, but he was well aware that doing something physical helped in changing people.

In this section we will go over some of the characteristics of ambiguous-function assignments. Since the Lanktons (1986)—who originated the name for this process—have developed this to a high art, their approach and commentary will be featured in the next section. Section 11.3 discusses some generic ambiguous-function assignments, and 11.4 contains some examples from the literature.

Ambiguous-function assignments work well with clients who are particularly stuck, and who are striving to do something about it, but who are *vague* about desired outcomes. These assignments can also work well for a therapist who is stuck in terms of what to do next with a particular client, but should always used as part of a conscious plan.

The following general guidelines for AFAs are paraphrased from Battino and South (1999, pp. 168–9):

1. Get the client to *do* something. The physicality of an action, of movement, of activity, breaks patterns. Although an AFA requires thinking by the client during the task, this is a focused thinking, and breaks away from introspection.

2. The task itself needs to be sufficiently ambiguous, enigmatic, puzzling, and even "ridiculous," that it will intrigue and hook the client into doing internal transderivational searches for the special significance of this task for her. Depending on the client, the task can be closely isomorphic to her concerns, or only vaguely related. If the task is transparently close, then the elements of surprise and ambiguity are lost.

3. The task itself cannot be harmful to the client or others. The actual taking on of the assignment involves a level of risk for the client, and that is the risk of learning things that will change her.

4. On the other hand, the AFA can be healthful and enjoyable and educational—in its puzzling way! Climbing Squaw Peak is good exercise.

5. The therapist implies and presupposes and expects that in doing the AFA the client *will* discover something (or several things) of

value by carrying out the task. This expectation can be implicit or explicit.

6. The follow-up, after the client has carried out the AFA—at this session or a later one—reinforces the therapist's expectation that something of value, something new and important, will have been discovered. "And, what interesting things have you learned from doing that? Anything surprising things come up?" The word "surprise" gives the client permission and direction.

7. The assigned AFA can be repeated as needed. Additional features may be added. "Did this task trigger any memories?" "Were you expecting too much the first time?" "Did you notice any particular physical sensations while you ...? What were they like? Is there anything special to learn from what your body was telling you?" "Were you open to surprise?" "How much change do you want, now?"

8. How do you get your client to actually carry out the AFA? You have to intrigue her, engage her curiosity, use her sense of adventure, and connect with a willingness to be scientific, to carry out an interesting experiment. What will she learn about herself? Of course, sincerity and congruity in presenting the AFA are essential. Without having first established rapport and trust, AFAs become a mechanical technique.

9. When you are "stuck" with a particular client, consider using an AFA. In a parallel way to guided metaphor, the client can be asked directly about what kind of intriguing task she senses would lead her to discover new things about herself, and/or useful solutions for her concerns. "Thinking about what is troubling you at this time, what sort of activity or task do you feel would help you discover what you need?" You can then suggest a number of possibilities, and let the client pick the AFA that is suitable, or co-create one. This goes along with the advice of, "When all else fails, simply ask the client what to do next that would help her."

11.2 The Lanktons on ambiguous-function assignments

Steve and Carol Lankton (1986, pp. 136–52) have provided the most complete description of AFA in the literature (in fact, a search of my library has unearthed no other sources for this kind of work—except for the mention in Battino and South (1999, pp. 168–9). In their Illustration 23 on p. 137 they give the characteristics of AFA, reasons for its use, and indications for its use. These will be presented in this section along with commentary (mine, and some taken from pp. 142–4). This is all within the framework of a book on family therapy, although the same conditions apply to individuals. They give eight components of an AFA. (Quotation marks are used whenever there is a direct quotation.)

1. "Stimulate the client's (or clients') thought about what the assignment will bring, what they will learn, and how it will reveal a therapeutic learning. Use indirect suggestion, metaphor, drama, and contagious delivery to hold interest. The most important aspect is that they have to return to therapy and explain what was learned and speculate why the therapist may have intended for them to have this (unstated) learning." This part is for implanting the seed for learning something useful from the task.

2. "Deliver with compelling expectancy. The seriousness with which you regard the assignment will necessarily be communicated with your voice tone, facial expression, and other nonverbal delivery." If you are not excited about the potential help of the task and communicate a "compelling expectancy" about helpful outcomes, why should the client be interested in carrying it out? What an interesting way to learn ...

3. "Be sure to imply that there is or will be value in the activity." Your expectation of value is the compelling reason for asking the client to do something that may appear on the surface to be absurd. The Lanktons suggest saying something like, "The more you wonder what you can learn, the more you are going to enjoy discovering exactly what it will be. But, of course, you can't know what you are going to learn until you have learned it ..." Expectation, mystery, surprise, drama.

4. "Assign a *specific* task (time, place, act) but *do not reveal its purpose.*" The *general* purpose is learning useful things. But, it is necessary to be ambiguous so the client can discover unique learnings from her own unique experience and background.

5. "Make use of an actual physical object." Examples of this are given in the next section. A physical object concretizes the experience and adds a kinesthetic component. This kinesthetic anchor is important since it provides a direct physical connection to the experience, and adds a touch of ceremonial myth, almost a hero's journey. Contrast this with a cerebral exercise to imagine carrying out an ambiguous assignment. Thinking can be easily distracted; an actual activity is much harder to sidetrack.

6. "Make sure the client is involved in active behavior and not merely fantasy work." This was commented upon in (5), but needs some expansion. To become a living metaphor, it is necessary for the client to actually physically carry out and live through the AFA. She is then in her own metaphor rather than observing it in some abstract manner.

7. "Place binds of comparable alternatives on the client's performance of the task." Would the task better be done in the morning, afternoon, or evening? On a week day, or a weekend day? With this or that object? The bind is that the client is considering how and when to do the task, but not whether or not he will do it.

8. "Maintain 'therapeutic leverage' while utilizing the client's responses.

   "a. Empathize and reinforce each learning.

   "b. Identify and accelerate the client's motivation.

   "c. Do not accept the client's initial thinking as complete.

   "d. Continue expectancy and imply the existence of more information.

   "e. Challenge or stimulate the client to do the continued thinking.

   "f. Continue the above until therapeutic receptivity is maximized."

These are all useful things to keep in mind while doing AFA work.

The Lanktons (1986, p. 137) list a variety of reasons for using AFA:

Reasons
- disrupts habitual conscious sets
- client will think deeply re: self
- client gives diagnostic information to therapist
- feeling and thoughts both elicited
- client attributes special "magic" to therapist
- client finds some refreshment and excitation about learning
- special rapport is created
- client focuses on any self motivation
- becomes aware of therapy as active
- becomes aware of therapy as something they do
- makes it meaningful
- stimulates a sense of curiosity
- increase sense of therapy's importance

AFA also leads to interesting new ideas. It is a kind of metaphoric reframing by the client's living through a challenge, and can be accepted as such since she is doing the actual work. Another reason to use AFA is that people have an innate drive to "understand" themselves and their behavior. An AFA gives them an opportunity to find meaning(s) in a given activity, "What can I learn from this ...?"

The Lanktons (1986, p. 137) list six indications for when AFA is appropriate:

Indications
- after rapport and credibility are established
- after resources are built by previous work or for diagnostic purposes
- with clients who have organized conscious minds (not with psychotics)
- when client manipulates or controls therapy
- when client's beliefs about therapy or therapist limit progress
- when client has seen many other therapists without success

The last item implies that AFA is useful with "therapist killers," i.e. clients who habitually defeat a therapist's helpful interventions. Again, AFA serves as a second-order-change tactic.

11.3 Some general ambiguous-function assignments

In this section many general or generic AFAs are listed with commentary. These AFAs are adaptable to particular clients and situations. They can also be adapted to couples and families. Add sufficient detail and binds about each AFA with respect to: time of day, location, duration of activity, how much to learn, physical effort involved, how much to remember, number of repetitions, whom to involve, when and how to report outcomes, and safety.

1. Carry an object on person
The client is requested to carry a particular object on their person (in a pocket or pocketbook or …) for a given period of time, such as one week. The object could be a stone or a book or a piece of fragile glassware or a piece of pottery or a wind-up alarm clock or some old holey socks or a photograph or an umbrella etc. The object should have some weight or bulk so that carrying it is inconvenient in some way. Choose the object so that it has potential significance, but not direct significance for the person.

2. Climb a hill, peak, mountain
We've already mentioned climbing Squaw Peak in Phoenix. Choose a readily available hill, peak, or mountain within the client's physical capability for her to climb. This assignment may also involve going to a site partway up a hill or mountain. This climb may be made with or without carrying extra weight in a backpack. At the top, some or all of the extra weight (a stone or stones or water) may be left as a symbolic offering. Where permissible, a stone or leaf or a bit of soil may be brought back down. Some significant words may be written on a scrap of paper and left buried under a stone or in the ground. A photograph may be taken. At the end of the climb, take some time to ponder its meaning. This

can also be done at rest stops on the way up or down. "What does this rest mean for the rest of your life?"

3. A walk in the woods

In a safe walking wood or forested area, stop at each place where the path branches and debate with yourself the merits of taking each path. Then take one of the paths (always the "right" one) and repeat the self-debate at the next choice point. You may wish to connect this AFA to Robert Frost's "The Road Not Taken."

4. Carry a heavy weight around the block

The client is asked to carry a heavy weight (such as a gallon of water) around the block or around several blocks while pondering on carrying a weight or a load on her shoulders. How much excess weight do we carry internally and externally and how can that burden be lightened? Distance and weight and route and object are adapted to the client. "And doing that again, how much more will you learn?"

5. Shopping malls

Spend one minute examining the window display of each store in a shopping mall. Pick a central location and study the variety of couples who walk past you. How are the couples different and the same? If you exchanged places with one of those persons and walked along with the other for a while, what would that be like for you? Study individuals as they pass by, noting their characteristics, similarities, and differences. Unobtrusively, follow some different people walking and moving as they do. What is it like to walk in someone else's footsteps or style?

6. Biblio AFAs

Give the client a particular poem/essay/book/article/chapter/children's story/magazine/Bible passage/religious writing to read. Why were they asked to read that writing? That author? What have they learned from that experience?

7. Random reading
Randomly open the Bible, other religious writing, unabridged dictionary, encyclopedia volume, thesaurus, or collection of poetry, and read what you find on that page. What is the significance for you of these randomly selected words? This can also be done with art books, such as one on Vincent van Gogh's paintings.

8. Museums and zoos and botanical gardens
Visit one and wonder why it was that you were asked to visit this particular place? Was it one specific exhibit that carried a special meaning? Or was it the totality of the collection? Or the environment? How much more would you learn about yourself by studying one exhibit in depth?

9. Browse the web
Give the client a specific topic to browse, but let her follow whatever links make sense to her.

10. Do a blind or deaf walk (safely)
Have a trusted person lead you on a blind or deaf walk for a given length of time. In any location where you can safely close your eyes for a few minutes, just listen intently. What have you been missing?

11. Write a letter
Write a letter to some special iconic figure such as: Santa Claus, a saint, Jesus, God, a philosopher, a guru, Buddha, a historical figure, a fictional person—and tell him/her exactly what you need to lead a satisfying life. A variant is writing to yourself what you imagine they would respond.

12. Random walk
In a safe, but unknown neighborhood, walk randomly for an hour and notice where your feet take you.

13. *Amusement park or circus*
Visit an amusement park or circus and discover for yourself some special significance in the rides, performances, events, or sideshows. Why were you told to do this?

14. *Symptom prescription*
Pick one of your symptoms and do it: in a different place, at a different time, in a different way, for a different duration. What has this taught you?

You can make each of the previous suggestions into an effective AFA by matching the client to the assignment. AFAs can be fun to carry out, but they also have the potential of being traumatic or leading to abreactions. Although AFAs appear to be simple on the surface, they must be used with skill and caution.

11.4 Six Erickson case studies

Erickson was a natural and consistent user and designer of ambiguous-function assignments for his clients. This usage grew out of his commitment to have his clients do something active in their own interests. The following six case studies are all taken from Rosen (1982) with the page numbers at the end of each case illustration. Some of the cases are clear examples of AFA, others are more subtle, but they are all stamped by Erickson's creativity. What other things was Erickson doing in each of these stories, since they are all "teaching tales" and hence metaphoric in nature? (The titles are those used by Rosen.)

Curious

A woman came to college always holding her left hand over her mouth. She recited in class holding her left hand under her nose, concealing her mouth. She walked out on the street with her left hand covering her mouth. She ate in restaurants concealing her mouth behind her left hand. When she was reciting in class, walking down the street, eating in restaurants, always the left hand was over her mouth.

218

Now that interested me. I made it a point to get acquainted with her. She told me, after much prodding, about a horrible experience she had when she was ten years old. In a car accident, she had been thrown through a windshield. A frightening experience for a ten-year-old girl. Her mouth was cut by the windshield glass and there was a lot of blood on the hood of the car. A lot of blood that was frightening to a ten-year-old could be a very small amount of blood, but, to her, it was an enormous quantity. She grew up with the idea that her mouth was terribly scarred—and that's why she kept her mouth covered, because she did not want anybody to see that horrible scar.

I got her to read a history of cosmetology and she came across beauty spots—spots that were crescent shaped, circles, stars, and so on. She read about how a woman would place a beauty spot near the feature she considered attractive. I induced her to draw me some beauty spots. Then I induced her, in the privacy of her room, to make a life-size copy of her scar—it turned out to be a five-pointed star, the size of a beauty spot. Yet she still saw it as larger than her whole face.

So I persuaded her to go on a date with one of the students. She was to carry two heavy handbags in order to keep her hands down, from her face. On this date, and on subsequent ones, she discovered that if she allowed a good-night kiss, the man would invariably kiss her on the scarred side of her mouth. Even though she had two sides to her mouth the man would always, invariably, kiss her on the scarred side. She dated one man but didn't have the nerve to let him have a good-night kiss. The second man kissed her on the right side of her mouth. So did the next, the third, the fourth, the fifth, and the sixth. What she didn't know was that she was curious and when she was curious she always tipped her head to the left, so that a man had to kiss her on the right side of her mouth!

Every time I tell that case history, I look around. You all know about subliminal speech, but you don't know about subliminal hearing. When I tell that case history, every woman puckers her lips—and I know what she is thinking of. You watch the neighbor come in to see the new baby. You watch the lips. You know just when that neighbor is going to kiss the baby. [pp. 64–5]

219

Cacti

Usually I send alcoholic patients to AA because AA can do a better job than I can do. An alcoholic came to me and he said, "My grand-parents on both sides were alcoholics; my parents were alcoholics; my wife's parents were alcoholics; my wife is an alcoholic and I have had delirium tremens eleven times. I am sick of being an alco-holic. My brother is an alcoholic too. Now, that is a hell of a job for you. What do you think you can do about it?"

I asked him what his occupation was.

"When I am sober I work on a newspaper. And alcohol is an occu-pational hazard there."

I said, "All right, you want me to do something about it—with that history. Now, the thing I am going to suggest to you won't seem the right thing. You go out to the Botanical Gardens. You look at all the cacti there and marvel at cacti that can survive three years without water, without rain. And do a lot of thinking."

Many years later a young woman came in and said, "Dr. Erickson, you knew me when I was three years old. I moved to California when I was three years old. Now I am in Phoenix and I came to see what kind of a man you were—what you looked like."

I said, "Take a good look, and I'm curious to know why you want to look at me."

She said, "Any man who would send an alcoholic out to the Botanical Gardens to look around, to learn how to get around with-out alcohol, and have it work, is the kind of man I want to see! My mother and father have been sober ever since you sent my father out there."

"What is your father doing now?"

"He's working for a magazine. He got out of the newspaper busi-ness. He says the newspaper business has an occupational hazard of alcoholism."

Now, that was a nice way to cure an alcoholic. Get him to respect cacti that survive three years without rain. You see you can talk about your textbooks. Today you take up this much. Tomorrow you take up that much. They say you do such and such. But actually you ought to look at your patient to figure out what kind of a man he is—or woman—then deal with the patient in a way that fits his or her problem, his or her unique problem. [pp. 80–1]

Skin Conditions

A woman doctor from the East called me up and said, "My son's a student at Harvard and he has an extremely bad case of acne. Can you treat that with hypnosis?"

I said, "Yes. Why bother bringing him to me? How are you going to spend Christmas vacation?"

She said, "I usually take a vacation from medical practice and go to Sun Valley and ski."

I said, "Well, this Christmas vacation, why don't you take your son with you? Find a cabin and remove all mirrors in it. You can eat your meals in that cabin, and be sure that you keep your hand mirror in the safety pocket of your purse."

They spent the time skiing and the son couldn't see a mirror. His acne cleared up in two weeks' time.

Now, acne can be cured by removing all mirrors. Rashes on the face or eczema often disappear in the same way.

Another patient, a woman with warts on both hands, deforming warts, came to see me. Her face was also a mess of warts. She said she wanted to get rid of them by hypnosis. If you know anything about medicine, you know that warts are caused by a virus and also that warts are very susceptible to changes in blood pressure.

I told the woman to soak her feet, first in ice-cold water, then in water as hot as she could stand, and then in ice-cold water again. She was to do that three times a day, until she was so annoyed that she'd give anything not to have to do it. When she had lost her warts she could forget about soaking her feet.

Now, it would be an annoying thing for her to have to interrupt the day's procedures to soak her feet and to keep this up in a scheduled manner.

Some three years later, this woman brought her son to me. I asked her about her warts. She said, "What warts?"

I said, "You came to see me, about three years ago, for the treatment of warts on your hands and face."

She said, "You must be mistaking me for another person." She had obeyed my suggestion. She had soaked her feet some months, as her husband confirmed. Then she got so disgusted by it, she forgot about soaking her feet, thereby forgetting about her warts. Since she was no longer worrying about her warts, their blood supply was cut down by the blood drawn to her feet and by her lack of attention to them. So she lost them all. [pp. 87–8]

A Flash of Color

A patient came to me and said, "I've lived in Phoenix for the past fifteen years and I have hated every moment of those fifteen years. My husband has offered me a vacation in Flagstaff. I hate Phoenix so much, but I have refused to go to Flagstaff. I prefer to stay in Phoenix and to hate being in Phoenix."

So I told her, while she was in a trance, that she would be curious about hating Phoenix and about why she punished herself so much. That should be a very big curiosity. "And there is another thing to be curious about—and very, very curious about. If you go to Flagstaff for a week, you will see, very unexpectedly, a flash of color." As long as she had a big curiosity about hating Phoenix, she could develop an equally large curiosity, just as compelling, to find out what that flash of color would be in Flagstaff.

She went to Flagstaff for a week, but stayed a month. What flash of color did she see? I had none in mind. I just wanted her to be curious. And when she saw that flash of color, she was so elated that she remained a whole month in Flagstaff. That flash of color was a redheaded woodpecker flying past an evergreen tree. This woman usually spends the summer in Flagstaff now, but she also has gone to the East Coast to see the color there. She has gone to Tucson, to see a flash of color. She has gone to New York, to see a flash of color. She has gone to Europe, to see a flash of color. And my statement that she would see a flash of color was based only upon the fact that you have to see a lot of things that ordinarily you don't see. And I wanted her to keep looking. And she would find something to translate into my words. [pp. 108–9]

Reduce-Gain-Reduce

A woman came to see me and she said, "I weigh 180 pounds. I've dieted successfully under doctors' orders hundreds of times. And I want to weigh 130 pounds. Every time I get to 130 pounds I rush into the kitchen to celebrate my success. I put it back on, right away. Now I weight 180. Can you use hypnosis to help me reduce to 130 pounds? I'm back to 180 for the hundredth time."

I told her, yes, I could help her reduce by hypnosis, but she wouldn't like what I did.

She said she wanted to weigh 130 pounds and she didn't care what I did.

I told her she'd find it rather painful.

She said, "I'll do anything you say."

I said, "All right. I want an absolute promise from you that you will follow my advice exactly."

She gave me the promise very readily and I put her into a trance. I explained to her again that she wouldn't like my method of reducing her weight and would she promise me, absolutely, that she would follow my advice? She gave me that promise.

Then I told her, "Let both your unconscious mind and your conscious mind listen. Here's the way you go about it. Your present weight is now 180 pounds. I want you to gain twenty pounds and when you weigh 200 pounds, on my scale, you may start reducing."

She literally begged me, on her knees, to be released from her promise. And every ounce she gained she became more and more insistent on being allowed to start reducing. She was markedly distressed when she weighed 190 pounds. When she was 190 she begged and implored to be released from her own promise. At 199 she said that was close enough to 200 pounds and I insisted on 200 pounds.

When she reached 200 pounds she was very happy that she could begin to reduce. And when she got to 130 she said, "I'm never going to gain again."

Her pattern had been to reduce and gain. I reversed the pattern and made her gain and reduce. And she was very happy with the final results and maintained that weight. She didn't want to, ever again, go through that horrible agony of gaining twenty pounds. [pp. 123–4]

A Different Shade of Green

I sent one of my patients, who is a heroin addict, to sit on the lawn until he made a fantastic discovery! He was an allergist and his perception of color was phenomenal. After about an hour and a half of sitting on the lawn, he came dashing into the house and said, "Do you realize that every blade of grass is a different shade of green?" And he arranged them from very light to very dark. He was so surprised! The amount of chlorophyll in each leaf differs. Chlorophyll differs according to the rainy season, to the fertility of the soil.

Another time I had him sit on the lawn facing east. He came in and said, "The cypress tree in the next lot is leaning toward the sun, leaning southward. I turned and looked and found that you have five cypress trees on your lawn and they are all leaning southward."

I told him, "I discovered that on my first trip to Phoenix, going all around the city, checking up on that. The first time I saw a heliotropic tree it amazed me. You usually think of trees growing straight up. And a heliotropic tree! By the sunflower you can tell the time of day."

Have you ever heard of a flower-bed clock? My grandmother had a flower-bed clock. Morning glories opened in the morning, certain other flowers opened at seven o'clock, others at eight, others at nine, others at ten, others at noon. And there were the evening primroses, for example. The night-blooming cereus opens at about ten-thirty or eleven o'clock at night. [pp. 186–7]

11.5 Concluding comments

Ambiguous-function assignments and ambiguous tasks certainly have their place in psychotherapy, but they are probably underutilized. Is there a reluctance to take the gamble that seems to be implicit in giving such assignments? Or do they require too much creativity to design? Or are "talking" therapists so enamored with their own words and working within the confines of their offices to risk involving activities "out there"? Yet, if metaphoric work makes sense, then this way of having a client live through and create a new life story is a method that needs to be used. When was the last time that ambiguity entered your life, and how did you use that experience to learn and to grow? What about those roads that you did not take?

Chapter 12

Ordeal Therapy as Metaphor

Toms: There are several elements in mythology: The Hero, for instance, and the Call. When did "the Call" first appear in mythology?

Campbell: In mythology? That's the *essence* of mythology, I would say. The theme of the visionary quest: The one who goes to follow a vision. It appears one way or another in practically every mythology I know of.

Toms: So it's the core of all myth.

Campbell: Yes, because the Hero is the one who has gone on the adventure and brought back the message, and who is the founder of institutions—and the giver of life and vitality to his community.

– Maher and Briggs, 1988, p. 23

12.1 Introduction

At the risk of exaggerating ordeal therapy to be synonymous with a Hero's Journey, this chapter is begun with an excerpt from an interview with the mythologist Joseph Campbell by Michael Toms. (For a scholarly study of the hero's journey see Campbell's book (1968).) The hero's journey is an *ordeal*, and the definitions in my unabridged dictionary are informative:

> *ordeal*. 1. A primitive means used to determine guilt or innocence by submitting the accused to dangerous or painful tests supposed to be under divine or superhuman control, escape from injury being ordinarily taken as a vindication of innocence. Ordeals are common to many peoples, and were a part of judicial procedure in Europe as late as the 13th century, and sporadically much later. The chief forms were the ordeals by battle, the ordeal by fire, the ordeal by water, used esp. when witchcraft was charged, and the ordeal by lots. In England the various forms were abolished in 1215–19, except the ordeal by battle. 2. Anything used to test character or endurance; any severe trial; a trying experience.

The early use of ordeals was to determine guilt or innocence. The second definition with respect to testing character and endurance is more germane to the use of ordeals in modern work as an agent of change.

Ordeals are *tests* whereby a person learns new things about himself. Since they involve the actual doing of a task—living through the ordeal itself, surviving it—the ordeal takes on the character of a living story, a metaphor for that person's life. It is in this sense that an ordeal is a metaphor, the actual acting out in a controlled way of a portion of a client's life. The therapist, rather than some "superhuman" being, is the control agent. There are expectations of learning and change. There is ambiguity, and it sometimes may be difficult to distinguish between an ambiguous-function assignment (see the previous chapter) and a therapeutic ordeal. Ordeals and trials are a continuing part of life, and are the metaphors by which we test ourselves.

Milton Erickson was a master of ordeal therapy, and his case studies are a rich source of his work in this area. The systematic exposition of ordeal therapy was done by Jay Haley (1984), a student, friend, and collaborator of Erickson's. His approach has been summarized by Battino and South (1999, pp. 162–4). The description of how to do ordeal therapy in the next section is based on Haley's book, but uses the format in Battino and South.

12.2 Haley's systematics of ordeal therapy

Haley (1984) systematically covers the elements of ordeal therapy in his introductory chapter (pp. 1–23). The remainder of the book illustrates the uses of ordeal therapy via his own and Erickson's cases. The creativity with which they apply this method is fascinating to follow. The basic idea is simple in itself: if you make it more difficult for the client to have a symptom than to give it up, then the client will give up the symptom. Although classic psychoanalytic theory indicates that "merely" giving up a symptom does not lead to significant change, Erickson and Haley and others found that giving up a symptom is a *change of behavior* that is both therapeutic *and* long-lasting. The client lives through and learns from the ordeal. This brings about permanent change because, in essence, an involuntary behavior (in the client's belief) is converted to voluntary behavior. Helplessness and hopelessness disappear (along with the symptom) due to actions.

Haley delineates several characteristics of an ordeal. These follow with some variants.

1. The ordeal must be more severe than the problem. That is, it should cause more distress than the symptom. If it turns out that the initial ordeal is not sufficient to extinguish the symptom, then it can be increased (within reason!) until it does so.

2. Generally, the ordeal should be related in some way to the symptom, in the sense that the "punishment" should fit the crime. On the other hand, totally unrelated ordeals also seem to work.

3. It is best if the ordeal is something good or beneficial or *healthful* to the client. These would include activities that the client would like to do (exercise, diet, reading, filing—see examples in next section), but has trouble making the time to do. The ordeal is then not seen as a waste of time, but as having useful side effects.

4. It is important that the ordeal be something that the client can do within the framework of his health, home, capabilities, and environment. The ordeal is then something the client cannot legitimately object to in terms of ability to carry out. (He may object to the time required, but that objection is not legitimate if he has already agreed to do the ordeal.)

5. A basic safety rule is that the ordeal should not harm the client, or other people, or do any damage.

6. For some clients, the ordeal may need to be repeated over a period of time. The client or the therapist may add appropriate variations.

7. It is crucial that the carrying out of the ordeal be *linked* to the occurrence of the symptom. This means that, on any given day when the symptom appears, the ordeal must be carried through if at all possible. Delays should be no longer than 24 hours. Immediate carrying out of the ordeal is preferable, if possible.

In his systematic approach, Haley also describes six stages of ordeal therapy. They are discussed in what follows.

1. The problem or concern must be defined in an *operational* way so that both the therapist and the client understand it. In effect, what kind of depression or anxiety or compulsion or whatever is it? When does it occur, under what circumstances, and for what duration?

2. It is essential that the client be a "customer," i.e. is committed to getting over the problem. He is ready to work; *he* is supplying the motivation, and *not* the therapist or some third party. The therapist may increase the client's motivation by stressing the gravity of the problem in terms of the client's past history, while being cognizant of realistic expectations. A standard "hook" is telling the client that there is a fail-safe cure, but that the client will not be told what this is until he agrees to follow the prescription. Of course, there must be mutual respect at this point. Some clients may carry out the ordeal to prove that the therapist is wrong! Remember to emphasize that it is the client who actually carries out the ordeal, although the therapist can certainly be sympathetic about the work involved.

3. The ordeal needs to be selected by the therapist, although this is best done with the client's collaboration and input so it can realistically fit his particular lifestyle. The ordeals need to be behaviorally specific with a clear beginning and ending. The time, location, activity, and duration need to be clearly delineated. Written directions may be needed by some clients and are generally a good idea.

4. It is quite important that the ordeal be described with a convincing rationale, i.e., one that is accepted by or acceptable to the client.

5. To be effective the ordeal is continued until the problem is resolved. To be sure, the typical contract for the ordeal is lifelong. If a physical exercise or physical component is involved, it needs to be sufficiently strenuous so that it can be felt in the muscles the next day. This provides a kinesthetic anchor.

6. Since neither the client nor the ordeal exists in a vacuum, the client's social context must be taken into consideration. The therapist needs some sense about the effect of the loss of the symptom on significant others, the workplace, social settings etc.

There are many factors to consider in using ordeal therapy and it should not be employed casually, but as part of a larger consciously designed therapeutic plan.

12.3 Types of ordeal

Haley discusses four categories of ordeal: (1) a straightforward task; (2) a paradoxical ordeal; (3) the therapist as an ordeal; and (4) an ordeal involving two or more persons. Remember that the ordeal is to be carried out every time the symptom appears.

1. Straightforward ordeals

a. *Exercise*—doing some form of exercise that day, that evening, or in the middle of the night. The exercise needs to be sufficiently active so it is felt in the muscles the next day—slight soreness rather than strain or sprain. This can be walking, jogging, push-ups, deep squats etc., all within the capability of the client. For the middle of the night an alarm must be set. If the client owns an exercise machine, such as a stationary bicycle, this can be used.

b. *Reading*—this is an opportunity to get that reading done that you've always wanted to do. But the ordeal is doing the reading standing up at 3 A.M. for one hour!

c. *Filing*—similar to (b), but can include sorting, pick-up, organizing contents of garage or attic or junk drawer or box of nuts, bolts, and nails. Middle of the night and for one hour.

d. *House cleaning*—a particular part of the house is cleaned for one hour at 3 A.M.: waxing floors, washing windows, thorough dusting, cleaning out a cupboard, polishing silver or glasses etc.

e. *Writing*—working on that paper or dissertation or correspondence or report for one hour or more.

f. *Financial*—doing income tax or income tax preparation, financial planning, balancing checkbook, sorting through and discarding old records etc.

Note: These tend to be the easiest to construct and convince the client to agree to do.

2. Paradoxical ordeals

a. *Symptom prescription*—these convert involuntary acts or symptoms into voluntary ones. These involuntary acts include behaviors and compulsions such as: impulsive eating or eating avoidance, overcleanliness or sloppiness, various aches and pains, anxiousness, depression, tension. The ordeal might be for the client to worry for exactly 30 minutes using a kitchen timer and at 3 A.M. Or to feel as depressed as he possibly can for a specific time period.

b. *Two symptoms*—"If a person has two symptoms, one can be required each time the other occurs, thereby introducing a paradoxical ordeal that is effective with two symptoms at once. For example, a person who has a particular compulsion and also suffers from extreme shyness can be required to socialize as an ordeal whenever the compulsion occurs." (Haley, 1984, p. 11.)

c. *Ambiguous-function assignments*—Most of the ones written about in the previous chapter can be adapted as ordeals. Their ambiguity actually works through paradox.

3. The therapist as an ordeal

All ordeals are in relationship with the therapist who is recommending them. So the ordeal is done to please or defy the therapist, or both. In a *reframe* the message that changes the client's perception can be considered to be an ordeal with which the client must grapple. Confrontation, as in bringing to the client's attention things he does not wish to acknowledge, has the character of an ordeal. An insight interpretation that the client doesn't like may be perceived as an ordeal. Haley mentions (p. 12) increasing the fee for as long as the person has the problem—an interesting approach, but not recommended. An alternative monetary ordeal is donating money to a disliked charity or organization (such as the KKK) whenever the symptom occurs. (It might be quite difficult to obtain agreement for this.)

4. Ordeals involving two or more persons

Erickson cleverly devised an ordeal for a bed-wetting child and his mother that involved her helping him practice his handwriting every morning the bed was wet. But, so that he would not miss school, the mother had to wake up the boy especially early. Both then participated in the ordeal. An entire family can do an ordeal when one member misbehaves. A couple have to go through a shared ordeal when one of them has a symptom that day.

12.4 Some literature case examples

An ordeal devised by Haley (1984, pp. 17–19) is instructive:

Things Up His Behind

Let me give an example that illustrates the procedures in designing an ordeal as well as the need to take the family organization into account when introducing a change. A sixteen-year-old youth recently out of a mental hospital had the distressing symptom of putting a variety of things up his behind. He would do this in the bathroom, inserting into his anus various vegetables, paper, Kleenex, and so on. He would then leave the bathroom a mess with all this material. His stepmother would have to clean it up, which she did furtively so the other children wouldn't know about his problem.

What ordeal might be appropriate for this unpleasant behavior? Not only should it be something more severe than the problem so he would abandon that behavior, but it should be good for him in some way. More than that, it should involve a change in the structure of his family organization.

What became apparent in a family interview by Margaret Clark, the therapist, was the way the stepmother was burdened by the problem, and the problems of all the children, while the father went about his business. She implied that when he had had several children to take care of after a divorce, he had married her and simply handed the children and their problems over to her. Clearly there was resentment on her part and a strain on the new marriage. The boy's problem became so severe that the parents did not have to deal with the marital issues between them; this appeared to be part of the function of the symptom.

The question was whether to arrange an ordeal with just the boy or to involve his family. It was decided to involve the family, partly because the boy did not seem motivated to get over the problem and partly to make a structural change possible so the symptom would be unnecessary. How to involve the family was the next step. It seemed logical to put the responsibility for an ordeal procedure in the hands of the father, since he should take more responsibility for solving the problem and burden his new wife less. Father and son could experience an ordeal together each time the symptom occurred. The next step was selection of an ordeal appropriate to the symptom.

The procedure decided on was as follows: Each time the boy put material up his behind and messed up the bathroom, the father would be told about it when he came home from work. The father would take the youth out into the backyard and have the young man dig a hole three feet deep and three feet wide. The boy would bury in the hole all the material that he had been messing up the bathroom with and then cover it up. The next time the symptom occurred, the behavior would be repeated and this would continue forever.

The father methodically followed the procedure with his son, and in a few weeks the symptom stopped. It was not merely that the boy did not do it; he lost enthusiasm for it, as is typical with the use of the correct ordeal. The father, pleased with his success with the boy, began to associate more with him. The wife, pleased with her husband for solving this awful problem, became closer to him, so that the boy's misbehavior to help them became less necessary. There were other problems with this boy and his situation, so that therapy continued, but the particular symptom was promptly ended and remained gone.

This ordeal had the preferred characteristics: It involved and changed the structure of organization in the family by getting an irresponsible father involved. It was more severe than the symptom, since digging a deep hole in hard ground in the fall in the cold is not a simple task. The father had to stand in the cold with the boy until the task was done, so that his attitude toward a repetition of the symptom became more negative. The boy got exercise, which he wanted, in digging the hole, and he was required by the therapist to put things in a hole. So the procedure involved not only an ordeal but a metaphor, a paradox, and a family organizational change. As with most therapeutic procedures, the more an ordeal deals with various aspects of a situation, the better.

Erickson used the *geometric progression* of doubling a fine for every occurrence of a symptom. Thus, for the first occurrence it would be 1 cent, the second 2 cents etc. This kind of fine escalates rapidly— for ten occurrences it is $5.12, for 15 it is $163.84, and for twenty it becomes $5,242.88. The following is another case where Erickson used money to stop a symptom (Haley, 1984, p. 59):

Urinating in Public and Drinking

A man once came to him asking him to cure his son of a problem of not being able to urinate in a public bathroom if anyone else was present. The son had had this problem all his life and in college had mapped out the bathrooms so that he could always be alone. He was to enter the Navy in thirty days. On a ship that kind of privacy would be impossible. So the man asked Erickson to cure the son. The father was a difficult man who was an alcoholic and was mean, as Erickson found out from the man's wife. He was also rude and insulting to Erickson, even though he was asking Erickson to cure his son. So Erickson told the man that he would cure the son on one condition: The father would have to post a bond of $3,000, which was to go to Erickson to use as he saw fit if the father took one drink. Erickson could give back the money, keep it and vacation, or do what he pleased with it. After soul searching, the father agreed because he wished to have his son cured.

Erickson cured the son within the thirty days, and the father did not take another drink. The mother reported to Erickson that the old man had even become a reasonable person since he had stopped drinking. At Christmas the man called Erickson and said, "I would like to have one beer, but I don't wish it to cost me $3,000. Can we arrange that I have one beer?"

"How big a beer?" asked Erickson.

"I thought you'd ask that," said the man.

They agreed on an eight-ounce glass of beer, and Erickson generously allowed him to have one on both Christmas and New Year's Day.

The following series of Erickson's use of ordeals in therapy are case summaries as given by O'Hanlon and Hexum (1990) with a page citation for their book at the end of each excerpt. See this book for full citations to original sources. For further study of Erickson's work, O'Hanlon and Hexum give a "technique index" in their book (pp. 349–50). The title for each case is RB's.

Quit Smoking and Lose Weight

Case Summary: A woman wanted to quit smoking and lose weight. She didn't like to exercise. MHE gave her two suggestions. First she was to keep her cigarettes in the attic and her matches in the basement. When she wanted a cigarette she was to do down to the basement, take a match and set it on top of the box. Then she was to go up to the attic, get a cigarette and bring it down to the basement. Second, MHE suggested that when she wanted some cake she should cut a thin slice and then run around the outside of the house as fast as she could before eating it. Each time she wanted another slice she had to run around the house twice as many times. She soon found that she wanted fewer and fewer cigarettes and snacks. [p. 20]

Picking Pimples

Case Summary: A boy compulsively picked a pimple on his forehead so that it turned into an ulcer that would not heal. Father had punished the boy by selling his bicycle and breaking his bow and arrow set in an attempt to get him to stop, but to no avail. The boy was angry at his whole family. The boy refused to see MHE, so he made a house call. MHE asked what the proper treatment for an ulcerated forehead was. Father and son both informed him that it involved bandages and salves. MHE asked how breaking a bow and arrow could be a treatment for the sore. Father acknowledged that it was inappropriate and MHE got the boy to agree that he could give his father credit for good intentions at least, even if his behavior was stupid. MHE found out that the boy dropped letters out when he wrote things, so he got the boy to agree to practice his handwriting by writing the sentence, "I do not think it is a good idea to pick at that sore on my forehead" (in another version, "I fully agree with Dr. Erickson and I understand that it is neither wise nor good, nor desirable, to keep picking at that sore on my forehead"), in order to eliminate the sore. The boy was to write that on weekends, during which time his father was to take over the boy's weekend chores. The boy was to count the number of lines he had written and was to bring them in to show MHE. His forehead was healed within a month and his grades had improved. [p. 40]

Compulsive Hair Pulling

Case Summary: MHE told a woman who compulsively pulled her hair out that she should pull one hair out per day and wrap it very tightly around a match stick for one month. She got so tired of having to do this that she asked MHE if she could stop. He told her she could pull out two or three hairs and wrap them around a match stick. She pleaded with him to let her stop. He let her substitute hairs that had naturally come out of her scalp while she was combing her hair and wrap them around a match stick. She quickly stopped pulling her hair out. [p. 44]

Bed Wetting—I

Case Summary: A 29-year-old man had wet the bed every night for 29 years. He lived in the guest house behind his parents' home and never dared to spend the night anywhere else. By 12 or 12:30 the bed would be wet and he would get up, change the linen and go back to sleep. In taking the man's history MHE learned that the man hated to walk. Erickson instructed him to get an alarm clock and set it for midnight or half past twelve or for one o'clock. When the alarm range, he was to get up and walk 40 blocks, regardless of whether the bed was wet or dry. The man told MHE he preferred a wet bed to this walking assignment and discontinued therapy.

Months later the man returned and agreed to carry out the task for two weeks (three in another version). After the two weeks were over he would have another week of walking at midnight if he ever found the bed wet again. After two weeks the man reported a dry bed. He returned again and reported that he still had not had to complete the third week's walking and that he had received a promotion and a long-needed transfer in his job. [pp. 104–5]

Bed Wetting—II

Case Summary: A mother and her 12-year-old son came to MHE because the boy wet the bed every night. MHE told the boy he had a solution for him which he wouldn't like but that his mother would like even less. Each morning at four or 5 a.m. the mother was to awaken the boy and check his bed. If it was wet he would have to copy out of any book he chose until 7 a.m. in an effort to improve his handwriting. The mother had to sit with him and encourage him. The father came in for one session during the course of treatment. In a very loud voice he told MHE that he had wet the bed until he was 16 [19 in another version] and that it was perfectly normal. He also told MHE that a man of any common sense would support a certain political party. When the mother and son came in the next they were clearly embarrassed by the father. [In another version the boy's father rejects him and refuses to come in to speak to MHE. When the boy stopped wetting the bed his father took him on a fishing trip.] In regard to the father's ideas, MHE said to the son, "I'm just going to forget them because it's the ideas that you and I and your mother have that are important." Then MHE turned to the mother and said, "It's the ideas that you and I have, and Johnny has, that are important." Johnny began wetting the bed less and less until he stopped wetting it altogether. He began developing friendships with kids his own age, his grades went up, and he was elected class president [captain of the baseball team, in another version]. [pp. 105–6]

Bed Wetting—III

Case Summary: A boy wet the bed every night at midnight, laid in it until 2 a.m. and then went to his parents' room, where he would receive a spanking. The parents had tried every possible bribe and punishment to get him to stop wetting the bed. MHE wondered about the boy's need to punish himself. He suggested that the boy take charge of his own punishment. The boy had a collection of

minerals and stones. MHE told the boy to spread them on a concrete floor and put a blanket over them. When he wet the bed at
midnight he was to sleep on the stones for the rest of the night.
After about a month he quit wetting the bed. [p. 106]

Insomnia—I

Case Summary: A 65-year-old man came to MHE for insomnia.
Fifteen years prior to seeing MHE, his physician had prescribed
sodium amytal for the mild insomnia the man was having. The bar-
biturates eliminated his insomnia so he continued to take them for
the next 15 years. Having habituated to the drug, the man found
that his insomnia returned with a vengeance when his wife died.
Each night he would toss and turn for hours, getting only one and
a half to two hours of sleep for all the time he spent in bed. MHE
learned from the man that his house had hardwood floors which he
hated to wax because he couldn't stand the smell of the floor wax.
MHE told the man that he could cure his insomnia if he was willing to give up eight hours of sleep. Each night the man was to pol-
ish the floors from 8 p.m. to 7 a.m. MHE believed he would be
cured in four nights. For the first two or three nights the man followed MHE's instructions. On the next night he told himself he
would just lie down and rest for 30 minutes before he waxed the
floors. He awoke at seven o'clock the next morning. On the succeeding night he told himself that he would lie down at 8 p.m. If he
could read the clock at 8:15 he would get up and wax the floors. [In
another version, MHE suggests the fifteen-minute contingency.] A
year later he reported that he'd been sleeping every night. MHE
mentioned that the man knew he still owed him two nights' sleep
and he would do anything to get out of waxing floors, even going
to sleep. [pp. 151–2]

Insomnia—II

Case Summary: A man came to MHE for insomnia. For 12 years he
had never fallen to sleep before 2 a.m. and had always awakened
at 4 a.m. The man was a busy doctor who worked erratic hours.
MHE learned that since college the man had been promising himself that he would read certain books but his busy lifestyle had prevented him from attaining this goal. MHE tried to make the man
feel guilty about his broken promises and then he offered the man
a cure for his insomnia. MHE told the man to read from 10:30 p.m.
to 5 a.m. each night. (In another version he told him to go to bed at

11 o'clock each night. If he was still awake at 11:30, he was to get out of bed and read [Dickens in one version] standing by the mantel for the rest of the night.) If he awakened during the night he would have to do the same thing. Later the man asked if he could read sitting down. Then he told MHE that he found himself reading one page and then falling asleep sitting up. MHE told him that he could go to bed and if he found himself awake 15 minutes later, then he should get up and read. One year later he reported that he was sleeping nights, that he was more successful in his practice, and that he was happier and healthier. [p. 152]

Ralph had Multiple Problems

Case Summary: A man named Ralph had attended medical school with MHE. Ralph quit his practice because he was "too neurotic." He came to MHE for help. Ralph gave MHE a long list of his problems: his mother dominated him; he wet his pants; he couldn't make decisions; and he couldn't play the cello in front of anyone, including his family. MHE saw the man's wife and daughter and they corroborated his story. The daughter particularly complained of the absence of affection and celebration of holidays in their family.

The first thing MHE did was to eliminate the urinating problem. The man had told MHE that as a child he had been made to dig huge bushels of dandelions for very little pay. MHE told the man to put on some old pants and to dig dandelions from 8 a.m. to 6 p.m. without leaving the lawn. During that time he was to drink two gallons of lemonade and to urinate on himself. MHE knew that the man would have to converse with passersby as he sat there in his wet pants. One day of dandelion-digging cured his urination problems.

MHE worked on the man's problems with women and making choices at the same time. He took the man shopping and had a pretty sales girl model underwear for him. He was then forced to make choices about what he would purchase. He made his choices regardless of size. MHE and the man went out to dinner, along with their wives. MHE had coached their waitress to make sure that the man considered all the choices carefully before making a decision.

MHE had Ralph learn to dance and he became very active in square dancing. He even tried calling a few dances. Ralph also was able to give a cello concert for his family.

MHE had Ralph sit out on his lawn with a couple of whiskey bottles, one empty and one half-full. He told his wife to put some rouge on Ralph's nose and cheeks. Ralph was to wear a straw hat and recline with his eyes half-closed and a cigarette dangling out of his mouth. Then his wife should take a picture of him and send it to his mother. After receiving the picture, his mother, who disapproved of drinking and smoking, stopped communicating with him.

The final phase of therapy came at Christmas time. The family had never celebrated Christmas so MHE and Ralph's wife got a tree and presents for everyone. On Christmas Day MHE instructed the family on the proper way to hand out presents: the person giving the present must say "Merry Christmas" and must kiss the receiver of the gift. After a couple tries Ralph mastered this behavior, to his daughter's delight.

A few months later Ralph came to MHE and said that he'd had a pain in his bladder for two months. MHE reprimanded him for not coming in sooner and said that he suspected malignant tumor in the pituitary. MHE's diagnosis was correct and Ralph died two years later. [pp. 240–242]

The possibilities appear to be endless.

12.5 Concluding ordeals and metaphors

Troubled Man Named George

Once upon a time there was a troubled man named George. His troubles were not of great concern to others, although they occasionally impacted on his family. George was a great student of history and noted how most of the famous from the past had troubles in their lives, too. Somehow, out of the suffering and travail and confusion and turmoil, a particular illness or trek led them to peace, tranquillity, understanding, and life. Their stories were inspiring. But how does an ordinary troubled man—that was the way George thought about himself—achieve the same ends? The days of heroic deeds and great adventures were over. Men have been to the moon, and the South Pole, and the top of Mount Everest. What was an ordinary troubled man to do?

Well, he thought, there were certainly things in his life that were challenging enough—lots of difficult and undone things around the house to do, that 100-mile solo bike trip he thought about, confronting his boss, getting closer to his wife and children, no longer having those occasional severe headaches, finding meaning for himself. Yet these were all, almost easily, attainable—all he had to do was do them, talk to someone, reach out.

In thinking about his troubles, George realized that so much depended on attitude. What had happened to his childhood and boyhood dreams? He needed to do something! The first step for George was his hardest—he called a family meeting and openly shared his troubles with them. Somehow, they all settled on the century bike ride as what he needed. He did some shorter trips with his wife and family, and on the appointed day he set out. He knew that it would be hard, but he expected something to happen.

And what happened was this—he fully experienced that day. There were the long uphill slogs, gearing down, but pedaling consistently. There were the joyous downhill speedings. There were the flat long sections. Some scenery was spectacular, other places ordinary, a few depressing. George drank it all in with the fresh energizing air. On a few stretches he knew the freedom of hands-free riding. His revelation, if you will, came during his lunch break, savoring every bite of the sandwich his wife had made for him. "I am," he thought. "I am loved," he thought. "I love," he felt.

The 100-mile bike ride didn't resolve all of George's troubles, since its end was more of a beginning. He did it, and he knew he could do it again whenever the troubles became too much, for those troubles have an interesting way of popping up.

And, where will you ride?

Chapter 13

As-If, the Miracle Question, and Metaphor

13.1 Introduction

It is difficult, if not impossible, to tell the difference between *acted* emotions and *real* emotions, between acting *as if* we believed something and genuine belief, between the story of our life that we tell ourselves and others and our historical story. The discovering of "truth" in human actions has been a central theme in the history of humankind. The movie *Rashomon* illustrated this by showing the "same" incident through the perceptions (not just the eyes) of several characters. The Heisenberg Uncertainty Principle in human terms states that what is observed depends on the observer, and that the observer has an impact on the observation. Given these comments about our perceptions and responses, how can these ideas be used therapeutically for mind and body concerns?

If an actor merges with his part as in "method" acting, the measured physiological signals for depression, rage, fear, peace, anger, meditative state, and anxiety are the same as for people who are depressed, fearful, angry, at peace or in a calm state. Acting *as if* you were stressed brings out the same reactions as actually being in a stressful situation. This is why you do not quiz a friend or a relative about her recent divorce or heart attack. She will relive, both emotionally *and* physically, the stresses of that event while she is talking about it. The relating of an incident, the recalling of the memory, "tricks" *both* the mind and the body into reliving that experience. This is what E. L. Rossi calls state-dependent-learning-and-behavior, or SDLB. Any time you ask someone to recall an event, SDLB is invoked in all of its dimensions. *We are what we think, and we are our (mutable) memories.*

The connection to useful therapeutic outcomes and healing is to get your client to act *as if* she were healed or was healing, and to act *as if* her concerns have been satisfactorily resolved. This mental trick fools the mind/body into responding positively. The power of guided imagery for healing is in congruently sensing the body's enhanced immune system. The power of the *miracle question* is in mentally rehearsing change so that the detailed description of life *after* the miracle becomes the new reality (see section 13.3 below).

The connection to metaphor is that within the mind we *associate* with the people, components, situations, and solutions in the stories we hear, and the stories we tell ourselves. People appear to actually live the parts of a story when they are wrapped up (rapt) in a story. This is why isomorphism and parallel situations are so important. But, since connections are made within the mind, it is important to provide many opportunities for a person to make her own unique connections. Being vague and permissive and open-ended provides more possibilities than being overly specific.

This chapter is written *as if* its content presents the value of "as-if" and the miracle question. The possibility of the placebo effect being an as-if intervention is also explored.

13.2 As-ifs

I have just spent considerable time looking through my library, particularly books that Watzlawick has authored or co-authored, for appropriate as-if interventions to include in this section. Perhaps this was an endeavor on my part to act *as if* I were a scholar—if I can cite a number of as-if interventions, then that shows that I am familiar with the relevant psychotherapy literature! Not finding any literature examples to cite in this section forces me to create some of my own from scratch, or to rely on my memory to give some credit to people I thought did these things. On the other hand, any of the ambiguous-function-assignment examples can be considered to be as-if behavior in the sense that the client is acting *as if* the activity has meaning. In a similar sense, a person carrying out an ordeal is behaving like a student on a journey of discovery. Both kinds of activities are play-acting—this personal drama requires the client to live and act in a new way, something foreign to her, but something with an implied learning. Also, behavior *as if* results in a *reframing* or a second-order change that is meta to normal behavior. This action reframing results in the same kind of changed perspective that verbal reframing produces. As-if change tactics are implicit in many interventions.

The case study that I was looking for in Watzlawick's work combined probability (a coin toss) with as-if behavior. The intervention relies on a coin toss done in the evening. If the coin comes up heads, then for the entire next day the client is to behave as if she is: feeling free of depression/helplessness/hopelessness/loneliness/despair *or* the reverse of feeling relaxed/energetic/active/hopeful/competent/up; free of her symptom(s) or compulsions or restrictive behaviors; warm and loving to her husband/children/parents; an active participant in household activities; really listening to her husband/children/lover/parents/workers/supervisor; drug- or substance- or alcohol-free; or physically taking care of herself. The coin toss is done every evening for one week. At the end of each day the significant others in the client's life are to make a note as to whether the coin came up heads or tails the previous day. All those involved can compare notes at the end of the week— was the client successfully faking altered behavior ... *or* was it genuine? The typical outcome is that the "faked" behavior becomes the norm, since it has produced desired outcomes for all involved. The client has been "tricked" into changing, yet all of the behavior, every action, is her own and is voluntarily conscious. Clients (couples and families) can be hooked into the coin-toss activity simply because it is intriguing, it is puzzling, it is a game, and it does not appear to be therapy, per se. "Here is an interesting experiment you can try. You might find this fun to do." Children, in particular, find the coin toss appealing.

All of the as-if behaviors listed in the coin toss can also be used independently of probability, that is, the client can be challenged to do the experiment of acting *as if* things had really changed for some specific time. Generally, the test period should be at least one week so that the client can discover what it is really like to live in this different way.

People who have been faced with the diagnosis of a life-challenging (versus life-threatening— very different emphasis) disease are forced to confront the probability of a foreshortened life. It is not unusual for them to consider this diagnosis at some time to be a "blessing" since they are forced to stop living *as if* they will die at some vague time in the distant future. Now, every moment, every breath, every experience becomes precious. With a potentially pro-scribed life span (remember that you may have to accept the diag-nosis, but you do not have to accept the prognosis!), life becomes the here and now, and people begin to live *as if* this were there last moment or day or week. They take the time to smell a flower, fully experience and enjoy each contact, really look at that cloud or painting, really listen to that person or music, really taste that bite of … *Really* or *as if*: for a person with cancer, is there any difference?

"And you can really sense what is going on right now, can you not? That touch, that flower, that smile, that billowing cloud, a sunset, a moonrise, the wind in your hair, rain, a glass of cold water, snug-gling down in bed, this moment, a deep breath, a smile, one blade of grass, that special music, a hug, laughter, and the moon in the morning."

13.3 Solution-focused therapy and the miracle question

At the Brief Family Therapy Center (BFTC) of Milwaukee (P.O. 13736, Milwaukee, WI 53213; (414) 302-0650; www.brief-therapy.org) they did an interesting experiment related to expectations. When clients asked the receptionist for an initial appointment, they were asked for a brief description of what they wanted to see a therapist about. The receptionist then told the client, "Oh, for that problem it generally takes five sessions." The next client was told *ten* ses-sions. So, alternate clients were told five or ten sessions with no connection to the presenting problem. The therapists did not know who was told five and who was told ten. The follow-up study showed that the five-session people typically started working seri-ously in about the fourth session, and the ten-session people typi-cally at about the eighth session. This bit of research is presented here for two reasons. The first is to emphasize the power of sug-gestion, expectation, and presupposition—all related, of course. The client acts *as if* her problem will be solved in five or ten ses-sions. The second is to indicate that the BFTC has a long history of doing research into its methods.

The approach that the BFTC pioneered is called solution-oriented therapy or solution-focused brief therapy (SFBT). Three useful references are de Shazer (1994), Miller and Berg (1995), and Berg and Dolan (2001). The title of the last-cited book is *Tales of Solutions. A Collection of Hope-Inspiring Stories.* The basic therapeutic approach is to emphasize *solutions* and not problems. Another study the BFTC did was to record the length of time a client would talk about problems if the language and orientation of the therapist was such as to elicit "problem" talk. By contrast, if the therapist's expectation and language had to do with solutions and what was going well in the client's life, then problem talk time was a fraction of that of the problem-oriented therapist. Indeed, it is possible to stretch out problem talk and its analysis almost ad infinitum. Would you rather spend your time listening to depressing details of problems, or about solutions and what the client feels good about? Expectations. From a behavioral viewpoint, problem talk reinforces problem behavior and solution talk reinforces solution behavior. The latter is presumably the goal of therapy!

Several quotations from Berg and Dolan (2001) connect SFBT to metaphor and guided metaphor:

> ... the more we repeat the same story, the more realistic it seems. [p. xiv]

> ... a distinguishing principle of the solution-focused approach is that the therapist empowers the client to retell their stories based upon their goals, rather than basing their goals upon their stories. [p. xiv]

> "Suppose you could understand your past right now. What difference would it make for you?" [p. 4]

> In contrast to problem solving, solution building as practiced in SFBT begins with client's descriptions of how they want their lives to be different. It can be understood as beginning with the end of the story rather than the beginning of the problems. [p. 5]

> The second step of solution building is to search for evidence or instances in which clients have experienced or are already experiencing bits and pieces of the desired life they identified in step one. [p. 5]

Notice the linguistic implications of the use of "problem-solving" versus "solution-building" language. The former is oriented to the past and the latter to the present and the future.

On pp. 12–14 of their book Berg and Dolan (2001) outline the seven steps of SFBT, and these are summarized here. See this book and the others cited above for more details. (Direct quotes are in quotation marks.)

Outline of SFBT approach

1. "Ask your client, 'What needs to happen that will tell you that today's meeting has been useful?' " (p. 12.) In the first session, after listening attentively to the client, the session immediately becomes solution- and future-oriented. This question also presupposes that there will be an end to her suffering, and that there will be markers for her satisfaction at termination. Therapy is not then endless, but rather it is focused toward solutions of the *client's choice*.

2. "One of the premises of SFBT is the idea that no problem happens all of the time—that is, there are exceptions, times when the problem does not occur." (p. 10.) As you elicit details about the client's solution to her problem(s), you also ask questions designed to uncover *exceptions*. It is a rare individual who has no time in her life only when the "problem" is paramount. For example, she may function reasonably well at work but not at home, or vice versa. Recall the figure in an earlier chapter of a black dot on an expanse of white—clients tend to be preoccupied with the black dot and not notice the white, the times and occurrences in their lives that are exceptions to the problem. Spending time on exceptions is essentially a *reframing* technique, and helps the client to become aware of competencies (versus involuntary undesired behaviors). The search for exceptions (which already exist!) is the foundation for change.

3. The next step is to ask the *miracle question*—the client's responses make real in the as-if mode her own unique solutions for her concerns. The following is a version of the miracle question (p. 7):

> I am going to ask you a rather strange question. [pause] The strange question is this: [pause] After we talk, you will go back to your work (home, school) and you will do whatever you need to do the rest of today … [Pause] It will become time to go to bed. Everybody in your household is quiet, and you are sleeping in peace. In the middle of the night, a miracle happens *and the problem that prompted you to talk to me today is solved!* But because this happens while you are sleeping, you have no way of knowing that there was an overnight miracle that solved the problem. [pause] So, when you wake up tomorrow morning, what might be the small change that will make you say to yourself, "Wow, something must have happened—the problem is gone!"

The therapist's task at this point is to lead the client through her day, asking for what *will be* different, due to the miracle. This is an as-if thought exercise of the client's creation and, since she creates it, the changes are unique, individual, and realistic. What would her spouse/children/parents/co-workers/boss/relatives/friends notice in her actions, behavior, and demeanor that would let them know that she has changed? If she were able to observe herself— from the back, the side, the front, through another's eyes—what would she notice that was different post-miracle? It is the build-up of detail that reifies this reframing of her life. And, once it is perceived in such profusion of detail, it is effectively impossible to go back to the old patterns. Responding to the miracle question is an as-if rehearsal that works. In effect, *the client is writing a new story of her life*.

Remarkably, the changed behaviors (be careful to elicit *observable changes* rather than feelings) are typically small, simple, and even mundane. Examples are: talking to each other over breakfast rather than reading, kissing spouse goodbye, washing the dishes, taking care of an oft-postponed task, reading to a child. It is these small realistic changes that are reported.

4. "Find out when the client has recently experienced even a little bit of the miracle day. This is crucial, because if a client has had even a half day of mastery over problems, he or she has the potential to extend the half day into a whole day, or into two days, and so on." (p. 13.) This validates that the miracle has its roots in current behaviors and is realistic. With respect to this current bit of the

miracle, "… ask about what other important people in the client's life would say if they were explaining how the client accomplished this small success." (p. 13)

5. "When you feel like you have sufficiently covered the exceptions, you can move into asking about the confidence scale." (p. 13.) SFBT makes much use of scaling questions. "Numbers are flexible and expandable. You can move up and down a numerical scale or multiply, divide, increase, or shrink a number. Words are not as flexible … Most of all, we like scaling questions because numbers tend to be more neutral than words." (p. 69) "We find them particularly helpful in gauging:

- a client's progress in treatment
- a client's level of hopefulness
- how much energy a client has to invest in making life better
- how much trust, willingness, confidence, and motivation a client has" (p. 70).

In this case the scaling question might be, "On a scale of 1 to 10 where 1 stands for having no confidence at all that you will overcome the problem(s) you talked about, and 10 stands for being completely confident of a successful outcome, where are you today?" Fractions are permitted, such as 4.5, and small incremental changes are encouraged—what would it take to move up to 4.7, or even 5.0? Scaling provides information for the therapist, and is the client's way of quantifying her status and progress.

6. "When the client is confident that he or she can repeat the successful strategies, the conversation should shift to, 'What will it take to make that solution happen again?'" (p. 14.) Elicit details to make this *new* story as real *as if* it actually occurred.

7. "At the end of the session, the therapist generally summarizes what he or she heard from the client about areas of competence, successes, positive intentions, and how the client overcame the odds against making it. This of course naturally calls for the therapist to give the client a compliment. This compliment is followed by a suggestion for homework. Most SFBT homework suggestions are along the lines of 'do more of what works.'" (p. 14) The summary ratifies the work of the session; the compliment is a reframe

about the client's work; and the homework continues the search for solutions. To continue this solution-oriented approach, the second session typically begins with something like, "What's changed for the better for you, even just a little bit?" Elicit details. The miracle question may need to be posed again; it certainly becomes the continuing theme.

The SFBT approach involves a *re-storying* of the client's life, and the future-orientation of the as-if process. There is also reframing and quantification via scaling. There is respect for the client as in, "A simple question such as 'you must have a good reason to ... (drink a lot, become angry, cut yourself, want to kill yourself, etc.)' can generate an amazing turn around in clients." (p. 97) There is an acceptance and an understanding in this "simple question" that leads to reasonable explanations and meaningful communication. Finally, here are the three simple principles of SFBT (p. 120):

1. If it is not broken, don't fix it.
2. If it worked once, do it again.
3. If it doesn't work, don't do it again. Do something different.

These three principles are the essence of common sense in doing effective therapy.

13.4 A few solution-focused case studies

To give you a sense of how the material presented in the previous section is used by SFBT practitioners, this section contains four case studies. The first three are from Miller and Berg (1995) and are transcripts from sessions. This particular book contains many other cases illustrations and also an excellent description of the SFBT approach, especially as applied to problem drinking.

Drinking on the Docks

By the time Lee came to see us, his job as foreman was in jeopardy. His performance had deteriorated over the last few months, and management had recently discovered that he was drinking on the job. After Lee had a chance to tell us his story, we asked him the "miracle" question.

Therapist: Lee, let me ask you a strange kind of question.

Lee: Okay.

Th: It takes some pretending on your part.

Lee: Yeah, shoot.

Th: Okay. Suppose tonight, after our meeting, you go home, go to bed, and fall asleep.

Lee: I'm with you so far.

Th: And while you are sleeping, *a miracle happens.*

Lee: Uh-huh.

Th: The miracle is that the problem or problems you are struggling with are solved!

Lee: I no longer have these problems.

Th: Yes. Just like that! Your problems are solved. Since you are sleeping, however, you don't know that the miracle has happened. You sleep right through the whole event. When you wake up tomorrow morning, what would be some of the first things that you would notice that would be different and that would tell you that a miracle has happened and that your problem is solved?

Lee (*pause*): I wouldn't feel like I am having to exert all of my energy to keep things in check.

Th: Uh-huh.

Lee: I would be living my life again. I wouldn't be so gloomy and negative. I would be more happy and positive. I would be smiling at work and maybe even laughing.

Th: Uh-huh. What else?

Lee: I wouldn't have this wrinkled brow and knotted-up forehead all the time, and I wouldn't have this ache in my chest. I would get out and move around again. Right now all I do is just stay at my desk. So I would go out and talk to the guys on the dock. No matter what they did. Nowadays I just hide, you see.

Th: Uh-huh.

Lee (*with surprise*): Oh, I know. I wouldn't come home from work and solve all my problems by drinking. Maybe I wouldn't stop by the bar and complain to Ted [the bartender] about the guys on the dock. "Oh, you shoulda seen those SOBs today," you know. My whole conversation wouldn't be negative.

Th: Anything else that would be different after the miracle?

Lee (*long pause*): Maybe work wouldn't be my entire life. Maybe, like I said, I would start living my live again. You know, I got this great job, and I haven't done anything for myself since.

Lee's answer continued for a while longer. As he continued to speak, he began to smile and his mood brightened considerably. [pp. 39–40]

Michelle
[This starts with just part of Michelle's background.]

Drinking was not the only problem that Michelle was struggling with. Prior to coming to see us, she had seen another counselor who told her that she had an eating disorder. She told us that she also felt unresolved about her past, in particular, her relationships with her mother and father as well as with her two siblings, with whom she had lost contact over the last few years. Both, she told us, had been struggling with alcohol the last time she saw them.

"There are so many problems to be dealt with," she said at one point in the session, "that I don't know where to start." We saw our opportunity and asked Michelle to imagine that a miracle had taken place and the problems that brought her to our office were solved. She responded by telling us that she had frequently imagined and fantasized about just such an occurrence as she was growing up. For this reason, perhaps, Michelle was able to answer the miracle question in considerable detail.

Therapist: Michelle, let me ask you a strange kind of question.

Michelle: Okay.

Th: It takes some pretending on your part. Here is how it goes. Suppose tonight, you go home, go to bed, and fall asleep. And while you are sleeping, a miracle happens, and the miracle is that these problems that brought you here today are solved. Just like that! But because you were asleep, you didn't know that this miracle had happened. When you woke up the next morning, what would be some of the first things that you would notice that would tell you that a miracle had happened?

Michelle: It's funny that you should ask me that question.

Th: Hmm. Why's that?

Michelle: Well, because I had this really, *really* bad childhood, I used to spend a lot of time alone in my room wishing a miracle would happen. It never did.

Th: Hmm. Suppose one did happen now, Michelle. Suppose you finally got your wish and the miracle did happen now. What would be different in your life tomorrow that would tell you that the miracle had happened?

Michelle: Well, I guess the first thing that I would notice if the miracle happened would be that my appearance would change.

Th: Okay.

Michelle: I would be taking care of myself. I would start wearing nice clothes again. Dressing up. Doing my hair and my nails. Eating right.

Th: Uh-huh.

Michelle: Right now I just eat whatever I feel like, and so after the miracle I would be watching what I eat. I wouldn't be going to all the fast-food restaurants and pigging out all the time.

Th: So you would be taking better care of yourself?

Michelle: Uh-huh, and that would make me feel better about myself. Because right now I have a really, *really* low self-esteem.

Th: No wonder.

Michelle: Right. And I would be more of a positive person. Put it this way: I wouldn't doubt myself so much. I would just go in there and do whatever I had to do whether in my job or with my family.

Th: What else?

Michelle: I wouldn't let others walk over me anymore.

Th: What would you do instead?

Michelle: I would just tell them they couldn't do that to me. Not in any mean way or anything, but I just wouldn't let people take advantage of me anymore.

Th: Uh-huh.

Michelle: I guess more of the real me would come out.

Th: Tell me more about that. How would you know that more of the real you was coming out?

Michelle: I'm a really friendly person. Nobody knows it, though.

Th: And so after the miracle?

Michelle: I would be getting out and meeting people, talking with people at work, you know, going out sometimes.

Michelle continued to describe her miracle for several minutes. Her description eventually included statements about how her use of alcohol would be different after the miracle. For Michelle, her miracle was that she would be completely abstinent from alcohol. She believed that the memories of her parents' drinking and the problems that alcohol had caused in her own life left her no other choice. Using Key 4, we helped Michelle specify what she would be doing instead of drinking. [pp. 107–9]

Key 4 is: Be sure you state what you *will* do rather Than what you *won't* do. (p. 52) The keys are six guidelines and are covered in Miller and Berg's chapter 3 (1995, pp. 32–65).

In and Out of The Toilet

Ronald had not had any problems with alcohol for nearly a year when he experienced his first setback. It was a particularly bad setback for Ronald. After a few weeks of problematic drinking, however, he finally picked up the phone and made an appointment to come in and see us. He was very discouraged when he arrived for his scheduled appointment.

Ronald (*tearful*): I feel like such a failure. A whole year down the toilet.

Therapist: Sounds like you're feeling pretty down about this.

Ronald: You know it. I just can't get it out of my head. I just keep going over and over it. Why? Why? I keep asking myself.

Th: Let me ask you something. *How* did you manage to pull yourself out of the toilet long enough to pick up the phone and call?

Ronald: I just did it. I knew I needed help.

Th: *How* is that different from what you might have done in the past?

Ronald: Before, I wouldn't have called, I don't think. I would've just wallowed in it and kept drinking.

Th: You would have wallowed in it and kept drinking?

Ronald: YEAH.

Th: You say you would have kept drinking?

Ronald: Yeah.

Th: Does That mean that you're not drinking now?

Ronald: I haven't had anything to drink for a couple of days now.

Th: Wow. *What* did you do to get yourself to stop like that?

Ronald: I just did it.

Th: You "just picked up the phone," you "just stopped drinking"? I don't believe it. You've been feeling really discouraged. It would have been really easy just to wallow around in it and keep drinking.

Ronald: I guess I didn't think about it like that, yeah.

Th: So *how* did you get yourself to stop like that? You must have done something.

Ronald (*Thinking*): I took this case of beer that I had bought and I gave it to my neighbor.

Th: Uh-huh.

Ronald (*smiles and laughs*): I was gonna throw it away, but I just couldn't get myself to do that.

Th (*laughs*): Okay, you couldn't throw it away so. . .

Ronald: I gave it to my neighbor.

The discussion continued, with the therapist and Ronald working together to identify "what had worked" to help Ronald stop his problem drinking. Considerable time was spent helping him identify the who, what, where, when, and how of his success. As this discussion took place, Ronald's mood and outlook began to change. By the end of the session Ronald felt better about himself and, more important, had identified what he could do if another problem arose in the future. [pp. 135–7]

In these three case studies there is also obviously much to learn from careful study of the therapist's language. There is much evidence of attentive listening and ratification of the client's statements.

Berg and Dolan's book (2001) is an inspiring collection of stories that they have garnered from SFBT practitioners around the world. These are stories and metaphors about change, and they cover a variety of client concerns. The subtitle of the book contains the words "hope-inspiring," and the tales within truly reflect those words. The following (pp. 145–6) was contributed by Robin McCarthy of Portland, Maine.

The Truck Driver Who Needed Help

Rachel brought her four-and-a-half-year-old son Timothy to see me because he was enuretic and encopretic. Rachel had left Arthur, Timothy's father, after he had beaten her in front of the children. Subsequently, Rachel found that when the kids were visiting Arthur, he spanked them and used other forms of corporal punishment that were unacceptable to her. Rachel decided to seek full custody of the children, with Arthur having supervised visits only. Arthur committed suicide. Following this event, Timothy lost control of his bowels and bladder.

Timmy didn't want to talk about any of it. At our third session, Timothy and I played in the sandbox with toy trucks. I was frantically thinking about how trucks could have a relationship to playing out encopresis or enuresis. Then I had an idea. I said in a "tough guy" truck driver voice, "Hey, buddy, let's take a coffee break." Timothy responded in a gruff tone, "Okay." Still using my truck driver voice, I asked where the bathroom was because "I needed to poop." I made loud (pretend) bathroom noises and pooping and farting noises. Then we got back into our trucks and back to work.

We continued playing with the trucks and using the voices for quite a while, until I felt we had bonded as fellow truck drivers. Then I said in my truck driver voice, "Hey buddy, I have a problem that's really embarrassing to talk about. Can I talk to you?" "Sure," Timothy responded. I continued with how embarrassed I was and how personal it was. Timothy continued to be open to hearing about it. Then I hesitantly said, "Well, the thing is, I keep peeing and pooping in my pants, and well, gosh, it's so embarrassing and I'm so ashamed telling you, but I just don't know what to do and I wondered if you could help me. Do you have any ideas about how I can stop peeing and pooping in my pants? What would you do? You gotta help me buddy. Please, tell me how you know when you start to have the feeling that you need to pee or poop?"

Timothy answered in his truck driver voice: "It's okay buddy, here's what you do. You just start to feel a funny feeling in your tummy and then you go right to the bathroom to see if it's pee or poop, and then you don't go in your pants anymore. That's what you do, now let's get back to work."

At Timothy's next session, Rachel told me he'd been using the toilet consistently. He solved his own problem by "helping his buddy."

We are indeed all miracles, and the SFBT approach provides an opportunity to achieve these small realistic miracles as we rewrite our stories and our lives. The miracle question provides The opportunity to convert thoughts to actions.

13.5 The power of as-if

In the realm of mind–body interactions, the scientific evidence for mind affecting body comes primarily from the field of psychoneuroimmunology. (An introduction to this work can be found in Rossi (1993) and in Battino (2000, pp. 15–27), and in the citations therein.)

As-if can be helpful for people undergoing chemotherapy or radiation treatments for cancer. The chemotherapy agent can be considered to be a noxious and toxic substance that poisons the body while it also kills cancer cells. The client then has a negative and noncooperative attitude toward the treatment, and is scared. I recall a member of our support group whose first round of

259

chemotherapy had rather uncomfortable side effects, mainly severe nausea. She was antagonistic to the treatment, and fought it. Her second round of chemotherapy was almost pleasant with only one time of minor discomfort. What was different (the treatment and side effect control agents were the same)? Mary was quite religious and had a deep faith. What was different for the second and subsequent rounds of treatment was Mary's attitude. She now perceived the yellowish chemotherapy fluid as being imbued with God's golden love, it was a sun-filled fluid that was full of God's healing power. She responded to this fluid *as if* it were a direct gift from God—of course, such a divine gift would carry no side effects with it. Her faith, her belief, and her conviction literally changed her body's physical responses. Lawrence LeShan's work (e.g. 1989) is a testament to the power of the mind when it acts in these as-if ways. Mary acted *as if* God had sent her a healing fluid.

Stephen Levine (1997) wrote a remarkable book about a self-imposed as-if experience—he assumed he had one year to live. In the first chapter (p. 6) he wrote:

> But all those who seemed to make the best use of a terminal prognosis began to change their relationship to relationship itself ... But almost all said that they would have slowed down and stopped to smell, if not plant, the roses.

Rather than "fight" whatever it is that troubles us, Levine recommends a kind of psychological judo where you use the troubles' strength—by incorporating it—to transform it into something harmless. This is a spiritual approach rather than a militaristic one—how commonly used are words such as defeat, destroy, battle, fight, war? This changed attitude reframes what transpires. Levine puts it this way (p. 19):

> When we begin to respond to discomfort instead of reacting to it, an enormous change occurs. We begin to experience it not as just "our" pain but as "the" pain. And it becomes accessible to a level of compassion perhaps previously unknown. When it's "the" cancer instead of "my" cancer I can relate to others with the same difficulty, and I can send compassion into the cancer rather than helplessly avoiding it and turning its pain to suffering.

Levine further observes (p. 18):

> Pity arises from meeting pain with fear. Compassion comes when you meet it with love. When we attempt to escape from our pain we feel a sense of helplessness. When we open to sensations at the very point of their origin, softening in to an awareness that embraces, rather than disclaims, its momentary inheritance, we experience compassion and even gratitude (more perhaps for the softening than the need it responded to).

Finally, a comment about healing that connects with the as-if theme of this chapter (p. 48):

> If there is a single definition of healing it is to enter with mercy and awareness those pains, mental and physical, from which we have withdrawn in judgment and dismay. Nothing prepares us so completely for death as entering those aspects of our lives that remain unlived ...

> Dying is the domain of the body. Death is the domain of the heart.

Becoming aware of, joining the pain and the treatment, acting *as if* they were part of you (rather than avoiding) heals.

13.6 Placebo as as-if?

As-if-ing involves faith and belief and hope. The essence of the placebo effect is that one *believes* in the efficacy of the particular treatment or drug. The placebo-taker acts *as if* the placebo were the "real" thing, the curative with all of its potency. Does this mean that the content of this chapter is about "mental" placebo effects? That conclusion is certainly warranted, since all as-if work can be considered to be placebo-related. The mental constructs that result from responding to the miracle question all involve a belief, a faith, that such change can occur. Aside from being an interesting intellectual exercise, is there any advantage to considering as-if as placebo? Probably not, but the connection needed to be mentioned. (An entrée to the considerable literature on the placebo effect, particularly as relating to guided imagery, may be found in Chapter 4 in Battino (2001).)

13.7 Concluding comments

The magical worlds of as-if are indeed metaphoric. Once upon a time there was a young _____ who set out on a journey of discovery. This young _____ had much book learning but little practical knowledge of the world. Tired and hungry at the end of the first day's travel, the young _____ came upon an isolated house. There was a person of great wisdom in this house, and this person set the young _____ several tasks. Upon their completion, the young _____ could have three wishes. Several years later the young _____ returned, and stated that the tasks, though challenging, had been completed. The young _____ described the heroic deeds in great detail, although it was difficult for the person of great wisdom to know if the deeds were actually accomplished or if the young _____ was an accomplished storyteller. Being indeed wise, the person of great knowledge granted the young _____'s three wishes, knowing not how to know what was known, and what not was known, for are not stories always true?

Chapter 14

Narrative Therapy

14.1 Introduction

Bill O'Hanlon (1994) is so impressed by White and Epston's narrative therapy (1990) that he suggests that this approach is so different from what came before that he calls it "The Third Wave of Psychotherapy." O'Hanlon considers the First Wave to have begun with Freud, that it laid the foundation for the new field of psychotherapy, and that it was pathology-focused and dominated by psychodynamic theories and also biological psychiatry. He considers that it was so heavily focused on pathology that it ended up skewing our view of human nature.

The Second Wave—or problem-focused therapies—arose in the 1950s but did not replace the first wave. On p. 22 of his article, O'Hanlon had the following to say:

> The Second Wave attempted to remedy the overfocus on pathology and the past. Problem-focused Therapies, including behavioral therapy, cognitive approaches and family therapy, didn't assume clients were sick. They focused more on the here-and-now instead of searching for hidden meanings and ultimate causes …

> Second wave therapists saw their clients as basically sound, just making a pit stop …

> Problems resided in small-scale systems; solutions still rested with the therapists. Few saw their clients as decisive agents in their own change.

In the 1980s there began a transition toward the Third Wave in what could be called the competence-based therapies. Therapists were no longer seen to be the source of the solution: rather the solutions resided in people and their social networks. These solution-oriented therapies were not focused on pathology and problem parts, but on what could enhance and enlarge people's lives utilizing their own resources.

The Third Wave, of which narrative therapy is an exemplar, has at its heart, "… its fierce belief in people's possibilities for change and the profound effects of conversation, language and stories on both therapist and client." (O'Hanlon, 1994, p. 28.) In Third Wave therapists there is, "… a willingness to acknowledge the tremendous power of the past history and the present culture that shape our lives, integrated with a powerful, optimistic vision of our capacity to free ourselves from them once they are made conscious. Third Wave approaches talk to the Adult Within." (O'Hanlon, 1994, p. 23.)

Narrative therapy works within and through the story that a person believes in about his own life. The guided-metaphor approach is also a personal-story-based approach. The literature or narrative therapy is extensive—you would best start with studying White and Epston's seminal book (1990). Freedman and Combs (1996) provide an excellent introduction to narrative therapy from the perspective of two well-trained Chicago-based therapists. Dulwich Centre Publications (Hutt St PO Box 7192, Adelaide 5000, South Australia, Australia. (61-8) 223-3966) is a source for many books, pamphlets, and articles on narrative therapy. A recent book edited by Monk, Winslade, Crocket, and Epston (1997) has individually authored chapters on theory and practice. Two other books that are useful to read are Epston and White (1992) and White (1995).

In this chapter all that can be really done about the richness and paradigm-shifting nature of doing narrative therapy is to present an abbreviated version of this approach with the hope that the reader will be sufficiently intrigued to study this work in depth. In particular, both White and Epston's first book (1990) and Freedman and Combs (1996) need to be studied. Both have many illustrative case studies and transcripts; the latter also contains a systematic description of narrative therapy.

14.2 Elements of narrative therapy

Before describing for the reader the many essential elements of narrative therapy, I need to point out that the originators proceeded in their work from a grounding in social, linguistic, and communication theory. That is, there is a solid theoretical base for narrative therapy. Freedman and Combs (1996) do an excellent job of summarizing this.

Perhaps some quotations from White and Epston (1990) can help.

> Social scientists became interested in the text analogy [where social organization is constructed as a behavioral test; problems are constructed as the performance of the oppressive dominant story or knowledge; and solutions are constructed in terms of opening space for the authoring of alternative stories] following observations that, although a piece of behavior occurs in time in such a way that it no longer exists in the present by the time it is attended to, the meaning that is ascribed to the behavior survives across time. [p. 9]

> Concluding that we cannot have direct knowledge of the world, social scientists proposed that what persons know of life they know through "lived experience." [p. 9]

> ... in order to make sense of our lives and to express ourselves, experience must be "storied" and it is this storying that determines the meaning ascribed to experience.

> In striving to make sense of life, persons face the task of arranging their experiences of events in sequences across time in such a way as to arrive at a coherent account of themselves and the world around them. Specific experiences of events of the past and present, and those that are predicted to occur in the future, must be connected in a lineal sequence to develop this account. This account can be referred to as a story or self-narrative (see Gergen & Gergen, 1984). The success of this storying of experience provides persons with a sense of continuity and meaning in their lives, and this is relied upon for the ordering of daily lives and for the interpretation of further experiences. Since all stories have a beginning (or a history), a middle (or a present), and an ending (or a future), then the

interpretation of current events is as much future-shaped as it is past-determined. [pp. 9–10]

White and Epston (1990, p. 83) consider that a therapy working within the narrative mode of thought would take a form that:

1. privileges the person's lived experience;

2. encourages a perception of a changing world through the plotting or linking of lived experience through the temporal dimension;

3. invokes the subjunctive mood in the triggering of presuppositions, the establishment of implicit meaning, and in the generation of multiple perspective;

4. encourages polysemy ["polyphonic orientation"] and the use of ordinary, poetic and picturesque language in the description of experience and in the endeavor to construct new stories;

5. invites a reflexive posture and an appreciation of one's participation in interpretive acts;

6. encourages a sense of authorship and re-authorship of one's life and relationships in the telling and retelling of one's story;

7. acknowledges that stories are co-produced and endeavors to establish conditions under which the "subject" becomes the privileged author;

8. consistently inserts pronouns "I" and "you" in the description of events.

Narrative therapy has a number of characteristic elements. A basic one is described as follows by O'Hanlon (1994, p. 24):

The hallmark of the narrative approach is the credo, "The person is never the problem; the problem is the problem." Through use of their most well-known technique, externalization, narrative therapists are able to acknowledge the power of labels while both avoiding the trap of reinforcing people's attachment to them and letting them escape responsibility for their behavior. Externalization offers a way of viewing clients as having parts of them that are uncontaminated by the symptom. This automatically creates a view of the person as nondetermined and as accountable for the choices he or she makes *in relationship* to the problem ...

Externalization also helps therapists quickly build alliances with difficult clients.

[The Canadian family therapist Karl Tomm is quoted as saying (pp. 24–5)]: "Ironically, this technique [externalization] is both very simple and extremely complicated. It is simple in the sense that what it basically entails is a linguistic separation of the problem from the personal identity of the patient. What is complicated and difficult is the delicate means by which it is achieved. It is through the therapist's careful use of language in the therapeutic conversation that the person's healing initiatives are achieved ... What is new about the narrative approach is that it provides a purposeful sequence of questions that consistently produce a freeing effect for people."

In practice narrative therapy involves a very careful use of language, and a sophisticated use of questions, which is designed to generate experience rather than to gather information. Chapter 5 (pp. 113–43) in Freedman and Combs (1996) provides a systematic development of the use of questions in narrative therapy, along with many illustrations. They discuss questions under five categories: deconstruction, opening space, preference, story development, and meaning. (It is beyond the scope of this book to even attempt to summarize the nature of questions.)

The process of externalization—with a person or a family—begins with coming up with a mutually acceptable *name* for the externalized problem. Are you being controlled or tricked by: Anger, Fear, Depression, Paranoia, Anxiety, Urine, Fatty Food, Bulimia, Panic, Anorexia? How long has this been going on? Have there been times when you were able to resist ____? put it in its place? ignore it? tell it off? This linguistically separates the person from the problem label, and clients soon perceived their problem in this externalized way. To aid in this separation the ogre or demon is made more real by attributing to it evil intentions and tactics. This is a nasty entity who has it in for you, and who has made your life a misery in many ways—elicit those ways from the client. O'Hanlon (1994, p. 26) has several comments on using externalization.

> ... the therapist starts talking to the person or family *as if* the problem were another person with an identity, will, tactics and intentions that are designed to oppress or dominate the person or family ... [Italics added.]

> The problem never *causes* or *makes* the person or the family to do anything, it only *influences, invites, tells, tries to convince, uses tricks, tries to recruit*, etc. This language highlights people's choices and creates an assumption of accountability, rather than blame or determinism. If the person is *not* the problem, but has a certain relationship to the problem, then the relationship can change ...

> Discovering moments when clients haven't been dominated or discouraged by the problem or their lives have not been disrupted by the problem ...

> Finding historical evidence to bolster a new view of the person as competent enough to have stood up to, defeated or escaped from the dominance or oppression of the problem ... Here, the person's identity and life story begin to get rewritten. This is the *narrative* part. The previous steps have been used to prepare the ground to plant the seeds for rewriting people's sense of themselves ...

> Solution-oriented therapists would quickly move on to the future once a past exception is discovered, content to use that exception to solve the problem. Instead, the narrative therapist wants to root this new sense of self in a past and future so bright the person will have to wear shades ...

> Next, the narrative therapist helps the person or the family to speculate on what future developments will result now that the person is seen as competent and strong, and what changes will result if the person keeps resisting the problems ...

> Since the person developed the problem in a social context, it is important to make arrangements for the social environment to be

involved in supporting the new story or identity that has emerged in the conversation with the therapist.

If the person is not the problem, and the problem is the problem, then separating the person from the problem via externalization is an essential step in moving from what the client considers to be involuntary, unable-to-control behavior to voluntary and controllable behavior. Narrative therapists cleverly personify the controlling element to make it real in an as-if sense. (Is this an adaptation of racial memories of being possessed by demons, dybbuks, and evil spirits? Certainly it connects with the hero's journey. Is, then, narrative therapy a kind of modern-day exorcism? These parallels make for useful speculation ...) Once the problem has been externalized, then in a solution-focused-brief therapy sense *exceptions* to being controlled are sought. These exceptions, times when the "demon" has been thwarted or resisted, are the basis for the client's new life story, that is, the new story is built on the client's proven strengths and resources. "What will let you continue to ignore/thwart/overcome/restrict Depression (for example)?" "What can you do to put Depression in its place so it will no longer bother you?"

Narrative therapy is very social-context and family-oriented. People do not live in the vacuum(!) of the therapist's office, but in a social context of family, friends, work, etc. The new story has to be acknowledged and ratified by this social network. This is called "creating an audience for perceiving the new identity and new story." Letters from former clients who have already overcome a particular problem are used. The client can "proclaim" in a public letter or document that he is now free of Depression (for example). This is a "coming out" and is an essential part of narrative therapy.

Letters are used extensively and with a variety of ways in narrative therapy. In fact an entire chapter (1990, pp. 77–187), the longest one in White and Epston's book, is almost entirely devoted to letters. Each of the following types of letters is illustrated in their book. Again, this chapter is but an introduction to the world of narrative therapy.

1. *Letters of invitation*—These are used to engage or entice people to enter therapy or to continue in therapy. The tone is respectful and

courteous, and generally involve "hooks" that are connected to externalizing the problems in the client's life. Of course, there is some relevant entrée to the client.

2. *Redundancy letters*—Since people get stuck in roles that they feel they cannot give up, a redundancy letter is designed to show the client that he is no longer needed (redundant) in a particular role. The roles may be: supermom, parentwatcher, sibling protector, marriage protector, family-problem fixer, sex object etc. This kind of letter evolves from knowledge of the client's situation.

3. *Letters of prediction*—David Epston writes (pp. 94–5), "Often at the end of therapy I ask permission to make my predictions for a person's, relationship's, or family's future. I regularly use the period of six months as my time-frame. I often refer to this time-frame as 'your immediate future.' I post these predictions in 'letters,' folded and stapled, with 'private and confidential' prominently displayed on them, along with 'Not to be viewed until _____ (date in six months' time).' My intentions in doing this are twofold: (1) the prediction proposes a six-month follow-up/review, and suggests that this would be an interesting exercise for both the person/family and therapist to undertake: and (2) since it is my suspicion that most people won't wait but will review their review prior to the specified date, then I expect that the prediction will function as a prophecy which may fulfill itself."

4. *Counter-referral letters*—These are letters of referral that emphasize the development in a narrative sense and refer to the externalization so that the referral person has a sense of the client's accomplishments and change vis-à-vis the problem.

5. *Letters for special occasions*—These letters *ratify* comment on the special occasion and ratify progress.

6. *Brief letters*—Brief, reassuring letters, that connect to people who are relatively socially isolated. Here is a letter from Michael White (p. 110) to Danny, who had just escaped a longstanding lack of interest in food.

Dear Danny,

After you left I found myself feeling very thirsty to know even more about how you did it. Did you get yourself into training first?

Now that I have written this I am more than thirsty to know more. In fact I'm very hungry—no, now I'm extremely hungry to know more. If you think of anything you could tell your Mum or Dad, they could then remind you to tell me the same the next time that we meet. This would help me a lot.

Yours voraciously,
M.W.

Under the category of brief letters are letters on: past session thoughts; therapist needs help; nonattendance; recruiting an audience; mapping of influence (to show progress); historicizing; challenging the techniques of power; challenging specifications for personhood and for relationship; that reminds me!; chance meetings.

The previous are just a sampling of the variety of letters that narrative therapists routinely use in their practice. Of course, you would have to consult the original to get the full impact and understanding of the use of letters. Typically, a letter is sent after every session—these letters serve as case notes, reminders to the client(s) of what has happened in the session, ratification of change, predictions of future behavior, and a way of continuing contact and maintaining rapport. People are so addicted to the mail and the special power of letters that letter receiving takes on extra significance in their lives.

There are a few more narrative-therapy practices to discuss. Clients can be asked to record their own stories via a wide range of media: videotape, audiotape, testimonial letters, in various genres, the telephone, and personal letters. The narrative structure is conventionally that of a success story. Narrative therapists also make creative use of certificates. These are printed in certificate format. One example is a certificate entitled, "Monster-Tamer and Fear-Catcher Certificate," and states, "This is to certify that _____ has undergone a Complete Training Programme in Monster-Taming and

Fear-Catching, is now a fully qualified Monster-Tamer and Fear-Catcher, and is available to offer help to other children who are bugged by fears." These certificates are dated and signed by the therapist. Powerful stuff! Diplomas are also awarded.

14.3 Summary

Narrative therapy builds on story and metaphor and the transforming power of retelling personal stories from new and changing perspectives. Since we are our own story, why not work directly on that story? In this chapter the power and scope of the narrative-therapy approach has been but briefly discussed—study it. The technique of externalization is simple on the surface, but requires sophistication in practice. I suspect that narrative therapists would recognize the usefulness of Kopp's Metaphor Therapy and my guided metaphor, and simply incorporate elements of these two approaches into their broader vision.

Chapter 15

The Arts as Psychotherapeutic and Healing Metaphors

15.1 Introduction

Chapter 13 in Battino and South (1999, pp. 341–56) is entitled "The Arts as Hypnotherapeutic Metaphors." The emphasis in that book was on hypnotherapeutic metaphors structured in a particular eight-step model that was described in great detail. The treatment in this book is both more general and briefer, and with a section on "guided" art therapy.

The *arts* are considered quite broadly and include drawing, painting, sculpting, drama and psychodrama, music, voice, dance, movement, body and family sculpture, writing, poetry, storytelling, and ceremonies. That is, the arts involve some form of creative expression, and being creative involves new forms, ideas, connections, images, and insights. There is much as-if activity in the arts, and that means metaphor—one thing is represented as another. I recall several wonderful (and even transformative) experiences where several hundred people were led in drumming on all sorts of percussive instruments. Where is the metaphor in a collective drumming experience? Or is it just being immersed in all of that sound and joy and community, and being a drummer yourself, that is the metaphor? That is, being transformed into a drummer in a drumming community as a kind of ambiguous function? Sometimes, the experience itself—really being in that experience—is sufficient!

The thesis of this chapter is that *any* art form can be considered for psychotherapeutic and healing work. The choice of art form for acting out in an as-if manner relates to the client's interests and background. Dance may be appropriate for one person and not another. But the appropriateness may have little to do with the client's skill in that area. You can work with music and be tone deaf, you can use drawing with a color-blind person, and you can use dance with a person who has "two left feet." Art therapists emphasize that drawings are just as impactful to the person who can draw properly proportioned people as well as to those whose skill extends only to stick figures. What is useful is engaging, perhaps intriguing, your client into expressing her concerns and their solutions in some artistic manner.

For simplicity, this chapter describes some ways of using drawing to represent the use of art therapeutically via metaphor. There is much to recommend other art forms, and the reader is encouraged to explore them. Drama and psychodrama, for example, add elements of three-dimensional kinesthetic experience through time. In an earlier chapter structured writing via workbooks was discussed.

15.2 Drawing

Basically, a four-step approach involving four different drawings or activities covers the essential elements. If drawings are being used, then the client is reassured that the drawings do not have to be "good" or "nice" or "artistic," but rather representative of how they feel, regardless of how they turn out. The drawings will not be graded—this is a projective and personal way of expressing themselves. Stick figures are fine, for example. Drawings should be dated. They can also contain written comments on the front or back; objects and characters can be given a voice in a balloon (as in comic strips).

The four approaches are:

1. Please make a drawing of yourself in your present condition or state. (For example, you can show yourself in a depressed state or as having lung cancer.)

2. Please make a drawing of whatever treatment or treatments you are now receiving. (These could be chemotherapy and radiation, or psychoactive drugs and psychotherapy.)

3. Please make a drawing of yourself after this particular state or condition is over, i.e., how you would like to be. (The cancer disappears or you go into remission; or you can function normally and are completely free of depression.)

4. Please make a drawing of how you get from (1) (current state) to (3) (desired state). Please note that this change may have occurred via the treatments in (2) or via other activities.

The client can make new drawings at any time as she progresses. It is of major importance that the therapist not interpret the drawings to the client. There may be some universally accepted symbols with "standard" meanings, but every person is unique. It is said that even Freud recognized that a cigar can be just a banana. Avoid the pitfall of leading questions about specific aspects of the drawings that have special significance to you. Open questions like the following can be useful:

- There is a lot of color in your drawings. Would you care to comment on that?
- This part of the drawing is interesting. Any comments?
- There are a lot of words in your drawing. Would you care to expand on any of them?
- This drawing must mean a lot to you. Yes?
- Anything you'd like to tell me about your drawing(s)?
- There is so much of you here, isn't there?
- So, what's going on now?

These kinds of questions are permissive and respectful.

The four-aspects approach is simple and it is adaptable to other media. Four clay figures, or four body postures (as in sculpting), or four dances, or four chants, or four sand drawings come to mind as possibilities. Would it be possible (and quite fascinating) to *laugh* or *make faces* in the four aspects? The possibilities are many, but need to match the client's proclivities and talents.

15.3 Guided metaphoric art therapy

In Metaphor Therapy and guided metaphor the client takes the lead in terms of her own particular story. A *guided*-metaphoric-art therapy would work in the same way. Simply ask the client how she would restructure or rewrite her story in some artistic medium. First, you need the client's story in a paragraph or a sentence. Then you need an indication of how that story would change to let the client attain what she wants out of life. The new (desired) story is then depicted in some way or acted out or rewritten or danced or sung or … The new story is given life via an artistic medium of the client's choice. This as-if new story has a way of becoming real. The therapist or the client can serve as the *director* of the new story.

15.4 Summary

This chapter has been rather short, as it is full of suggestions of ways to use artistic media therapeutically. Since the artistic media *represent* situations and conditions, they are in essence metaphoric in nature. There is much room for experimentation and exploration along these lines.

Psychodrama has been singled out for separate treatment in the following contributed chapter by the New Zealand psychiatrist Joan Chappell Mathias, an expert and trainer in the field of psychodrama.

Chapter 16

Psychodrama and Metaphor

Joan Chappell Mathias, M.D.

16.1 Introduction

A. Metaphor

Metaphor is a word that is not often used in training for psychodrama, but we frequently use the concept. In real life metaphors are often shared. Family therapists refer to "family myths," and double-binds are frequently noted in unhappy families. Many of the disagreements between religious and cultural groups are about metaphorical aspects, and symbols. The same applies in national and international political scenes.

B. Psychodrama action and words

Psychodrama is an action rather than a verbal method and was developed by Jacob Moreno in American. We need few props for this work, so any enclosed and reasonably private space can be used. It takes place in a group setting, though it can be utilized in a family or a dyadic scene. It was developed in Australia and New Zealand by Max Clayton (see Holmes, et al., 1994), and ANZPA (Australia New Zealand Psychodrama Association) has just passed its 21st anniversary.

Some people believe that in the beginning was the word, but my interest in therapy is about problems that start before verbal fluency is achieved. The child who has what Winnicott described as "good enough mothering" will learn to speak by listening to and then copying the mother's speech, much of which will be metaphorical language, as she plays with her infant. Effective teachers, therapists, politicians, preachers, and comedians are usually masters of the art of using metaphors. In due season the child learns to speak in adult terms and to separate "fact" from "phantasy," and direct from indirect communications.

We like to think of early childhood as fun and we call it " Play for Adults" in psychodrama.

C. The role of metaphor in propaganda, religion, or therapy

Unfortunately, not all children have that good enough start to life and may have been terrified most of their early days. Some will not even survive; others will make it to adult life but they may have ongoing problems, call "unfinished business," from their early adverse experiences. The outcome may be virtuous, and many of them join the helping, educating, pastoral, and judicial professions. Some, however, move into vicious circles. In vicious circles metaphors can be used to propagate theories like those of the Nazis and the Marxists. In a home where there is dysfunction such as alcoholism, or when the grown-ups engage in physical or verbal sparring, the child will develop a distressing rather than a happy outlook of life.

D. Actions speak louder than words

By their deeds shall ye know them! Using metaphor in verbal counseling and therapy is usually a "safe" and useful technique. When there is enactment this is no longer always so. Acting out is avoided in most approaches to therapy and counseling. Touching of any sort can be labeled "sexual abuse." In psychodrama we study how to make enactment as safe as in a theatre, but without the use of footlights or separating the players from the audience. Those who become interested in psychodrama usually start with role-playing their clients during sessions with their supervisor. They then reverse roles, using an empty chair, as in Gestalt work, or have an auxiliary play the original role.

E. In the beginning was the word

The use of metaphor necessarily requires that both parties have achieved sufficient verbal efficiency. My special interest is on the problems that start in the preverbal aspect of an individual's life, especially the "missing elements" from the process by which inter-action between infant and caregiver assists the child to move from what Bion (1974) called beta elements of knowing to alpha elements that are more effective in communication. He makes the suggestion that, if in the international scene people were more fluent in alpha language, there could be more diplomatic discussion and fewer aggressive acts.

We are aware today that many adults of the world are deprived and live under rigid regimes. Moreno's best known work is *Who Shall Survive?* (1934) and much of his work was with disadvantaged individuals, be they adults or children or both.

For the individual who has had a tough time, the labels and descriptions used by writers can be unhelpful. Winnicott (1986) would have used the metaphor that an obedient or overcompliant child had a false self, albeit, a self that protests the true self. I believe that this description is incomplete and needs a third metaphor to cover the concept of the adverse experiences of an abused child and the attunements missed in "Not Good Enough Experience Mothering." I designated the missed experience the Black Void. The late George Thomas, from the TA (transactional analysis) and Gestalt therapy fields, referred to the lack of a father figure as a Black Hole (personal communication while I was in training with him). We need yet another metaphor to cover the cumulative trauma of less obvious deprivations and minor abuses. A resilient child may mature prematurely and cope by becoming a "Parentified Child."

In the opposite scenario the spoiled, pampered or overmothered, overfathered child may well be like Peter Pan and never grow up. All or any of these aspects can be displayed and enacted on a psychodrama "stage." The memories from these "difficult" starts to life appear to have an overriding power, in terms of "once bitten, twice shy," or never really forgetting how to ride a bicycle or swim, a sort of rubber-band effect. This is such that, during excess of stress, fatigue, or confusion, the long-term memories emerge, the more recently learned skills being pushed aside by the alarm engendered by "not understanding" and the ensuing adrenaline-flow message to freeze, fight, or flee.

The more that therapeutic work is with the healthy coping neurotic, the less likely are we to depend upon an action method, and the more likely to use direct and crisp communications in a dialogue between the client and the therapist—metaphorical language will be little used. Transactional analysis uses metaphors in terms of ego states, Parent, Adult, and Child—similar to but not the same as Freud's Superego, Ego, and Id. These are used to map the "internal" dialogue of the self. The uses of metaphor with a relaxed recipient client—in its various forms, such as hypnotic processes, narrative therapy, and musical-, art-, and body-therapy approaches—are well-established disciplines, and often effective with the motivated client who is only moderately or temporally dysfunctional. Talking approaches are probably the most utilized aspects of therapy and counseling.

Metaphor is a significant part of our daily use of language, and can be a significant part of the therapeutic process. In real life our ritual greetings are largely metaphorical, and we often have playful or formal "pastime" phrases that we use after the ritual opening. Thereafter we may well involve ourselves with social comment or playful exchanges and may not reach formal adult-to-adult communication.

16.2 *Training in psychodrama*

Psychodrama in Australia and New Zealand has four main subdivisions: role training, sociometry, sociodrama, and psychodrama. In this chapter I will be referring to psychodrama unless I indicate otherwise. An advantage of psychodrama, especially the sociodramatic form, is that we can get ourselves set for "co-creation" with the protagonist, the group members and the producer, working together to find workable creative solutions to problems and disagreements. In our training we talk about *general systems theory*, emphasizing that "any change" can promote "change" in other people and things, even many things. In this sense the drama itself is but a "system."

All branches of psychodrama require that the trainee hold a tertiary qualification in an appropriate subject, and have many hours of supervised training and experience. Those who are already trained in psychological and pastoral disciplines and counseling techniques may find that they need a shorter time before they can complete the requirements.

The first written requirement is about work with a single patient using a format developed by Moreno known as a Social Atom. We have codes for recording this, somewhat like strip cartoons. After this trainees write a thesis. During this period they have a contract with a "primary trainer," and may take supervision with any suitable and available practitioner, preferably another trainer.

When the thesis is accepted trainees will produce a session for ninety minutes in front of two or three examiners. Those who have achieved a "practicing certificate" are expected to undertake ongoing supervision and training. Yet further training is required before trainers are granted certification as a TEP (trainer, educator, and practitioner) and they, too, are expected to go to at least one residential training-for-trainers workshop of three to five days, to comply with the ongoing supervisory requirements of their primary discipline, to involve themselves with the work of their local training institute and to attend the annual conference.

The more that we work alongside the "sad, the mad, the had and the bad," the more we will need to tune into their irrational beliefs and denials and voids in language and experience, and forge a means of communicating with them. Franks stated that warm, well-intentioned listening is perhaps 50 percent of the benefit of a therapy session. The challenge comes when client or therapist realizes that significant change is required. There are two aspects to this: the actual behavior, when the client is alone, in a dyad, a threesome, or a larger group; and the individual's internal experience. Some people tend to treat their internal stress, depression, or anxiety by "self-medication" with alcohol, tobacco, and/or caffeine, or to consult their doctor for prescribed medication. A surprising number will take banned substances, risking legal proceedings, as well as uncertainty about dosage and contamination and addiction. It is becoming more accepted that counseling has its place after any stressful and challenging experience.

Psychodrama focuses not so much on counseling and support as on "change" and "growth" and "development" and "creativity."

16.3 A psychodrama session

A session is often over an hour long. Our metaphor for opening each session is "warm-up." The focus of the warm-up is on the group members, why they have come to group, and what they hope to achieve. A "leader-focused" warm-up is sometimes used. We emphasize safety and confidentiality. When contributions are made by group members, the leader may respond by inviting the speaker to "concretize" the ideas involved. Sometimes this will be a concrete object such as a brick wall, but may be something intangible, such as "my bad luck" or "the fear I experienced" or "what my guts told me." We tend to keep our metaphors, as in transactional analysis, to a noun and a descriptive word. The TA jargon refers mainly to ego states (Parent, Adult, Child) with descriptions such as "Nurturing or Critical Parent," "Computer," "Pathos and Ethos Adult," "Little Professor," "Natural and Adapted and even Vengeful Child." In psychodrama we refer to roles, and use words that point to whether or not the roles are underdeveloped, overdeveloped, absent, or dysfunctional. We might talk of an Angry Teacher, a Frightened Schoolboy, or an Arrogant Bully. Williams in *Forbidden Agendas* (1991) notes that in psychodrama we use mainly "overt metaphors" such as a "brick wall between me and my husband." We are less likely to use long, descriptive, goal-oriented metaphors as described by the Lanktons in *Tales of Enchantment* (1989), at least in the early stages of a drama.

Once the group is "warmed-up," the leader will endeavor to find which group member is most warmed up in terms of working to change or to grow, and then warm up the rest of the group members to that person, their theme or objective, and invite them to be the "protagonist" for the group. This is followed by a short dialogue aimed at identifying the relevant scene or the time (past, present, or future) for the ensuing enactment. When possible, we define the objectives and what is necessary as in the Gouldings' "redecision model" (1997). When a tight contract is not obtained we encourage the protagonist to set the scene, a process that assists the individual's recall. The main work follows with the protagonist choosing group members, now known as auxiliaries, to be part of their scene, and then to become the characters in the drama. Role reversing is directed when the protagonist asks a question. If auxiliaries are not available, we will use a chair or a cushion. Moreno often used *trained* auxiliaries. The producer can use many "tools," such as asking the protagonist to maximize or minimize any aspect of the work (and we have techniques to make aggressive and sexual enactments safe). A valuable feature is to be able to "bring on stage" people who are deceased, inanimate objects such as the TV set, or concepts such as "the power of evil" and the "power of suggestion."

We frequently have several scenes. We may start with what happened last week. The protagonist may say, "This keeps happening," and the producer will ask, "When did this happen first?" When this is identified the opening scene is cleared and the new scene is set.

Metaphor is sometimes considered to be about identifying affinities, but in our dramas we are likely to identify and display the differences and blockages, and then investigate their interaction. One function of a warm-up is to establish a sense of a safe place for exploration of dysfunctional events of the past, as well as a "play area." Then the "bad objects," the real and unreal hazards, and our reactions to those hazards are represented by auxiliaries or "props." The auxiliaries are given time to "derole" at the conclusion. Williams (1991) described how we often define our reality in terms of metaphors and then behave as though the metaphors were fact. These metaphors can be information givers, or information hiders.

A brick wall may be a valid problem—like the Berlin wall—or it may represent an idea that, using "as-if," can be made to disappear, having been merely a representation of "feeling scared to death," being fearful of an armed authority figure, or being fearful of an out-of-control parent. We can explore the "future," such as what might happen at a job interview. If a protagonist opens by talking about a brick wall between him and his partner, we would expect most directors to use either chairs or a row of auxiliaries to represent the brick wall. Then the protagonist is invited to become that brick wall or part of that wall, and he gets a glimpse of how he is seen or heard or felt by his partner. That may leave him less inhibited, and able to develop his own development in the next scene. Sometimes people's personal dramas are reminiscent of Dickens's *A Christmas Carol*—and the Spirit of Christmas Past or Christmas Future—or other classical stories. Useful metaphors about survival in my childhood were to be found in *The Count of Monte Cristo*, *Robinson Crusoe*, and *Tom Brown's Schooldays*.

Drama is a way of clarifying "cognitive dissonance" and displaying the factors involved in being stuck, being at an impasse, being on the horns of a dilemma. I find in supervising health workers that this is a useful way for them to deal with the ongoing tension between service to patients and the finance available; or between compliance and individuality by the clients. The use of metaphors is a means of attempting to find a bridge between the dissonant concepts.

Some people define a metaphor as a novel representation of something old. I do not see why we should restrict its use to the "old." The objective of therapy is growth, development, creation, research, and the development of something new, so the past and the future are both involved. Catharsis or abreaction is sometimes sought in psychodrama, but mainly as a step toward reaching a catharsis of integration. Unlike the theater, opera, ballet, and other "entertainment" modalities, psychodrama is never rehearsed, and each drama or vignette is "written" largely by the protagonist.

"Hypnosis" and "trance states" are words rarely heard in psychodrama training, and not mentioned in the training manual. We endeavor first to have the protagonists access their own ideas, their own creative genius. If they get stuck and the drama ceases to flow, the producer may provide metaphors. Our metaphor for that role is "therapeutic guide." We also have the roles of Spontaneous Actor, and Artistic Producer. Sometimes we invite members of the group to enact suggestions. Sometimes we deliberately use a guided metaphor in a guided phantasy. More usually we would watch for gestures or posturing or eye movements and alert the protagonist to what we have seen, and invite him to "put words to what you are experiencing" or "put words to what your hands are telling you." We refer to this approach of encouraging the protagonists to find their own solutions as spontaneity, that is, a new solution to an old problem or an appropriate response to a new problem. When a protagonist has achieved a shift in his role or their script, we usually have a final scene or role test, which, apart from the safety and feasibility aspects, helps to re-enforce any new insights achieved by the protagonist. The final stage is sharing, in which the group members share with the protagonist their own experience during the drama. If need be, the auxiliaries derole themselves from challenges they faced during the drama.

16.4 *It's never too late to learn to play*

Winnicott, Bowlby, Guntrip, Klein, and Fairbairn (see Guntrip, 1973) are among the many therapists who have written about therapy with dysfunctional adults, suggesting that their problem is often rooted in the "pre-oedipal," preverbal usually dyadic period of life. I was born before many of their seminal works were published.

I was expected to be totally obedient until I was 21 (in those days not unusual) and even in the 1960s some women were still expected to promise to "obey" their husbands. I learned to comply with my parents' regime by day and listened to stories of life in the trenches in France at the dinner table; but I had my own private life in bed. I was re-enforced in my attempt to be "myself" and to think for myself by "this above all, to thine own self be true, thou canst not then be false to any man" and the religious notions that I was taught.

Life today is very different, though the "old order" still reigns in fundamentalist families and throughout many of the Islamic regimes. Meanwhile, the tendency for entertainment to be more and more about aggression, crime, and pornography today is being followed by some of the young and not so young, as they attempt to enact what they have seen on the screen. "Copycat" crimes often surfaced during my forensic work.

My background of Balint groups, based on the work of Bion (1974), followed by psychoanalysis has ensured that I am comfortable with metaphors such as "the unconscious" and the "conscious mind." The behaviorist approaches tend to minimize the possibility of "unconscious" activity. Words such as "metapsychology" and many other ideas have been discussed in recent years, but metaphors have been part of religion and philosophy for centuries. Berne, in "What Do You Say After You Say Hello?" (1973), suggested that metaphors are used when the scene or context of our communications is changed.

The Lanktons (1989) suggest that we can use metaphors to help others change their lives. When we are with our clients, we need to identify if the client is warmed up to "listening" to our metaphors. Any form of interaction can be used, but for the severely dysfunctional individual such as the schizoid types described in *Transactional Analysis Journal* of January 2001 even the well-motivated client may withdraw if we make a suggestion for which he is not yet ready. If, however, we choose the right moment we may help him to claim some hope and respect for himself. I find it useful to hold on to my own metaphor of having a "wastepaper basket" by my side, and allow any unsuccessful response or intervention on my part, as it were, to drop silently into it!

16.5 Empathy and attunement

TA uses diagrams featuring circles divided radially, or circles within circles, labeled Parent, Adult, and Child, together with the OK or non-OK descriptions. These are useful for those who prefer a visual to an auditory representational system. Freud refers to metaphors in his *Jokes and Their Relation to the Unconscious* (1963).

In our clinical work using psychodrama we tend to "stream" our clients: women only; men only; A and D cases; business and managers; trainee nurses; therapy trainees.

All these treatment regimes are complex multifactoral activities and difficult to fit into a linear, on-and-off, direct cause-and-effect paradigm. The "scientific approach" is attempted by the behaviorist schools and their search for measurable treatment outcomes. The medical professions require double-blind tests for pharmaceuticals. However, it seems unlikely that "scientific" proof about the use of metaphor will be forthcoming.

Despite this lack of "scientific proof," I believe that metaphor continues to be a large part of our life at home, in our professional, commercial, political, and entertainment activities of life, and does have a high potential for healing.

16.6 Commentary (by RB)

Psychodrama is obviously a structured and systematic way of using drama to help people in distress. It takes skill and experience to "direct" a psychodrama. Yet these are playlets about the central protagonist's life, and these playlets are enacted in real time with the client's participation in many roles. It permits the client not only "to see ourselves as others see us," but also to live as *both* how others see us and we see ourselves. These psychodramas can be powerful change agents for *all* participants living through the client's as-if world. Stories are enacted, and told and retold.

Chapter 17

Guided Metaphor for Healing

17.1 Introduction

The presumption in using psychotherapy for healing is that the mind can have profound effects on how you *feel* and *think* about what is going on in your life, particularly about physical ailments. Recall the distinction made earlier between a *disease*, which is the physical manifestation of something that is wrong with the body, and *illness*, which is how you feel about the disease, that is, what it *means* to you. Diseases are *cured*, i.e. the physical problem goes away. Illnesses are *healed*, which means that you now feel comfortable and at ease and settled. Healing is in the realm of the mental, the spiritual, the religious—it is *meaningful*. The fascinating thing that LeShan (1989) and Spiegel et al. (1989) found in their work was that, frequently, healing (via psychotherapy or support groups) was accompanied by some degree of significant improvement in the disease. That is, healing can and does have physical effects as well as spiritual ones. Healing does not necessarily result in physical improvement, but neither do standard medical interventions such as surgery, radiation, and chemotherapy. People are rather individual in their responses to medical and mental processes.

Is there a difference between guided imagery and guided metaphor? In individual guided-imagery work (see, e.g., Battino (2000)) a healing metaphor is developed collaboratively with the client, i.e. the client's metaphor uniquely matches her. In generic guided-imagery work, a healing image, such as healing light, is presented with vague and open-ended language designed to let the listener fill in personally relevant details. A guided metaphor is developed collaboratively, but specifically utilizes the client's *story* of her life as well as her personalized healing metaphor. Thus, a guided metaphor for healing incorporates a narrative element.

Before an outline of the elements of a guided-metaphor session, those for guided imagery are presented as a review.

Components of a guided-imagery session

1. Elicit the client's healing image.

2. Elicit the client's special healing haven.

3. Introduction and relaxation: 5–7 min.

4. Transition to healing haven: 1–2 min.

5. Delivery of guided imagery: 8–10 min.

6. Affirmations and suggestions for continuance: 1–2 min.

7. Closing and reorientation: 1–2 min.

8. Overall session: 15–20 min.

17.2 Elements of guided metaphor for healing

Everybody grows up with healing and curing stories that they have learned and incorporated from family and friends. Some of these stories are legends within the family or the neighborhood. There may be traditional routes to healing and curing that are part of the ethnic group or religion. In designing a guided metaphor it is important to know of these stories, and the depth of the client's belief in the stories. These stories control the way that a person goes about helping herself, and also the extent of her involvement in this work. If the story in your family is that all cancer is painful and terminal, then that influences the outcome. If your family story is that all Smith men die young of a heart attack, or die "with their boots on," or never show pain, or are survivors, or are fighters, or are weaklings when ill, or ..., guess how they will approach the diagnosis of a life-challenging disease. An atheist approaches death differently from someone who believes in heaven and hell, or in reincarnation. In a sense, *all* of metaphor-related work is *cross-*

cultural, even if you think you grew up in the same sub-sub-sub-culture. The more of this cross-cultural knowledge you have about your client, the better.

With this in mind, the following is an outline for guided-metaphor work for healing.

1. Gather information
The following questions are the starting point:

    a. Why me?

    b. Why now?

    c. Why this particular disease?

    d. Why am I doing better or poorer or staying the same at this time?

    e. What options do I believe I have?

    f. How much more time do I believe I have?

    g. How capable am I of coping?

    h. Will I break down?

    i. What do I believe about this disease and its likely course?

    j. What does my family, spouse, friends, religion, culture say about this disease?

The answers to these questions involve a soul-searching that will undoubtedly be difficult. The questions are put gently and with much concern, and need not all be asked at one time. The list is comprehensive—as a therapist you need a *sufficient* amount of information to design an intervention. This process should take 15–30 minutes with the interviewer taking notes.

2. The healing metaphor(s)

With the information gathered, the client is asked:

    a. Please summarize the story of how you got to this point briefly in five to ten sentences.

    b. Please boil that down to one sentence.

    c. Assuming you could describe yourself in a word or two, what would that be?

    d. Thinking over the story of your life to this time, how would you change that story so you would be the way you want to be now?

    e. From this point forward, how would you change your evolving life's story? What would be different so that you become who you want to be? What will be the form of these changes? What particular healing images do you sense would work for you? What is your new story?

    f. Please tell me your new story briefly in a few sentences.

    g. Please summarize your new story in a sentence.

    h. Please choose a word or two to describe yourself in your new story.

Use the client's healing metaphor(s) and changing story to devise a guided-healing metaphor.

3. Delivery of the guided-healing metaphor

This follows the standard steps of:

    a. Relaxation.

    b. Going within the mind to a safe haven that is a personal healing place.

c. Telling sufficient parts of the old story to establish connection, followed by the telling of the new healing story with much detail to make it compelling and appealing. The client's special words and phrases and sentences—the self-descriptives used by the client—are woven into this new story. Wordplay and confusion and the use of grammatical tense are all employed to convincingly establish the new story as a *fait accompli*. This is *the client's* story you are telling.

d. Compliments, affirmations, and continuity. The client is complimented on her courage in confronting her old story and creating a new one; affirmations are given about the appropriateness of the new story in the client's present life and social context; statements are made about how the new story will be the continuing new pattern for the client's life, and with a built-in capacity to adapt and change.

e. Re-entry. The client is reoriented to the present time and place and thanked for her courage and trust.

This is a client-generated approach, as in Metaphor Therapy and guided metaphor. As such, there is an implicit belief on the part of the therapist that the client already has the resources to find creative solutions to her concerns, whether they be mental or physical. The therapist mainly serves as a *guide*.

17.3 Generic healing metaphors

In addition to the client-generated healing metaphor as utilized in guided metaphor, there are a number of general healing metaphors that can be suggested to the client. "Some of my clients use an image of ____ as a healing metaphor. Others have used ____ or ____." The client may adapt one of these metaphors to her own circumstances, or simply like a general image that actually has a highly specific meaning for her.

The following are some possible adaptable generic healing metaphors—they are essentially self-explanatory:

• magician, wizard, magic potion, magic, miracle, ceremony

- relative—mother (usually), father, uncle, aunt, grandparent, older sibling, cousin
- healing hands, healing light, healing music
- healing presence—angel, god, goddess, Jesus, saint, Holy Spirit, power animal, pet, nurse, doctor, teacher, guru, spirit, psychotherapist, benevolent alien, character from fiction or the movies or television or cartoons or history
- prayer, faith
- Nature in any manifestation or location, Gaia

There are obviously many choices to build upon. But, even if a client selects one of these general healing metaphors, it needs to be adapted to the client and her circumstances.

17.4 Two case examples

Some background information is given for each case to set the stage. I worked with Jeri a few years ago and I have permission from her widower to use her name and some elements of her story. As of the present writing, I am working with Dorothea and have her permission to base the case study on parts of her life. Many details have been altered, though.

Jeri's angels and Indians

Background—Jeri had lung cancer and was a recovering alcoholic and a regular attendee at AA meetings. She was in her second marriage and had a slew of children and grandchildren in the blended family. She was one tough lady with lots of fire and laughter and spirit. She was also quite religious. She might have told her story as, "Led a hard life with many ups and downs, good kids, and a lot of love." I expect she would have described herself as a "warrior angel." I suspect her changed story would have included much quality time with her husband, her family, and being there for her AA friends.

In our early guided-imagery work she used a group of healing angels until one day, when she said that the angels were not sufficient and she needed something much stronger. This turned out to be her own tribe of fierce Indians, who were ruthless trackers and fighters. At the beginning of each session I would ask her whom she wanted that day—sometimes it was angels, sometimes Indians, and sometimes both. Jeri died peacefully about eleven months after we started working together—this was about two to three times longer than her doctor's prognosis, and I have no way of knowing what our work contributed to that. After all, she was a warrior angel! Here are Jeri's stories as I would tell them now:

Hello, Jeri. We'll start as usual with your paying attention to your breathing. Just noticing each breath as it comes in, and goes out. Slowly, easily, naturally. Just one breath at a time. Your time now, with nothing at all to bother you or disturb you. Any little background sounds that you hear will help you to be even more comfortable. If any stray thoughts should wander through, notice them, thank them for being there, and simply go back to paying attention to your breathing. Enjoy the way your familiar couch and cushions support and relax you, finding, perhaps, an even more comfortable position. Your time now, your healing time.

And now, within your mind, just drifting easily off to your safe healing place, that quiet serene place, your personal shrine. Enjoy its familiar surroundings, sights, odors. Your place. And almost on the wings of a soft gentle breeze comes the sounds of your angels nearing, laughing, singing, joy, serenity—your healing angels. And with a whisper of wings they are with you, each with an assigned task, softly melting, fusing, merging with your body. And you can feel their presence within you, can you not? At all of those places that need their healing love, their ministrations, gently persuading those old weak cancer cells to go away, to vanish, to disappear, just as fast as your body can remove the debris. And they are special warrior angels fighting for you in their gentle ways. Some of the angels are restoring, reconstructing, rejuvenating, rebuilding, reconnecting angels, each with her own rehabilitative strengths. Your healing angels.

And while they continue to do their work Chief Fire-in-the-Sky and his fierce warriors ride in. They have already sent in their scouting party and know just where, all the places, to attack straight on, or where to ambush a particularly resistant group of cells. Sensing, feeling the warriors move within you, scalping, spearing, destroying the enemy cells without mercy—your Indian warriors. And Chief Fire-in-the-Sky rains down arrows and destruction, a firewater washing all those unwanted cells away, a water fire clearing and cleansing and preparing the way for your healing angels.

And there is joy here, and rejoicing, and song and love, and the wonder of family, your family, with you, around you, you with them, them with you, happiness, helping each other to live and learn and grow. And mother, grandmother, wife Jeri is there for them as angel, as warrior, as angel warrior, as protector, continuing her life with them, for them, for herself, too.

And you know that this work of your healing angels and Chief Fire-in-the-Sky and his tribe will continue and continue and continue. They leave for now, and will return whenever you need them, as you need them, being there for you whenever you close your eyes and take a few deep breaths.

Jeri, thank you for letting me spend this time with you and your angels and Indians. You are indeed a warrior angel and an angelic warrior. Whenever you are ready, just take a few deep breaths, blink your eyes, and come back to this room. Thank you.

The preceding is one example of a healing guided metaphor. In the delivery, of course, there would be many pauses, and certain words and phrases would be emphasized.

Dorothea's Thea-ology

Shortly after her fiftieth birthday, Thea (her preferred name) was diagnosed with breast cancer. As one of my former students in guided imagery and the wife of an old friend and colleague, she, with her husband, sought me out for assistance. They have two grown daughters; the married one has a child. Thea was brought up as a Catholic; her husband Larry is strongly Jewish, but not orthodox. Their daughters were raised in the Jewish faith. Thea wears a cross on a chain. She has retired from active work as a counselor.

When asked about her hopes and dreams, what she wanted to do with the rest of her life, what would give it meaning, she responded that she wished to return to being a practicing Catholic and to use her skills in volunteer pastoral work. Her brief life story is: born and raised Catholic, happy childhood, fulfilling marriage to a Jewish man, loves her children and grandchild, completed a satisfactory career as a counselor, and now ready for giving back via volunteer pastoral counseling work. Larry is very supportive. She is finding her way to being a "Thea-logian." Here is the guided metaphor for healing that we developed together:

> Hello, Thea. This is the special healing tape we talked about. It repeats on the second side. Please be sure to be in a comfortable quiet place where you will not be disturbed for the next fifteen minutes or so. This is your time, a time for healing. This is your continuing story. You can start as usual with paying attention to your breathing, noticing each breath as it comes in, belly and chest softly rising. And, with each exhale, a release, with belly and chest easily relaxing. Just one breath at a time, your time now, with nothing to bother or disturb you. And, if a stray thought wanders through, notice it, thank it for being there, and go back to observing your breaths. Softly, easily, naturally. Just let any background noise help you relax even more. Your time, your story.
>
> And within your mind you can just drift off to the special safe healing place that is uniquely yours. Enjoy being there—the peace, the calm, the odors, the sounds, the sights, being among familiar things. And, as of old, the Holy Spirit is with you at this time. Sensing it there with you, around you, in you. That calm and reassurance of old, being immersed in the safety of your spiritual roots. Creating your own Thea-ology, with its special meanings of old, with its new meanings, transformations, transcending and transcendental, being, just being with the Central Being, the One, the Holy, the Holy Healing Spirit. Sensing the power of that all-encompassing love and caring, moving wherever in your body you need its healing spirit, power, action. Cleansing, cleaning, clearing, eliminating. Rebuilding and strengthening. Empowering and making more efficient your own immune system so that it can continue and continue to do this healing/curing work whenever you need it, and as you need it. Automatically.

The Holy Spirit is with you as you begin to live through this next chapter of your life. Developing and creating your new story of volunteer pastoral counseling, within the church of your heritage. Such an interesting new Thea-ology. Giving back and receiving, forgiving and being forgiven. A time for new stories and parables growing naturally out of your life. Finding joy with Larry, and family and friends and those you work with. Touching and being touched, loving and being loved, laughter, accomplishment, peace. Returning home to your new/old home.

Just one breath, one moment, one experience at a time. This precious breath, this precious moment, this interesting experience.

And I want to thank you for your trust and letting me share in your dream, your life, being curious as to how it will unfold, develop, grow. Thea and her Thea-ology. Yes. Yes. Yes.

And whenever you are ready, you can simply blink your eyes, stretch, and return to this room. Thank you.

Everyone is so unique, so special. I had always thought that Thea was Jewish. Her emergence into her own way of living was a surprise and a reward. Once again, there is the discovery of a central humanity, a genuine person, without the labels. Thank you, Thea.

17.5 Summary

There are many routes to personal healing. This chapter has presented one. It is always important to work within belief systems and design interventions with and for a unique individual. Imagination and belief and faith are powerful change agents. Always having hope and believing in miracles is a basic element of helping others. Is the placebo effect involved in this work? Of course—yet there is no need to single it out. Perhaps you will find your own healing angels, or Indians, or Thea-ology …

Chapter 18

Preparation for Surgery and Other Interventions

18.1 Introduction

Modern surgical procedures are among the wonders of our times, with complex operations such as organ transplants, hip replacements, heart bypass procedures, and the removal of brain tumors being done routinely and with excellent success rates. We all know people whose lives have been extended and improved by surgery. There is generally little to fear, even though we all read and sign those "informed-consent" forms that relate all of the possible difficulties for a particular surgery. Yet many people fear surgery, an invasion of their body, the loss of a body part, and the potentially painful recovery period. In these fears we may be the victims of all of the stories that we've heard, and the ones we've written for ourselves.

Preparation for surgery and other physically invasive interventions (chemotherapy, colonoscopy, angiograms, endoscopic work, dialysis etc.) has been found to be quite helpful. The ways I prepare people for surgery are described in Chapter 10 of my book on guided imagery (Battino, 2000, pp. 149–62). This preparation is done in collaboration with the client so that the helpful imagery, the safe haven to dissociate to, and other details are his. This preparation work then becomes his new story of how he will get through the surgery experience. Ideally, the client will accept the posthypnotic suggestions built into the delivery to effectively go into trance, and be pleasantly dissociated for the entire experience from entering the hospital to returning home. In this section some of the relevant literature will be reviewed. The next section gives details on the methods of preparation for surgery, including a letter to the surgeon. A sample script is presented.

Judith B. Petry, M.D., in an article entitled, "Surgery and Complementary Therapies: A Review" (Petry, 2000), has summarized the available literature on the use of complementary therapies in surgery. Petry examined the following with respect to improving surgical outcome: relaxation techniques, hypnosis and suggestion, imagery, acupuncture, therapeutic touch, Reiki, music, massage therapy, and herbs and supplements. Of these, the reported effects of hypnosis and suggestion in surgical patients:

- decreased hospital stay
- decreased sedation/narcotic requirement
- decreased intra- and postoperative pain
- decreased patient interference with surgery
- decreased postoperative anxiety
- decreased postoperative nausea and vomiting
- decreased postoperative complications
- decreased blood loss
- decreased time to return to gastrointestinal function
- increased patient satisfaction
- increased surgeon satisfaction
- effected more stable intraoperative vital signs

Hypnosis and suggestion appeared to be the most effective of the complementary therapies. Imagery was useful, but Petry stated (2000, p. 68), "… it is debatable whether it is different from hypnosis." To accurately report Petry's work, her summary (2000, p. 73) is cited:

> Improvement in surgical outcome measures including anxiety, blood loss, postoperative pain levels, pain medication requirements, postoperative nausea and vomiting, recovery of bowel function, length of hospital stay, cost of care, and patient satisfaction have been documented in a variety of studies—some well controlled—using relaxation techniques, hypnosis/suggestion, and imagery. Effects of these and other complementary therapies on immune function, stress hormone levels, and wound healing are suggested by some studies, but require more careful investigation. Further research into the mechanism of action and specific physiologic changes in relation to surgery attributable to the complementary therapies discussed in this paper is needed to clarify their role in the surgical setting.

The article by Bank (1985) is specifically on the use of hypnosis for controlling bleeding in the angiography suite, but it also contains references for controlling bleeding, anesthesia, blood pressure, skin temperature, salivation and heart rate. The use of hypnosis for these purposes is well documented, and is related to metaphoric work.

Enqvist and Fischer (1997) report on the use of preoperative hypnotic techniques and their abstract states in part:

> Thirty-six patients in the control group were compared to 33 patients in the experimental group. Anxiety before the operation increased significantly in the control group but remained at base-line level in the experimental group. Postoperative consumption of analgesics was significantly reduced in the experimental group compared to the control group.

The above-cited studies show that preoperative hypnotic and suggestive work can have profound beneficial effects on anxiety, rate of healing, and the use of medications. This means that it makes sense to do hypnotic/suggestive/guided-imagery/metaphoric work with surgery patients. Details on preparing people for surgery are in the next section. A special letter for surgeons is in the following section, and a sample script ends this chapter.

18.2 Preparing for surgery

Generally, preparation for surgery—this is similar for other medical procedures—involves two sessions. The first session starts with an exploration of previous experiences with surgery. What was the client's reaction and how did he feel about it then? Does he feel differently now? What is he *telling* himself about the upcoming surgery and the outcomes and recuperation? Knowing what he knows now, how would he change the story about the planned surgery so he would get through it in the most comfort, and with the most rapid recovery? It is explained that there are two parts to this preparation work: (1) preparation of a tape designed to put the client into a relaxed and dissociated state for the procedure, along with suggestions for comfort and rapid recovery; and (2) a letter to his surgeon suggesting that he/she (or someone in the operating room, such as the anesthetist) make positive and healing state-ments to him during the actual surgery.

Since I am a practicing hypnotherapist, my approach is based on hypnosis. The basic concept is to provide posthypnotic suggestions for the client to go into a dissociated or trance state from a time of his choosing (e.g. on the way to the hospital, during the pre-op preparation time) until his arrival at home or whenever he feels comfortable after the operation. His preferred story for this is elicited—where would he like to go within his mind for the dura-tion, and what would he be doing there? Details of this safe haven are requested and a narrative for his sojourn is created. Time dis-tortion is built in so that his "time away" will be stretched out, while the actual hospital experience is compressed. In effect, the experience will appear dreamlike. He is also instructed to respond appropriately to requests made by hospital staff, and conversation with family and friends.

The audio tape usually runs about thirty minutes, and is repeated on the second side. It is suggested that he listen to the tape once or twice each day for one to two weeks before the surgery. The five components of the tape and individual sessions are:

1. induction and relaxation

2. preoperation experience

3. during the operation

4. postoperative recovering period

5. returning home and to normal functioning

This is done at the end of the first session, usually in a shortened form of about twenty minutes. The client is asked if anything should be changed before making the tape. He is given the tape several days before the second session.

At the second session, feedback is obtained on the content of the tape, and information on anything that has changed in the client's life. There is another delivery of the content of the tape, but generally the client is encouraged to do the induction and relaxation on his own for practice and confidence. Some details about the five parts of the tape follow:

1. Induction and relaxation
The simpler, the better, usually focusing on breathing. The client is instructed to just do this relaxation portion on his own for five to ten minutes whenever he feels the need. No more than five minutes is spent on this part.

2. Preoperative experience
Within the client's mind the preoperation experience begins at a time of his choosing—be it the night before (or earlier), the morning of the surgery when entering the hospital, or when the pre-op preparation is begun by the nurses. The suggestions at this time are to "drift off to your safe haven," enjoy being there, observe from time to time what is going on "over there" where he is in competent hands, and to respond appropriately. This is the beginning of the dissociation.

3. During the operation
Three things are provided here. The first is continued enjoyment of the safe haven while competent and skilled and caring "things" are going on "over there." The second is time distortion: long internal time versus short external time. The third is the helping, healing, and comforting statements made by the surgeon or anesthetist.

4. Postoperative recovery period
This is generally in three parts: recovery room, hospital room, and home recuperation. The dissociation and time distortion continue with suggestions for comfort (but requesting whatever medications are needed), healing, rapid recovery, and rapid return to bowel functions if there was abdominal surgery. In fact, he will be "surprised" (as will others!) at how comfortable he is, how few medications he needs, and his rapid recovery. Responses are appropriate.

5. Returning home and to normal functioning

It is his choice as to when he returns to normal full awareness to be able to *look back* on this experience. The experience was somewhat like a mildly pleasant dream where all of these other things were happening.

The narrative and metaphoric parts of this as-if experience involving surgery are in the new story of how he has gotten through this experience, and in the "adventures" in his safe haven.

18.3 Hearing under anesthesia and the doctor's letter

There is a significant amount of evidence (Pearson (1961), Cheek (1959, 1960a, 1960b, 1961, 1964, 1965, 1966, 1981), Rossi and Cheek (1998, pp. 113–30), Dubin and Shapiro (1974), Liu, Standen and Aitkenhead (1992), Clawson and Swade (1975), Bank (1985), and Bonke et al. (1986)) that people can hear what is said in an operating room, even under the surgical plane of anesthesia. So it behooves operating-room personnel to be both careful about what they say during procedures and to take the opportunity to say healing and helpful things. Bonke et al. (1986) had the following to say in the summary of their study: "Results showed that exposure to positive suggestions during general anesthesia, as compared with noise or operating theatre sounds, protected patients older than 55 years against prolonged postoperative stay in hospital."

If it appears that the surgeon may be open to making healing statements during surgery, or that he/she may ask the anesthetist to do this, then I send the following letter to the surgeon, or have it hand-delivered at least a few days or a week in advance of the scheduled surgery. The statements are in large type and on a laminated 5" × 8" index card so it can be taken into the operating room. Feel free to adapt the letter and the statements to match the needs of your client and the particular surgery.

Battino Counselling Services

440 Fairfield Pike   (937) 775-2477 (work)
Yellow Springs, Ohio 45387   (937) 767-1854 (home)
October 21, 2001   FAX: (937) 775-2717
                     E-mail: RUBIN.BATTINO@WRIGHT.EDU

Dr. Cynthia Jones
Dayton, Ohio

Dear Dr. Jones:

I am writing this letter on behalf of my friend Dorothea M. She has consulted with me concerning her breast cancer and the kinds of things I can do to help her at this time. I have been working for nine years now as a leader or co-leader of support groups based on Bernie Siegel's principles for people who have life-challenging diseases and those who support them. I do individual work with some of our members which involves teaching them guided imagery for healing, relaxation methods, ways for resolving unfinished business in their lives, and preparing them for surgery and other medical interventions. As to my credentials, I am a licensed professional clinical counselor (LPCC) in Ohio, and a national board certified counselor. I recently authored books on guided imagery and coping skills, co-authored a book on hypnosis and hypnotherapy, and have taught courses for many years for Wright State University's Department of Human Resources (counseling) as an adjunct professor.

There is a great deal of evidence that patients, even under the surgical plane of anesthesia, can hear what is said in the operating room. It is believed that if the surgeon (or a designated person in the operating room) makes encouraging and healing comments directly to the patient during the surgery, that this has a beneficial effect on outcomes and recovery. This has been both my personal experience and the experience of the people I have prepared for surgery. To this end you will find enclosed a brief set of directions and some simple statements that we hope you will be willing to say to Dorothea at appropriate times during the surgery. These statements need to be made only a few times, and should always be prefaced by using Dorothea's name so that she knows the message is directed to her; and ended with a "Thank you," so that she knows the message is over. By the time of the surgery I will have spent some time with Dorothea preparing her for the surgery and the recovery period. She will have an audiotape to listen to in advance of the surgery. She prefers being called Thea. I would certainly be willing to talk with you or your staff about my preparation methods.

Sincerely yours,

Rubin Battino

MS, Mental Health Counseling
Licensed Professional Clinical Counselor (Ohio)
National Board Certified Counselor

copy to D.M.

* * * * *

Dear Dr. Jones:

I would be pleased if you would make the following statements (and/or other relevant statements) to me at appropriate times during my surgery. So that I know you are talking to me, please preface each statement with my name, and end each statement with, "Thank you."

1. Thea—please slow down (or stop) the bleeding where I am working. Thank you.

2. Thea—please relax your muscles in this area. Thank you.

3. Thea—this is going very well. Thank you.

4. Thea—you will heal surprisingly quickly. Thank you.

5. Thea—you will be surprisingly comfortable and at ease after this. Thank you.

6. Thea—your recovery will be very rapid. Thank you.

18.4 Thea's surgery preparation tape

This script was prepared with Thea's assistance so that it matched her needs and story and expectations. Pauses and their duration and words or phrases for marking are not explicitly indicated, except for the use of ellipses for pauses in a number of places. The tape runs about thirty minutes. It is for the reader's guidance in preparing tapes. Thea's safe haven is a tree house in a sturdy old oak tree, but the location of the tree was left open.

Thea's surgery preparation

Thea, this is the special tape I told you I would make for you so that you will be able to go through your upcoming surgery in surprising comfort, and so you will be able to recover as quickly as possible.

Just start with paying attention to your breathing, being sure that you are in a comfortable position ... and that your head and neck are free and easy ... jaw loose and relaxed ... knowing that at any time you can move a little bit to become even more comfortable. Noticing each breath as it enters, and leaves. Belly and chest softly rising, and then relaxing. Your time now, with nothing at all to bother you or concern you. Your time, a special quiet peaceful time. One breath at a time. Perhaps counting your breaths ... one ... two ... three ... four ... five ... and back to one ... two ... easily and simply. Any pattern of numbers. Breathing softly.

And if a stray thought happens to wander through, notice it, thank it, and go back to paying attention to your breathing. One ... and two ... and three ... and back to ... Just one soft easy breath at a time, your time, relaxing even more. That's right. Softly and gently.

And your inner mind will let you know just when it is the right time for you to drift away within your mind, to your own special, safe, and secure, place—your own tree house. This may be the night before, or the morning, or when you enter the hospital, or when they start to prep you. You'll know just when to start paying attention to your breathing, easily counting your breaths, and then just drift away to your tree house. And yet, at the same time, you'll know that you'll be able to respond appropriately to those people who have questions, assist them in any way, so that all of this goes smoothly, comfortably, quickly. And wouldn't they be surprised to know that you were already in your tree house, enjoying being there? One part of your mind is perhaps dealing with all those mechanical details, competently, while you settle down for a nice long stay in your tree house.

And, I don't know exactly what the first thing will be that catches your attention there ... perhaps it is the texture of the tree bark, or the wind gently rustling the leaves, branches swaying lightly, dappled sunlight, a bird singing, maybe one, two, three birds in chorus. The sounds of cicadas calling for mates, the smells of tree and leaf and grass and woodlands. Some clouds floating by, and passing shadows. Your tree house. Just continue to enjoy the peace of being there, and knowing that at this time you are being prepared for the surgery, yet that all seems to be happening somewhere over there. You are so engrossed in where you are, perhaps reading an absorbing book, or sipping a drink, just being in your special place. The time goes so quickly, almost as if the minute hand on the clock were moving as fast as the second hand; and yet, strangely, your time in your tree house seems to go on and on and on, peace, quiet, tranquility.

And then your other mind knows that you're now in the operating room ... while you continue to enjoy the tree house, observing, sensing, being. Perhaps you respond to a comment of the surgeon or anesthetist over there, I don't know who. And now all is really quiet within your body. Being so strongly alive, and yet willing to assist them in any way, so that this experience goes successfully, and rapidly. And I don't know when you become aware of the antics of those squirrels, chattering at each other, playing squirrel tag, jumping, leaping from one branch to another, scurrying sounds, tail sometimes high, stopping still and tall, alert for a moment, and then dashing off. From somewhere near there is the sound of flowing water, rippling, splashing, sparkling, clear clean flow. In the midst of Nature, so pleasant and peaceful.

And Thea, you should know that the procedure is going very rapidly, very well. Thank you. Thea, you should know that you will be recovering from this rapidly, easily, simply faster than you could ever have believed. Thank you. And what is that over there? Two butterflies. What wonderful colors in their wings. Just dancing around each other, fluttering, flitting in the air. And they settle inches from you, so still and calm, resting. Then darting off to find a flower, floating, shimmering in the sun. Iridescent.

And Thea, you know that you'll be very comfortable after this is all over, being able to request whatever medications you need, and yet, surprisingly needing very few, being very comfortable within yourself, knowing that the healing has already started. Your body regenerating, reconstructing, rebuilding, pulling together, healing, knowing just what to do, automatically, without any awareness on your part. So rapid, so simple. Thank you.

Thea, now that the procedure is over you sense somehow, with some deep internal knowledge, that it has been successful. You have been in the care of competent, concerned, and caring professionals all of this time. They have been using their skills at peak efficiency, and that is comforting, isn't it? While you continue enjoying your tree house with its familiar comforts. Perhaps you glance up through the branches of this mighty oak, its roots so solidly embedded in the ground, its thick trunk, old and yet so sturdy. Through the branches bits of sky and cloud, light trickling down, changing patterns of shadows. So entrancing, so peaceful, so quiet. Your time, a safe and a quiet time. Bird song, the sound of insects buzzing on their way, perhaps the rat-a-tat of a woodpecker, a crow's call. And this time, your time, is moving so slowly, slowly in your enjoyment, while that external time out there goes so fast, so very fast.

And, before you know it, that other part of your mind knows that you are in the recovery room, healing continuing, responding appropriately to any comments or questions, aware of who is there and being with them. Yet, at the same time, continuing to be in your tree house, a bit above it all, looking down at the ground, leaves and twigs and grass and flowers. Noticing one plant in particular, marveling at its uniqueness, its form, its colors. One plant and many. Here and there a bee buzzes, gathering pollen, hovering, darting, following its own path, its own destiny, so many byways, so many things, gathered, collected, nourishing. And over there is

309

a shrub, solitary, sturdy, glorying in its size and shape, robust, being in its place in the world.

And soon, you know, in that other part of your mind, that you are now in a regular hospital room, feeling ever so comfortable, asking for what you need, as you need it, and sensing within just how rapidly the healing is going on, mending, rebuilding, connecting, strengthening. Perhaps there are little sensations of warmth or coolness or tingling. I don't know exactly how your body will be speaking to you, Thea, some internal way, letting you know just how fast this is going on, how much you have already been helped by this procedure, looking forward to going home to familiar surroundings, so that you can be both within your mind as you are now, and physically home again.

All of this, all of this is going on within an awareness of comfort, calm, ease, peace, simply and rapidly. And at some point, whenever you choose and it is appropriate to do so, you become aware that time is now again at its regular pace, state. Wondering, just wondering with some surprise, that this episode is already all over, done, and you're home again. Almost like awakening from a dream, one where you've been at peace, calm, where within your mind you have lived and relived many enjoyable and peaceful moments. Your time, this moment, now, so restful, the healing continuing automatically, naturally, rapidly.

And you know that your mind is somewhat like a tape recorder; so you will recall and remember whatever I've said that's helpful, that you need; and you can play those words over and over as you need to in preparation, in wonder, in looking back at how simple and fast this has all been.

Now, when you know in some way inside that it is now OK to be fully conscious and aware of whatever place, whatever way you are, with this all over at this time, will you find yourself taking a deep breath or two, blinking your eyes, stretching a bit, feeling very rested, and yet somehow full of energy? Just come back to this room, here and now. Thea, thank you. Thank you for your trust and letting me spend this time with you. Yes and yes and yes ...

18.5 Summary

There are just too many studies that show that the kinds of psychological supportive preparations discussed in this chapter shorten hospital stays, speed up recovery, and have the patients using less medication, that it is a wonder that this is not routinely done for all surgical procedures (and other interventions). Both the "cost" to the patient and those to society are decreased—insurance companies should find this work to be cost-effective. Some of this, of course, is making its way into our medical systems. More needs to be done. The story of a hospital stay can be rewritten, shortened, and with a happier ending.

Chapter 19

Metaphors for Meaning and Spirituality

19.1 Introduction

One of the features of talks by Bernie Siegel and Carl Hammerschlag is the recounting of tales of heroism of people they know or have read about. Bernie's stories tend to be about people who have survived various cancers and are now in long-term remission. He also talks about the incredible spirit and will to live he has found in paraplegics and quadriplegics, and even those on total life support. Carl tells stories and shows pictures. One I recall was of a mountain climber who lost both of his legs after being caught in a freak storm and then rescued. After a long recuperation, this young man went back to mountain climbing with the use of artificial legs. These true stories provide models and hope and inspiration for the listener; these heroes and heroines are not fictional, they are real. If they can do it, and have done it, then it is *possible* for any of us faced by disastrous events.

We read biographies and autobiographies and see movies of true-life stories, and we are uplifted by the spirit and courage of the heroes and heroines. Some may find such real-life stories intimidating: how could *I*, an ordinary person, do such things? What would I do when suddenly faced with tragedy? Do I have the strength, the willpower, the faith to see me through? We can speculate endlessly on how we would respond. Yet I have written elsewhere about the universal response of people I know—who were "ordinary" until disaster struck—who have stated about having cancer, "You know, this has been a blessing." Paradoxical? Startling? Unexpected? Yes. Then they go on to explain that the cancer (or other serious disease) has resulted in their being more alive, more in love, more aware than in their "routine" lives, which they were living rather mechanically. Now, each moment, each

313

breath, each touch and smile, were consciously and intensely lived. We all have that capability, we all have a choice in how we respond to the seeming capriciousness of life.

Children are always looking for role models. Their first are their parents. Then there may be older siblings and teachers. There are always the heroes and heroines in books and TV and movies. There are even ritualized fantastical "superheroes," as if ordinary heroes were not sufficient! For many children sports stars become role models. When I was younger, politicians were frequently looked up to.

For many it is religious figures who are revered and respected as role models. They are often examples of selflessness and sacrifice and faith and compassion and love. There are many saints and historical figures, priest and rabbi, minister, imam, and guru. In recent times Albert Schweitzer, Mahatma Gandhi, and Mother Theresa inspired millions. You do not have to look far to see that same spark of selfless humanity in all of us.

There are many real-life stories that can be incorporated into a meaningful metaphor. The ones you choose to tell your client need to connect with her in terms that fit in with her belief system. Tailor the tale to the person. Be sure to reframe by telling her how much courage she has already exhibited in coming to see you, or in facing her challenges. Some nasty comedian has said that you can never be a heroic figure to your spouse or grown children. Not true. That is both part of my personal belief system and my observation.

In the next two sections I will recount briefly the stories of two of my heroes: Professor Viktor E. Frankl and Gerald Mawson, Ph.D.

19.2 Professor Viktor E. Frankl

You can read Frankl's autobiography (1997) for his description of his life. The book he wrote about his concentration-camp experiences (1984) has a final section on logotherapy. An authorized biography has been written by Klingberg (2001), and it is well worth reading. Frankl's most acclaimed book is *Man's Search for Meaning* (1984), which has sold over nine million copies and been translated into more than twenty languages. How can a book that is mostly about his three years in Nazi concentration camps during World War II be so popular? The book tells the story of his unwavering faith in people and in life, and expresses his philosophy of life. In essence, his philosophy, which has sustained millions of people, is relatively simple: we may have no control over certain hardships that life seems to give out in somewhat capricious ways, but we always have the *choice* of *how we respond* to those challenges. One example is the actor Christopher Reeve, who became a quadriplegic in a freak horse-riding accident. Somehow, he has worked out ways to be alive each day, and even to continue acting. Frankl's achievement was in retaining his humanity while surviving the hells of those concentration camps. He was also lucky on a number of occasions—random events and choices contributed to his survival. He started young, as indicated in this quotation from his autobiography (1997, p. 56):

> When I was 15 or 16 I gave a lecture there; the subject was "The Meaning of Life." Even at that early age I had developed two basic ideas. First, it is not we who should ask for the meaning of life, since it is we who *are being asked*. It is we ourselves who must answer the questions that life asks of us, and to these questions we can respond only by being responsible for our existence.

> The other basic idea I developed in my early years maintains that the ultimate meaning is, and must remain, beyond our comprehension. There exists something I have called "supra meaning," *but not in the sense of something supernatural*. In this we can only believe. In this we must believe. Even if only unconsciously, essentially we all do believe in it.

> It must have been at that time, at the same age, that one Sunday I was on one of my typical walks through the streets of Vienna. At a certain spot on Tabor Street, I pondered what I almost might call a hymn-like thought: *Blessed be fate, believed be meaning.*

> By this I meant that, whatever we have to go through, life must have ultimate meaning, a supra meaning. This supra meaning we cannot comprehend, we can only have faith in it. In the last analysis this was only a rediscovery of Spinoza's *amor fati*—the love of fate.

The following are a few quotations from *Man's Search for Meaning* (1984) with a page reference at the end of each:

We who lived in concentration camps can remember the men who walked through the huts comforting others, giving away their last piece of bread. They may have been few in number, but they offer sufficient proof that everything can be taken from a man but one thing: the last of the human freedoms—to choose one's attitude in any given set of circumstances, to choose one's own way.

And there were always choices to make. Every day, every hour, offered the opportunity to make a decision, a decision which determined whether you would or would not submit to those powers which threatened to rob you of your very self, your inner freedom; which determined whether or not you would become the plaything of circumstance, renouncing freedom and dignity to become molded into the form of the typical inmate ... [p. 75]

If there is a meaning in life at all, then there must be a meaning in suffering. Suffering is an ineradicable part of life, even as fate and death. Without suffering and death human life cannot be complete.

The way in which a man accepts his fate and all the suffering it entails, the way in which he takes up his cross, gives him ample opportunity—even under the most difficult circumstances—to add a deeper meaning to his life. [p. 76]

As we said before, any attempt to restore a man's inner strength in the camp had first to succeed in showing him some future goal. Nietzsche's words, "He who has a *why* to live for can bear with almost any *how*," could be the guiding motto for all psychotherapeutic and psychohygienic efforts regarding prisoners. [p. 84]

What was really needed was a fundamental change in our attitude toward life. We had to learn ourselves and, furthermore, we had to teach the despairing men, that *it did not really matter what we expected from life, but rather what life expected from us*. We needed to stop asking about the meaning of life, and instead to think of ourselves as those who were being questioned by life—daily and hourly. Our answer must consist, not in talk and meditation, but in right action and in right conduct. Life ultimately means taking the responsibility to find the right answer to its problems and to fulfill the tasks which it constantly sets for each individual.

These tasks, and therefore the meaning of life, differ from man to man, and from moment to moment. Thus it is impossible to define the meaning of life in a general way. [p. 85]

Frankl developed the psychotherapeutic approach of *logotherapy* as a way of helping people find meaning in their lives. He spoke of medical doctors tending the body, psychologists the mind, and that there was a gap that needed to be filled by helping the spirit, the soul, the essence of a person to find meaning. Without a goal, a direction, meaning, life becomes mechanical and pointless. Out of his suffering and humanity he provided meaning for many.

19.3 Dr Douglas Mawson

The beginning of the twentieth century was a time for heroic exploration and adventure in Antarctica. I became interested in these exploits during my visits to New Zealand—the jumping-off point for most of the early trips. The names of Robert Falcon Scott, Ernest Shackleton, and Roald Amundsen are well known, and their deeds are well worth reading about. In particular, Shackleton's extraordinary leadership in the 1914–15 trip in the *Endurance*, when the ship was trapped in ice for 281 days, crushed by the ice and sunk—an adventure that ended without the loss of a single man—is one of the great sagas of heroism under adverse conditions. (You may read about this trip in the wonderfully illustrated book by Alexander (1999).)

Yet I choose to write here about the story of Dr Douglas Mawson, an Australian professor of geology. Mawson was a scientist and explorer first—the other three men cited above were more interested in "glory" and adventure than scientific exploration. Mawson turned down an invitation to join Scott, on what proved to be a fatal expedition to the South Pole, to head up his own scientific trip. In 1908, Mawson and Edgeworth David and Alistair Mackay man-hauled a sledge to the south magnetic pole. The 1911 to 1913 expedition explored and mapped the geology, geography, and meteorology of a large part of the continent in the Cape Adare area. The story of this trip is told in detail by Bickel (2000).

After landing and setting up a base (a second base was established several hundred miles away on the coast), they sent out several exploratory teams at appropriate times. Dog sleds were used for supplies. Mawson led a three-man team with himself, a Swiss doctor and skier named Xavier Mertz and Lieutenant Belgrave E. S. Ninnis of the Royal Navy. Six weeks and 320 miles into the journey, Ninnis and one team of dogs with most of the supplies disappeared down a crevasse. Mawson and Mertz had no tent and one week's supply of food. They started back. The dogs were sacrificed one at a time and Mawson gave Mertz most of the dog liver, since Mertz was the weaker of the two and liver was considered to be especially nourishing. Mertz died of a vitamin A poisoning from the dog livers. Somehow, Mawson fought his way back to the base camp, enduring freezing winds, snow, cold, thirst, starvation, disease, and snowblindness. In addition to his own survival instincts, he was powerfully motivated to rejoin the wife he had wed shortly before the expedition began—to see her again gave meaning to his ordeal.

Although the ship turned back to pick him up, it couldn't land and Mawson spent about one year recuperating with his comrades at base camp. He wrote later that this saved his life since he probably would not have survived the boat journey. Mawson went on to lead several other Antarctic expeditions.

19.4 The meaning of meaning

There are many whose lives have been extended and enriched by finding meaning. It is well known that "terminal" cancer patients will live beyond prognosis to be able to be at especially significant events such as a daughter's wedding or graduation, a first grandchild, the completion of a book or a degree, or to attain a particular birthday. Meaning is meaningful—it is what we live *for* that matters. And what we live for generally involves love of others, concern for others, people values. Studies of concentration-camp survivors all point out that a deep faith—that which provides meaning—was central for almost all survivors. This deep faith was religious, familial, and political because "devout" communists were also survivors.

If your life is humdrum and routine and dull, read a story about people like Frankl and Mawson. Indeed, we all have the potential to make our own lives, our own stories, heroic.

Chapter 20

Rituals and Ceremonies

20.1 Introduction

Hammerschlag and Silverman (1997) make a useful distinction between rituals and ceremonies. *Rituals* are routine activities such as habits in the sense that they are repetitive and part of everyday life. We all have morning "rituals" in terms of the order we do things: shower, toilet, dress, shave, or put on makeup, and whether you put items of clothes on with left or right limbs first. Evening rituals involve the sequence of getting ready for bed, getting in bed, and what we do to fall asleep. These activities tend to be unique and individual and routine. Some may be related to a particular spiritual or religious practice. Rituals are in effect *ordinary* activities.

On the other hand, *ceremonies* are *special* events and have a connection to the spiritual or sacred or religious. Where and when and how you brush your teeth is a ritual; getting married, graduating from school, being baptized or circumcised, a memorial service, an initiation, an inauguration, and burning your lost love's letters are ceremonies. In essence, ceremonies are designed to give meaning to special occasions. Different religions have their own traditional ceremonies for the end-of-life memorial service, interment, mourning. Within a given religion these activities are ritualized, but the totality of the special events surrounding death are a ceremony. There is certainly room for other interpretations of ritual and ceremony—however, the presented distinctions are useful.

Since rituals are routine, it is ceremonies that are more connected to metaphoric work. Ceremonies tend to be structured stories relating to life transitions—the "rites of transition" are a basic part of everyone's life story. In a sense, we live from ceremony to ceremony, each one a special marker on our life's journey.

Ceremonies may be created for specific purposes (see below). A ceremony typically incorporates the following elements:

- leader(s) to facilitate
- specific goal
- significant or sacred object
- group of select people
- particular site
- mutual respect/reverence
- special timing
- specific order of service or components

For example, a wedding ceremony involves: a rabbi or priest or minister; the religious and/or civil legality of the state of matrimony; wedding ring(s); family and friends of the bride and bridegroom; church or hall or synagogue or temple; exchange of solemn vows; particular date; and order of service prescribed by the religion, the civil office, or, frequently in modern American weddings, by the bride and bridegroom. In the last case, those weddings create their own ceremony, their own story.

20.2 *Navajo Talking Circle*

This is a ceremony used by Navajos and other Native Americans. It incorporates the elements cited above, and may be adapted to many circumstances. There is a person who is the focus of the circle, which may have been convened for his healing, or some other known purpose. There is a leader who facilitates, and who explains the goal of the meeting. The focal person provides an object sacred to him, which is passed around the circle. You may talk only when you are holding the object. When you finish talking, you pass the object on to the next person until all have had a chance to speak. The rules are:

- whatever is said and shared in the circle is confidential and may not be repeated outside of the group
- each person talks about his or her own *personal* experience, from the heart, for as long as he or she wishes
- when the person has finished, the next person has the attention of the group

- there is *no* cross-chatter, interruption, or commenting on what others have said
- everyone listens attentively and respectfully to whoever is speaking

Generally, each person speaks only once—time permitting, and if it is appropriate, a person may speak again for him- or herself. Non-Native American groups may dispense with the use of a sacred object and just go around the room, or permit a random order of speaking. Hammerschlag points out that, in Native American tradition, when you "speak from the *heart*," you are considered to be telling the truth. The expectation is for heartfelt personal statements rather than intellectual commentary. Thus, it is personal stories that are shared.

20.3 Rachel Naomi Remen's wisdom

Remen, who is an M.D., is the medical director of Commonweal (www.commonweal.org), a residential treatment center in Bolinas, CA, where people with serious diseases can spend a week. Her books (1994, 1996, 2000) speak to the human spirit in poems and stories, the stories mainly drawn from her own life. In thumbing through her two books of stories (1996, 2000), I was looking for one to reproduce here to give you some sense of this remarkable woman and her own story. There were dozens that I wanted to include—you really have to read her books and spend time with her. So, here is a small sample (2000, pp. 337–8):

Mystery

The first time I heard the word *Mystery* I did not understand what it meant. As an avid reader of mystery stories, I had the idea that something is a mystery only because its solution has not yet been found. But mystery is different from Mystery. By its very nature Mystery cannot be solved, can never be known. It can only be lived.

We have not been raised to cultivate a sense of Mystery. We may even see the unknown as an insult to our competence, a personal failing. Seen this way, the unknown becomes a challenge to action. But Mystery does not require action; Mystery requires our attention.

Mystery requires that we listen and become open. When we meet with the unknown in this way, we can be touched by a wisdom that can transform our lives.

Mystery has great power. In the many years I have worked with people with cancer, I have seen Mystery comfort people when nothing else can comfort them and offer hope when nothing else offers hope. I have seen Mystery heal fear that is otherwise unhealable. For years I have watched people in their confrontation with the unknown recover awe, wonder, joy, and aliveness. They have remembered that life is holy, and they have reminded me as well. In losing our sense of Mystery, we have become a nation of burned-out people. People who wonder do not burn out.

Everything and everyone has a dimension of the unknown. Mystery helps us to see ourselves and others from the largest possible perspective, as a unique and possibly endless process that may go on over lifetimes. To be living is to be unfinished. Nothing and no one is complete. The world and everything in it is *alive*.

A sense of Mystery can take us beyond disappointment and judgment to a place of expectancy. It opens in us an attitude of listening and respect. If everyone has in them the dimension of the unknown, possibility is present at all times. Wisdom is possible at all times. The Mystery in anyone may speak to them and heal them in the grocery store. It may speak to us and heal us too. Knowing this enables us to listen to life from the place in us that is Mystery also. Mystery requires that we relinquish an endless search for answers and become willing to not understand. That we be open to witness. Those who witness life may eventually know far more than anyone can understand.

Perhaps real wisdom lies in not seeking answers at all. Any answer we find will not be true for long. An answer is a place where we can fall asleep as life moves past us to its next question. After all these years I have begun to wonder if the secret of living well is not in having all the answers but in pursuing unanswerable questions in good company.

More germane to the subject of this chapter is Remen's story, "Making Caring Visible," (1996, pp. 151–3). Here, she gives details about a healing circle that is designed to prepare a person for surgery or radiation or chemotherapy. This group usually consists of a few family members and close friends, and is convened solely for this purpose. The meeting is a few days or a week or so before the surgery or the beginning of the treatment. The central person brings along a small stone that is symbolically important to him. The stone should be flattish and no larger than an inch or so. The rules are explained, the central person does not speak, but hands the stone to a person seated next to him.

In this, Navajo Talking Circle rules apply. The person holding the stone tells a personal story about a trauma or difficult time in his life. Then he describes what personal characteristics, attributes, or actions helped him through that time. These could be courage, strength, faith, love, persistence, belief in a divine being, stubbornness, prayer. This personal tale is concluded with, "I put *love* and *prayer* into this stone so you may have it with you." The stone is passed on. In this manner each person ends with a similar statement, endowing the stone and imbuing in it his or her way of coping and surviving. When all have spoken, the stone, which is now the repository of all of these personal gifts, is given to the central person. He would tape the stone to a hand or foot, and inform the medical staff about its sacred significance.

Remen has used this ceremony for over twenty years with much success. In fact, she has received positive feedback from area surgeons. One said (1996, p. 153), "Listen, I have seen people do badly after surgery and even die when there was no reason for it other than the fact that they believed they wouldn't make it. I need all the help I can get." Ceremonies can be lifesaving.

20.4 Other uses of ceremonies

Ceremonies can be used in large groups for particular purposes such as grief work. Some general comments about grief, grieving, and traditions start the session. It is also useful to have two to four people talk *briefly* about their own personal losses and their way of grieving. Navajo Talking Circle rules are explained—a handout with the rules and some references would be helpful. The large group is divided into smaller groups of four to six each, with six as a maximum. Chairs are rearranged to form small circles. Each small group member speaks in turn about his or her own personal experiences of grief and the ways he or she coped. About 35 minutes is allotted to this sharing. About halfway through it is advisable to remind people about confidentiality within each group and no interruptions of the speaker. A two-minute warning is given. The instructions state that, if a group finishes early, members can enlarge on their comments, but still without cross-chatter and commentary by other group members. This is a *personal sharing* time and not a discussion group. At the end, the members of the small groups hold hands and the facilitator does a 5–7-minute grief-oriented healing meditation for the entire group. Depending on time and the group, the facilitator may lead a general group discussion on grief and how the participants experienced this process.

LeShan (1989) has written about the importance of hopes and dreams and cleaning up unfinished business for people who are seriously ill. This, too, can be the subject of a large group meeting. In this instance, rather than have a few people publicly share their hopes and dreams, the facilitator reads Minnie's story in LeShan's book (1989, pp. 48–54). Her story sets the stage for the formation of small groups. Again, circles are formed and people share their hopes, dreams, what would give meaning to their lives, and any significant bits of unfinished business. Confidentiality is requested. At the end, the facilitator leads the entire group (small groups holding hands) in a healing meditation centered on the subject of the day.

Ceremonies may be used as part of a psychotherapeutic treatment plan. Gilligan (1987, pp. 177–95) has written and lectured on helping his psychotherapy patients through critical points in their lives by using ceremonies (he prefers "ritual"). If a marriage or a long-term relationship breaks up, then the person may be able to put the experience behind him by burying or burning or throwing out in the trash symbols that maintained connections. It is now time to put these things out of mind, "bury" them and go on. Another way is to write about the old feelings and connections and dependencies and other debris from a relationship, and then to ceremoniously burn or destroy the writing. This is almost a kind of exorcism. Long-term grief may be assuaged and shortened by planting a memorial tree or shrub or flower bed.

The therapist can mention the value of a ceremony to mark an important transition. Rites of passage come in many varieties. If the client is open to devising a ceremony, then the therapist follows the client's lead in terms of symbols and actions. Although, to help out, the therapist may describe several possible kinds of ceremonies used by previous clients. Only the client knows the significance and appropriateness of objects and acts. Narrative therapy makes use of declarations, proclamations, and certificates to mark changes. This is akin to the award of a diploma on graduation. Computer graphics programs and parchment papers and color printers make it easy to produce such documents. Ceremonies for change can be cathartic and are powerful ways of ratifying change.

For people who have life-challenging diseases ceremonies can be of special importance. They can be used for resolving unfinished business, ending old and unneeded feelings and attitudes and habits, marking a new phase of life, and for celebrating the end of radiation or chemotherapy treatments. Ceremonies can also be developed with a client for that final change from life to death. The Chalice of Repose project uses harp music and singing during the last stages of life. It is important to involve family members in the design and execution of these ceremonies—the therapist is a guide.

20.5 Connections to metaphor

Ceremonies are both as-if and also invariably realistic. We can mark out our lives in terms of ceremonial occasions. The power of these ceremonies is related to the specificity of the symbols, symbolic actions, and traditional associated rituals. Some traditions invoke religious figures, angels, spirit guides and helpers, power animals, particular readings, and special sites and trappings. The respectful therapist works within the client's belief systems, actions being consistent with those beliefs.

Symbols imply stories. Ceremonies are symbolic. Metaphors are an interesting form of ceremony.

Chapter 21

Closing Thoughts

21.1 Metaphors for special purposes and populations

In the initial outline for this book there was going to be a penultimate chapter with the catch-all title of this section. There were to be sections on post-traumatic stress disorder, geriatric, sleep, children, pain control, and substance abuse—each with illustrative metaphors for particular (or general) cases. This no longer makes sense, since a central thesis of this book is that everyone is unique, everyone has his or her own story, and that metaphoric work needs to fit that particular person. Metaphors for children and geriatric clients will perforce be different, *but* they will also change with each child or each person who is "chronologically advantaged." This is the essence of Erickson's *utilization principle*.

I just thumbed through Hammond's encyclopedic tome (1990), which is titled *Handbook of Hypnotic Suggestions and Metaphors*. The index under "metaphor" lists more sixty entries—three that caught my attention are: jazz band for family interaction, lake for managing nausea, and ranch for behavioral problems. Burns's book (2001) contains 101 healing stories. Chapter 1 cites many other sources. These can all be gainfully studied to find out how other people use and create metaphors. *Yet, it is always better to tell your own stories.*

21.2 A story

Mikey—a story

Once upon a time there was a young boy who dreamed, and he dreamed of faraway places and doing heroic deeds. He was a pretty ordinary boy with an ordinary name like Michael. His family called him Mikey and that was OK, for that was all he knew.

Now, Mikey's parents were ordinary loving parents with all the limitations those parents have. They provided and cared and were full of their own "shoulds" and "need tos" and "musts." Mikey was a dreamer and it seemed like his family was all dreamed out. Impossible, you say! Everyone dreams. Everyone has hidden hopes and dark secrets and delicious desires. What are yours? What are mine? Can adults have dreams, too?

But Mikey was a boy whose job it was to grow up, to learn, to be a man, to maybe follow in his father's footsteps. Perhaps Mikey was different, for he continued to daydream of those faraway places and daring deeds. The faraway places came from books and movies and the TV—full of fabulous fascinating sights and sounds and smells and tastes. Well, not all tastes—mushrooms and liver were still on the yucky side. But, a lot. Growing up there were a whole bunch of daring things that Mikey and his friends did—they were secret because if their parents found out ... You know all about keeping secrets when you're young, and there are a whole bunch of things you can't tell your parents. After all, they're so old and stuck in their ways, aren't they? But kids, well, they are made for adventures of any size. Sometimes, sometimes those dreams come true.

Here is Mike now—he's no longer Mikey—as a young man, having survived the dangers of teenage, still dreaming of faraway places. He goes away to college, not too far, and yet far enough. More learning, more experiences, more dreams open up from the profs and the readings and from his friends. Some of them are really from far away. Some of them have already done daring deeds. Mike dreamed on and graduated and married and had children and found a fulfilling enough job.

He changed. His dreams changed a wee bit. They now included his family at times. His personal dreams never changed. He wondered how far away faraway was. He wondered how much courage it took to love and care for one person, then another and another. What were the dangers in intimacy and commitment and in being a parent?

Then one day the sky fell in: his young wife Joan was diagnosed as having breast cancer. Unfair. Not in his dream or hers. Yet how much did he know about her dreams, the dreams Joan had as a child, a teenager, now? As a family they did all the appropriate medical things. It wasn't enough. They needed more for themselves. So, one evening, they all sat together after dinner and held hands and told dream stories. Faraway places, daring deeds, discovering, exploring, trying, being, doing. Hopes and fears and magic and dreams. Was this where Mike's dreams were supposed to go? and Joan's? and the children's?

Where have your dreams gone? Are they still buried in the vault of "shoulds and shouldn'ts?" Or, are they still viable, accessible, doable? Dreams are, are they not? And, hopes are, too. Miracles are also for grown-ups. Yes? Yes and Yes and Yes.

Thank you.

Bibliography

Achterberg, J. (1985) *Imagery in healing: shamanism and modern medicine.* Boston: New Science Library.

Achterberg, J., Dossey, B. & Kolkmeier, L. (1994) *Rituals of healing: using imagery for health and wellness.* New York: Bantam Books.

Alexander, C. (1999) *The Endurance. Shackleton's legendary Antarctic expedition.* New York: Alfred A. Knopf.

Bandler, R. & Grinder, J. (1975) *Patterns of the hypnotic techniques of Milton H. Erickson, M.D.* Vol. 1. Cupertino, CA: Meta Publications.

Bandler, R. & Grinder, J. (1975) *The structure of magic.* Palo Alto: Science and Behavior Books.

Bandler, R. & Grinder, J. (1982) *Reframing: Neuro-linguistic programming and the transformation of meaning.* Moab, UT: Real People Press.

Bank, W. O. (1985) "Hypnotic suggestion for the control of bleeding in the angiography suite," in S. R. Lankton (ed.) *Ericksonian Monographs, No. 1.* New York: Brunner/Mazel, pp. 76–88.

Barker, D. (1985) *Using metaphor in psychotherapy.* New York: Brunner/Mazel.

Bateson, G. (1979) *Mind and nature: A necessary unity.* New York: E. P. Dutton.

Battino, R. & South, T. L. (1999) *Ericksonian approaches: A comprehensive manual.* Carmarthen, UK: Crown House Publishing.

Battino, R. (2000) *Guided imagery and other approaches to healing.* Carmarthen, UK: Crown House Publishing.

Berg, I. K. & Dolan, Y. (2001) *Tales of solutions. A collection of hope-inspiring stories.* New York: W. W. Norton & Company.

Berne, E. (1973) *What do you say after you say hello? The psychology of human destiny.* New York: Bantam Books.

Bickel, L. (2000) *Mawson's will. The greatest polar survival story ever written.* South Royalton, Vermont: Steerforth Press.

Bion, W.R. (1974) *Experience in groups: And other papers.* New York: Ballantine Books.

Bodenhamer, B. G. & Hall, L. M. (1999) *The User's Manual for the Brain. The Complete Manual for Neuro-Linguistic Programming Practitioner Certification.* Carmarthen, UK: Crown House Publishing.

Bonke, B., Schmitz, P. I. M., Verhage, F. & Zwaveling, A. (1986) "Clinical study of so-called unconscious perception during general anesthesia," *British Journal of Anesthesia,* 58, pp. 957–64.

Brewer, W. (1986) "What is an autobiographical memory?" in D. C. Rubin (ed.), *Autobiographical memory.* New York: Cambridge University Press, pp. 25–49.

Buber, M. (1947) *Tales of the Hasidim.* New York: Schocken Books.

Burns, G.W. (1998) *Nature-guided therapy.* New York: Brunner/Mazel.

Burns, G.W. (2001) *101 Healing stories using metaphors in therapy.* New York: John Wiley & Sons, Inc.

Cade, B. & O'Hanlon, W. H. (1993) *A brief guide to brief therapy.* New York: W. W. Norton & Company.

Campbell, J. (1968) *The hero with a thousand faces,* 2nd edn. Princeton, NJ: Princeton University Press.

Capra, F. (1988) *Uncommon wisdom: Conversations with remarkable people.* New York: Simon and Schuster.

Cheek, D. B. (1959) "Unconscious perception of meaningful sounds during surgical anesthesia as revealed under hypnosis," *American Journal of Clinical Hypnosis,* 1, pp. 101–13.

Cheek, D. B. (1960a) "Preoperative hypnosis to protect patients from careless conversation," *American Journal of Clinical Hypnosis,* 3(2), pp. 101–2.

Cheek, D. B. (1960b) "What does the surgically anesthetized patient hear?" *Rocky Mountain Medical Journal,* 57, January, pp. 49–53.

Cheek, D. B. (1961) "Unconscious reactions and surgical risk," *Western Journal of Surgery, Obstetrics, and Gynecology*, 67, pp. 325–8.

Cheek, D. B. (1964) "Further evidence of persistence of hearing under chem-anesthesia: Detailed case report," *American Journal of Clinical Hypnosis*, 7(1), pp. 55–9.

Cheek, D. B. (1965) "Can surgical patients react to what they hear under anesthesia?" *Journal American Association Nurse Anesthetists*, 33, pp. 30–8.

Cheek, D. B. (1966) "The meaning of continued hearing sense under general anesthesia," *American Journal of Clinical Hypnosis*, 8, pp. 275–80.

Cheek, D. B. (1981) "Awareness of meaningful sounds under general anesthesia: Considerations and a review of the literature," in H. J. Wain (ed.), *Theoretical and Clinical Aspects of Hypnosis*. Miami: Symposia Specialists, Inc.

Cheek, D. B. (1994) *Hypnosis. The application of ideomotor techniques*. Boston: Allyn and Bacon.

Clawson, T. A. & Swade, R. H. (1975) "The hypnotic control of blood flow and pain: The cure of warts and the potential for the use of hypnosis in the treatment of cancer," *American Journal of Clinical Hypnosis*, 17, 160–9.

Clayton, M. (1994) Role theory and its application in clinical practice, in P. Holmes, M. Karp, and M. Watson (eds), *Psychodrama since Moreno: Innovations in theory and practice*. New York: Routledge, pp. 121–44.

Close, H. T. (1998) *Metaphor in psychotherapy. Clinical applications of stories and allegories*. San Luis Obispo, CA: Impact Publishers.

Cohen, T. (1979) "Metaphor and the cultivation of intimacy," in S. Sacks (ed.), *On metaphor*. Chicago: University of Chicago Press, pp. 1–10.

Combs, G. & Freedman, J. (1990) *Symbol story & ceremony. Using metaphor in individual and family therapy*. New York: W. W. Norton & Company.

De Shazer, S. (1994) *Words were originally magic*. New York: W. W. Norton & Company.

Dubin, L. L. & Shapiro, S. S. (1974) "Use of hypnosis to facilitate dental extraction and homeostasis in a classic hemophiliac with a high antibody titer to factor VIII," *American Journal of Clinical Hypnosis*, 17, pp. 79–83.

Enqvist, B. & Fischer, K. (1997) "Preoperative hypnotic techniques reduce consumption of analgesics after surgical removal of third mandibular molars," *International Journal of Clinical and Experimental Hypnosis*, Vol. XLV, No. 2 (April), pp. 102–8.

Epston, D. & White, M. (1992) *Experience, contradiction, narrative, & imagination. Selected papers of David Epston & Michael White. 1989–1991.* Adelaide: Dulwich Centre Publications.

Erickson, M. H. (1958) "Pediatric hypnotherapy," *American Journal of Clinical Hypnosis*, 1, pp. 25–9. (Also reprinted in Rossi, E. L. (ed.) (1980) *The Collected Papers of Milton H. Erickson, Vol. IV: Innovative Hypnotherapy.* New York: Irvington, pp. 174–80.)

Erickson, M. H., Rossi, E. L. & Rossi, S. I. (1976) *Hypnotic realities.* New York: Irvington Publishers, Inc.

Erickson, M. H. & Rossi, E. L. (1979) *Hypnotherapy: An exploratory casebook.* New York: Irvington Publishers, Inc.

Esterling, B. A., L'Abate, L., Murray, E. J. & Pennebaker, J. W. (1999) "Empirical foundations for writing in prevention and psychotherapy: Mental and physical health outcomes," *Clinical Psychology Review*, 19, pp. 79–96.

Frankl, V. E. (1959, 1962, rev. 1984) *Man's search for meaning*, 3rd edn. New York: Simon and Schuster.

Frankl, V.E. (1997) *Recollections. An autobiography.* New York: Insight Books, Plenum Press.

Freedman, J. & Combs, G. (1996) *Narrative therapy. The social construction of preferred realities.* New York: W. W. Norton & Company.

Freud, S. (1963) *Jokes and their relation to the unconscious.* New York: W. W. Norton & Company.

Gergen, M. M. & Gergen, K. J. (1984) "The social construction of narrative accounts," in K. J. Gergen & M. M. Gergen (eds), *Historical social psychology.* Hillsdale: Lawrence Erlbaum Associates.

Gilligan, S. G. (1987) *Therapeutic trances, the cooperation principle in Ericksonian hypnotherapy.* New York: Brunner/Mazel.

Gordon, D. (1978) *Therapeutic metaphors. Helping others through the looking glass.* Cupertino, CA: Meta Publications.

Goulding, M. M. & Goulding, R. L. (1997) *Changing lives through redecision therapy*. New York: Grove Press.

Graham-Pole, J. (2000) *Illness and the art of creative self-expression*. Oakland, CA: New Harbinger Publications, Inc.

Grinder, J. & Bandler, R. (1976) *The structure of magic. II*. Palo Alto: Science and Behavior Books.

Grinder, J., DeLozier, J. & Bandler, R. (1977) *Patterns of the hypnotic techniques of Milton H. Erickson, M.D.*, Vol. 2. Cupertino, CA: Meta Publications.

Grinder, J. & Bandler, R. (1981) *Trance-formations: Neuro-Linguistic Programming and the structure of hypnosis*. Moab, UT: Real People Press.

Guntrip, H. (1973) *Psychoanalytic theory, therapy, and the self: A basic guide to personality in Freud, Erikson, Klein, Sullivan, Fairbairn, Hartmann, Jacobson, and Winnicott*. New York: Basic Books.

Haley, J. (1984) *Ordeal therapy. Unusual ways to change behavior*. San Francisco: Jossey-Bass Publishers.

Haley, J. (1986) *Uncommon therapy. The psychiatric techniques of Milton H. Erickson, M.D.* New York: W. W. Norton & Company.

Hall, E. T. (1959) *The silent language*. New York: A Fawcett Premier Book (Doubleday & Co., Inc.)

Hammerschlag, C. A. & Silverman, H. D. (1997) *Healing ceremonies. Creating personal rituals for spiritual, emotional, physical and mental health*. New York: A Perigree Book.

Hammond, D. C. (ed.) (1990) *Handbook of hypnotic suggestions and metaphors*. New York: W. W. Norton & Company.

Havens, R. A. & Walters, C. (1989) *Hypnotherapy scripts. A neo-Ericksonian approach to persuasive healing*. New York: Brunner/Mazel.

James, T. & Woodsmall, W. (1988) *Time line therapy and the basis of personality*. Cupertino, CA: Meta Publications.

Klingberg, S. H. (2001) *When life calls out to us. The love and lifework of Viktor and Elly Frankl*. New York: Doubleday.

Kopp, R. R. (1995) *Metaphor Therapy. Using client-generated metaphors in psychotherapy.* New York: Brunner/Mazel.

Kopp, S. B. (1971) *Guru. Metaphors from a psychotherapist.* Palo Alto, CA: Science and Behavior Books.

Kopp, S. B. (1972) *If you meet the Buddha on the road, kill him! The pilgrimage of psychotherapy patients.* Palo Alto, CA: Science and Behavior Books.

L'Abate, L. (1992) *Programmed writing: A self-administered approach for interventions with individuals, couples, and families.* Pacific Grove, CA: Brooks/Cole.

L'Abate, L. (1997) "Distance writing and computer-assisted training," in S. R. Sauber (ed.), *Managed mental health care: Major diagnostic and treatment approaches.* Bristol, PA: Brunner/Mazel, pp. 133–63.

Lackoff, L. & Johnson, M. (1980) *Metaphors we live by.* Chicago: University of Chicago Press.

Lankton, S. R. & Lankton, C. H. (1983) *The answer within. A clinical framework of Ericksonian hypnotherapy.* New York: Brunner/Mazel.

Lankton, S. R. & Lankton, C. H. (1986) *Enchantment and intervention in family therapy. Training in Ericksonian approaches.* New York: Brunner/Mazel.

Lankton, C. H. & Lankton, S. R. (1989) *Tales of enchantment. Goal-oriented metaphors for adults and children in therapy.* New York: Brunner/Mazel.

LeShan, L. (1989) *Cancer as a turning point.* New York: A Plume Book (Penguin Books).

Levine, S. (1997) *A year to live. How to live this year as if it were your last.* New York: Bell Tower Crown Publishers, Inc.

Lewis, B. A. and Pucelik, F. (1982) *Magic demystified: A pragmatic guide to communication and change.* Lake Oswego, OR: Metamorphous Press.

Liu, Y. K., Standen, P. J. & Aitkenhead, A. R. (1992) "Therapeutic suggestions during general anesthesia in patients undergoing hysterectomy," *British Journal of Anesthesia*, 68, pp. 277–81.

Lowen, Alexander. (1975) *Bioenergetics.* New York: Coward, McCann & Geoghegan, Inc.

Maher, J. M. & Briggs, D. (eds) (1988) *An open life. Joseph Campbell in conversation with Michael Toms*. Burdett, NY: Larson Publications.

McLauchlin, L. (1992) *Advanced language patterns mastery*. Calgary, Canada: Leading Edge Communications.

McNeill, D. (1992) *Hand and mind: what gestures reveal about thought*. Chicago: University of Chicago Press.

Miller, S. D. & Berg, I. K. (1995) *The miracle method. A radically new approach to problem drinking*. New York: W. W. Norton & Company.

Mills, J. C. & Crowley, R. J. (1986) *Therapeutic metaphors for children and the child within*. New York: Brunner/Mazel.

Monk, G., Winslade, J., Crocket, K. & Epston, D. (eds) (1997) *Narrative therapy in practice. The archeology of hope*. San Francisco: Jossey-Bass Publishers.

Moreno, J. L. (1934) *Who shall survive? A new approach to the problem of human interrelations* Washington, D.C.: Nervous and Mental Disease Publishing Co.

Mosak, H. (1958) "Early recollections as a projective technique," *Journal of Projective Techniques*, 22(3), pp. 302–11.

O'Hanlon, W. H. (1987) *Taproots. Underlying principles of Milton Erickson's therapy and hypnosis*. New York: W. W. Norton & Company.

O'Hanlon, W. H. (1994) "The third wave," *Family Therapy Networker*, Nov./Dec., pp. 19–29.

O'Hanlon, W. H. & Hexum, A. L. (1990) *An uncommon casebook. The complete clinical work of Milton H. Erickson, M.D.* New York: W. W. Norton & Company.

Pearson, R. E. (1961) "Response to suggestions given under general anesthesia," *American Journal of Clinical Hypnosis*, 4, pp. 106–14.

Pennebaker, J. W. (1997) *Opening up: the healing power of confiding in others*. New York: Guildford.

Petry, J. J. (2000) "Surgery and complementary therapies: A review," *Alternative Therapies in Health and Medicine*; 6(5), pp. 64–76.

337

Pribram, K. (1971) *Languages of the brain: Experimental paradoxes and principles in neuropsychology*. Englewood Cliffs, NJ: Prentice-Hall.

Pribram, K. (1978) "Our brain: the holographic theory," *On the nature of reality*. Los Angeles: UCLA Extension (audiotape).

Pribram, K. (1985) "What the fuss is all about," in K. Wilder (ed.), *The holographic paradigm and other paradoxes: Exploring the leading edge of science*. Boston: New Science Library, pp. 27–34.

Pribram, K. (1990) "Prolegomenon for a holonomic brain theory," in H. Haken and M. Stadler (eds), *Synergetics of cognition*. Berlin, Germany: Springer-Verlag.

Pribram, K. (1991) *Brain and perception. Holonomy and structure in figural processing*. New Jersey: Lawrence Erlbaum Associates.

Remen, R.N. (1994) *Wounded healers. A book of poems by people who have had cancer and those who love and care for them*. Bolinas, CA: Wounded Healer Press.

Remen, R.N. (1996) *Kitchen table wisdom. Stories that heal*. New York: Riverhead Books.

Remen, R.N. (2000) *My grandfather's blessings. Stories of strength, refuge, and belonging*. New York: Riverhead Books.

Ricoeur, P. (1979) "The metaphorical process," in S. Sacks (ed.), *On metaphor*. Chicago: University of Chicago Press, pp. 151–57.

Ricoeur, P. (1984) *The rule of metaphor: Multi-disciplinary studies of the creation of meaning in language*. Toronto: University of Toronto Press.

Rogers, C. R. (1994) *Freedom to learn*. New York: Merrill Publishing Co.

Rosen, S. (1982) *My voice will go with you. The teaching tales of Milton H. Erickson*. New York: W. W. Norton & Company.

Rossi, E. L. & Cheek, D. B. (1988) *Mind-body therapy. Methods of ideodynamic healing in hypnosis*. New York: W. W. Norton & Company.

Rossi, E. L. (1993) *The psychobiology of mind–body healing*, 2nd ed. New York: W. W. Norton & Company.

Rossi, E. L. (1996) *The symptom path to enlightenment. The new dynamics of self-organization in hypnotherapy: An advanced manual for beginners.* Pacific Palisades, CA: Palisades Gateway Publishing.

Siegel, B. (1986) *Love, medicine and miracles.* New York: Harper and Row.

Siler, T. (1987) *Metaphorms. Forms of metaphors.* New York: The New York Academy of Sciences.

Siler, T. (1990) *Breaking the mind barrier: the artscience of neurocosmology.* New York: Simon and Schuster.

Snyder, E. D. (1971) *Hypnotic poetry. A study of trance-inducing technique in certain poems and its literary significance.* New York: Octagon Books.

Spiegel, D., Bloom, J. R., Kraemer, H. C. & Gottheil, E. (1989) "Effect of psychosocial treatment on survival of patients with metastatic breast cancer," *Lancet*, 2 (Oct. 14), pp. 888–91.

Talmon, M. (1990) *Single-session therapy. Maximizing the effect of the first (and often only) therapeutic encounter.* San Francisco: Jossey-Bass Publishers.

Wallas, L. (1985) *Stories for the third ear. Using hypnotic fables in psychotherapy.* New York: W. W. Norton & Company.

Wallas, L. (1991) *Stories that heal. Reparenting adult children of dysfunctional families using hypnotic stories in psychotherapy.* New York: W. W. Norton & Company.

Watzlawick, P., Weakland, J. & Fisch, R. (1974) *Change. Principles of problem formation and problem resolution.* New York: W. W. Norton, & Company.

White, M. (1995) *Re-authoring lives: Interviews & essays.* Adelaide: Dulwich Centre Publications.

White, M. & Epston, D. (1990) *Narrative means to therapeutic ends.* New York: W. W. Norton & Company.

Williams, A. (1991) *Forbidden agendas: Strategic action in groups.* New York: Tavistock/Routledge.

Winnicott, D. W. (1986) *Home is where we start from: Essays by a psychoanalyst.* New York: Viking Penguin.

Zeig, J. (1980) "Erickson's use of anecdotes," in: J. Zeig (ed.), *A teaching seminar with Milton H. Erickson, M.D.* New York: Brunner/Mazel, pp. 3–28.

Zeig, J. K. (1999) "The virtues of our faults: A key concept of Ericksonian hypnotherapy," *Sleep and hypnosis*, 1, pp. 129–138.

Index

Ericksonian Approaches
A Comprehensive Manual
Rubin Battino, M.S. & Thomas L. South, Ph.D.

Many books have been written by and about Milton H. Erickson and his unique contribution to the field of hypnotherapy. Very few are designed as training resources in Ericksonian hypnotherapy. None of them provide the comprehensive training program that is *Ericksonian Approaches.*

The definitive training manual in the art of Ericksonian hypnotherapy, this easily-accessible book provides a systematic approach to learning the subject, set against a clinical background. A thoroughly practical resource that assumes no previous knowledge of the field, it develops the subject over twenty-two chapters that include:

- the history of hypnosis
- myths and misconceptions
- traditional vs non-traditional inductions
- rapport-building skills
- language forms
- basic and advanced inductions
- hypnotherapy without trance
- utilization of ideodynamic responses
- basic and advanced metaphor
- Ericksonian approaches in medicine, dentistry, special populations, substance abuse and life-challenging diseases
- ethical and legal considerations.

"Students delight! Fundamentals of the Ericksonian approach have never been so easy to learn. Tom South and Rubin Battino offer an eminently comprehensible training manual abounding with illustrations and exercises."
—*Jeffrey K. Zeig, Ph.D., Director, The Milton H. Erickson Foundation.*

CLOTH   560 PAGES   ISBN: 1899836314

Guided Imagery
And Other Approaches To Healing
Rubin Battino, M.S.

An essentially practical and accessible healing manual, *Guided Imagery* presents a breakdown of published guided imagery scripts, while investigating the language used in guided imagery, the skills required in rapport-building, and the most effective methods in inducing a state of relaxation. Pioneering new bonding and fusion healing methods, *Guided Imagery* also incorporates a useful section on preparing patients for surgery, and a chapter on Nutrition and Healing, by nutrition expert A. Ira Fritz, Ph.D., plus a chapter on Native American Healing Traditions, by Native American healer Helena Sheehan, Ph.D. Designed as a resource for health professionals, *Guided Imagery*, meticulously researched and authoritative, is essential reading for doctors, nurses, psychologists, counselors and all those involved or interested in healing.

"Well chosen, illuminating clinical examples abound, with eminently useful imagery suggestions for practitioner and patient."
—*Belleruth Naparstek, L.I.S.W., author of Staying Well with Guided Imagery.*

Also available: 2 audiotape set of guided imagery scripts, 113 mins. ISBN: 1899836594

CLOTH   400 PAGES   ISBN: 1899836446

Coping
A Practical Guide for People with
Life-Challenging Diseases and their Caregivers
Rubin Battino, M.S.

Coping is a practical guide for those living with or dealing with
life-challenging diseases. Detailing the many effective coping strategies
that Professor Rubin Battino has encountered during his extensive
professional experience—from friends and support groups, from
research and from practice—it is written to be thoroughly accessible
and informative, inviting you to explore a wide range of techniques and
methods that have proved to have a healing influence.

"Coping is an excellent source of information and wisdom, and when
  they are combined with action and inspiration wonderful things
  happen."
  —*Bernie Siegel, M.D. author of Love, Medicine & Miracles and
    Prescriptions for Living.*

PAPERBACK   192 PAGES   ISBN: 1899836683

Meaning
A Play Based on the Life of Viktor E. Frankl
Rubin Battino, M.S.

Meaning: a play based on the life of Viktor E. Frankl is a biography in play form. Using many of his own words, the play focuses on the key moments in Frankl's life, it explores his experiences in a Nazi concentration camp, his development of Logotherapy and his insights into the human condition. His book *Man's Search for Meaning* has influenced millions of people worldwide.

Richly illustrated with photographs of Frankl's life and times, including both painful images of imprisonment in the camps and joyful family portraits, *Meaning* presents this extraordinary man's life in a dramatic and readable style. It will appeal to those familiar with Frankl's work, and inspire new readers to learn more about this remarkable man and his contribution to the cause of humanity.

"*Meaning* brings Frankl to life in full dimension—his spirit, determination, wisdom, and integrity."
—*Jeffrey K. Zeig, Ph.D., Director, The Milton H. Erickson Foundation.*

"The passionate and poignant bleakness of this magnificent play paints vivid pictures with both precision and grandeur. Each person realizes anew, the humanness as well as the inhumanity of mankind. Frankl's own words responding to the questions we all still have, gives wiser and more deeply profound understanding to the meaning of life, then, now and for the future. Seeing Frankl's life, in this setting—love and life juxtaposed with suffering and death, brings somber joy as we realize once again we all can be free, as Frankl always was."
—*Betty Alice Erickson*

PAPERBACK   128 PAGES   ISBN: 1899836837

USA & Canada *orders to:*

Crown House Publishing
P.O. Box 2223, Williston, VT 05495-2223, USA
Tel: 877-925-1213, Fax: 802-864-7626
www.CHPUS.com

UK & Rest of World *orders to:*

The Anglo American Book Company Ltd.
Crown Buildings, Bancyfelin, Carmarthen, Wales SA33 5ND
Tel: +44 (0)1267 211880/211886, Fax: +44 (0)1267 211882
E-mail: books@anglo-american.co.uk
www.anglo-american.co.uk

Australasia *orders to:*

Footprint Books Pty Ltd
101 McCarrs Creek Road, P.O. Box 418, Church Point
Sydney NSW 2105, Australia
Tel: +61 2 9997 3973, Fax: +61 2 9997 3185
E-mail: footprintbooks@ozmail.com.au